VE DAY

THE PEOPLE'S STORY

About the Author

Russell Miller is the author of *Nothing Less Than Victory, The Oral History of D-Day*; *Magnum, Fifty Years at the Front Line of History*; *Behind the Lines, The Oral History of Special Operations in World War Two*; and *Codename Tricycle, The True Story of the Second World War's Most Extraordinary Double Agent*.

VE DAY

THE PEOPLE'S STORY

RUSSELL MILLER
WITH RENATE MILLER

TEMPUS

'Let war yield to peace, laurels to paeans'
Cicero (106-43 BC)

Front cover illustration courtesy of the Imperial War Museum.
  (Image no. HU49414.)
Back cover illustration courtesy of Steve Nicholas.

First published 1995 by Michael Joseph Ltd
This edition first published 2007

Tempus Publishing Limited
The Mill, Brimscombe Port,
Stroud, Gloucestershire, GL5 2QG
www.tempus-publishing.com

British Library Cataloguing in Publication Data.
A catalogue record for this book is available from the British Library.

ISBN 978 0 7524 4312 6

Typesetting and origination by Tempus Publishing Limited
Printed in Great Britain

Contents

Illustrations

(*Copyright holders are indicated in italics*)

Permissions

The author and publishers would like to thank the following for permission to reproduce copyright material: British Broadcasting Corporation for extracts from the BBC Radio Collection tapes, *Victory in Europe*; the Trustees of the Mass Observation Archive, University of Sussex for Mass Observation Archive material reproduced by permission of Curtis Brown Group Ltd, London; Imperial War Museum for material from their Sound Archives; Falling Wall Press for *Nella's Last War: A Mother's Last Diary* by Richard Broad and Susie Fleming; Heinemann Ltd for *Three Years with Eisenhower: The Personal Diary of Captain Harry C. Butcher*; Little Brown Ltd for *Will the Real Ian Carmichael ...* by Ian Carmichael; S. Fischer Verlag GmbH for *Zwischenbilanz* by Guenter de Bruyn; Hodder Headline Ltd for *Richard Dimbleby* by Jonathan Dimbleby; HMSO (Crown copyright is reproduced with the permission of the Controller of HMSO) for *History of the Second World War, Civil Affairs and Military Government in North West Europe 1944 46* by F.S.V. Donnison; Gollancz Ltd for *Paris Journal 1944 65* by Janet Flanner; Macmillan Publishing Co., Inc. for *The War 1939 45* by Desmond Flower and James Reeves; Virona Publishing for *Helga* by Helga Gerhardi; André Deutsch Ltd for *The Sheltered Days: Growing Up in the War* by Derek Lambert; Hutchinson for *When We Won the War* and *How We Lived Then* by Norman Longmate; Chatto and Windus Ltd for *The Home Front* by Norman Longmate; Granada Ltd for *I Play as I Please* by Humphrey Lyttelton; HarperCollins Ltd for *The Memoirs of Field Marshal the Viscount Montgomery of Alamein KG*; the Estate of Alan Moorehead for *Eclipse* by Alan Moorehead; Hamish Hamilton Ltd for *The Moon's a Balloon* by David Niven; Stephen Schimanski and Henry Treece (eds) for *Leaves in the Storm: A Book of Diaries*; and Heinemann Ltd for *Wartime Women* edited by Dorothy Sheridan.

(For specific reference to the above material please refer to the Notes and Bibliography. Every effort has been made to trace or contact copyright holders. The publishers will be glad to rectify, in future editions, any amendments or omissions brought to their notice.)

Acknowledgements

One of the problems about writing an oral history of VE Day is that 50 years have passed and memories are fading. It was not a difficulty with our oral history of D Day because many of the veterans who took part in such a dramatic moment of history had an extraordinarily clear and detailed recall of everything that happened to them on that day. Being in Normandy on 6 June 1944 was something you did not forget.

VE Day is different, as we rapidly discovered. Denis Norden, for example, could remember nothing except being 'maudlin in a tent on Lüneberg Heath'. Lord Hailsham, perhaps understandably, could only recall that his son, Douglas, was christened in the crypt at the House of Commons on that day. Sir John Mills said he was too young to remember anything and Donald Sinden explained he was so busy entertaining the troops he didn't even know it was VE Day! Sir Robin Day's one memory is of being on a troopship and being allowed a single beer, 'a rare treat', to celebrate. Raymond Baxter, who was a Spitfire pilot, recalls giving joy rides to WAAFs in a little Auster; Sir Hugh Casson only remembers leaving a Ministry of Planning conference in Edinburgh and finding all the street lamps on for the first time in years. David Kossof vaguely recalls a 'prolonged knees-up' in Lincoln's Inn Fields; Lord Carrington, with his battalion somewhere near Freiburg, claimed VE Day was completely unexceptional, just another working day.

It is the fallibility of memory that makes the Mass Observation archive at the University of Sussex such an invaluable resource for any author embarked on a project such as this. Mass Observation was set up in 1937, by the poet and journalist Charles Madge and the anthropologist Tom Harrisson, to 'record the voice of the people'. At the time of VE Day its volunteer observers were out and about recording extraordinarily detailed contemporary accounts of what was happening, what people were saying and thinking. Unfortunately, a condition of being able to make use of the archive is that all contributors remain anonymous, but the authentic colour they provide is irresistible.

The staff at our local library in High Wycombe considered it a personal challenge to seek out every one of the multitude of books we requested and proved, once again, that our library service is second to none and needs to be protected against philistine governments looking for budget cuts.

We would also like to thank the courteous and helpful staff of the Sound Archives and the Department of Documents at the Imperial War Museum; the London Library, particularly Joy Eldridge of Mass Observation; Martin Tapsell and staff of the Inter-Library Lending Department of Bucks County Library; members of the National Federation of Women's Institutes, the Royal British Legion, the War Widows' Association and the Burma Star Association. A special word of thanks, too, to John Frost, who manages to keep track of his historic collection of newspapers in a small suburban house in north London and who also wrote a fascinating letter to his mother from Germany on VE Day.

Finally, we must express our gratitude to all those who offered up their diaries, letters and memories and for everyone who agreed to be interviewed. Not everyone could be included in this book, but all the material will be lodged in a suitable archive for the benefit of those people who will undoubtedly be writing about the centenary of VE Day in the year 2045.

Russell and Renate Miller,
Buckinghamshire, 1994.

Introduction

It is a cherished legend in my family, at least cherished by me, that on the night of VE Day my mother was brought home from the pub in a wheelbarrow. I was only six at the time (well, six and three-quarters), so took no part in the celebrations, but I was thrilled beyond belief when, the following morning, I heard what had occurred. Nothing so risqué, so, so … scandalous, had ever happened in the family to my knowledge and I kept pressing various aunts and uncles for more information. Did my mother willingly get into the wheelbarrow? Why? Where did it come from? Who pushed it? Did anyone see?

The ending of the war in Europe meant little to a six-year-old; but his mother coming home from the pub in a wheelbarrow made a deep impression. I suppose in the end I realized that my Mum had been 'tipsy' (the rather charming euphemism then in use for being completely plastered) and that probably everyone else had been tipsy, too.

I knew my Dad went out for pint in the local on a Saturday night and my Mum liked a Guinness—she believed the advertising that it was good for her—but I had never seen or heard of either of them having too much to drink, even at Christmas or family parties. It never crossed my mind that my quiet and very conventional parents, who cared a great deal about keeping up appearances, would ever risk getting drunk. So it was the thought of them merrily weaving home from the pub, with my Dad pushing my Mum in a wheelbarrow, that brought home to me the realization that something truly significant had happened.

If further confirmation was needed that historic events were taking place it came shortly afterwards when I arrived home from school to find a glass bowl in the middle of the dining table containing three curious curved yellow tubes. My older sister, who knew about such things, announced that they were bananas. That evening my mother peeled one of the exotic tubes and my sister and I shared the literal fruits of victory. I declared it to be delicious, although actually I was a bit disappointed.

Two days after VE Day, there was a party on our street. We lived in a working-class neighbourhood on the east side of London, but my Dad was a white-collar clerk and we aspired to middle-class values. Consequently I was the only boy present wearing a tie. I know this because I have still got the black and white group picture of our scruffy little group. There I am, sitting cross-legged in the front row, still apparently unable to grasp the victory concept. All the other kids are giving the victory sign in the approved Churchillian fashion; I, alone, have got it the wrong way round and appear to be making a very rude gesture at the photographer.

Years later, whenever the family got together, my mother, whose name was Queenie, would be teased about VE night: 'I don't suppose you remember much about that night, do you, Queen? You know, that night they brought you home in a wheelbarrow.' My mother would blush and pretend to be cross, but I always had the feeling she was secretly rather proud that she had celebrated the end of the war in Europe with such ostentatious and uncharacteristic abandon.

Interviewing people for this book reminded me very forcibly of how different times were then, how curiously innocent life was. Everyone knew, beyond any shadow of doubt, that we were involved in a just war. The issues were clear: we were fighting on the side of good against the forces of evil, therefore we must, in the end, win. Whatever the price that had to be paid, whatever sacrifices it required, it was worth it. No war has ever been fought so unequivocally.

If anyone did harbour any doubts about the Allied cause, or the necessity for war, they were surely swept away when, in April 1945, the first reports began filtering back to Britain of the discovery of the concentration camps. Most people knew about the existence of the camps, and something of the Nazi persecution of the Jews, but until the advancing Allies had overrun places like Belsen and Dachau and Nordhausen, no one appreciated the sheer scale of the horror. Here, alone, was justification for the war.

A few days later came news of the death of Hitler. By then everyone guessed the end was near and that it was only a question of time before the war in Europe would conclude in victory for the Allies. There was still the war against Japan to be won, but peace in Europe was the first priority. The days of waiting were tense but, like the times, strangely disciplined. Even though we knew the Germans had surrendered on Lüneburg Heath, we waited patiently for the official declaration of VE Day and for permission to celebrate.

When it came there was an outpouring of rejoicing and relief and patriotism, the like of which the world will never see again. In these depressing days of social decay and drugs and violence, when large public gatherings frequently end in pitched battles with the police, it is hard to imagine that thousands and thousands of people jammed the streets of London well into the night on 8 May 1945 and those who were there, in that swirling mass of humanity, remember it as an unforgettable experience, one of the happiest days of their lives.

The most common crime of the night was to knock a policeman's helmet off; the most frequent act of vandalism was to climb a lamp post.

Total strangers linked arms in the comradeship of their happiness, kissing and hugging was the order of the night, there was dancing on the streets whenever and wherever space could be found, when the crowd was not singing it was cheering, when it was not cheering it was laughing. The pubs ran dry, but who cared? This was a celebration driven by communal joy; no other stimulants were needed.

There were similar scenes in other cities around the world, in Paris, New York, Melbourne, Copenhagen … In rural areas, village communities lit huge bonfires and danced around the flames … And everywhere people drew back their curtains and let their lights blaze out into the night to mark the end of the blackout.

No, there will never be another day like it.

Tuesday 1 May

The Death of Hitler

At 10.30 p.m. on the evening of Tuesday 1 May 1945 the familiar voice of Stuart Hibberd interrupted a programme from Glasgow, called 'Piping' on the BBC's Home Service: 'This is London calling. Here is a newsflash. The German radio has just announced that Hitler is dead. I repeat, the German radio has just announced that Hitler is dead.'[1]

There was no further comment, no speculation about whether or not the report was correct and no change to the normal schedule of programmes. 'Evening Prayers' followed immediately after the announcement.

Elsie Brown regularly listened to 'Evening Prayers' and was making a cup of tea in her terraced house in East London. 'I never missed "Evening Prayers" because my husband, Bert, was in the artillery somewhere in Germany and, it's silly I know, but I thought that "Evening Prayers" was a way of staying in touch with him. I imagined him, wherever he was, listening too and thinking about home. 'Course I didn't even know if they broadcast it over there; probably they didn't.

'Anyway, this night I was still warming the pot when I heard the news that Hitler was dead. At first I didn't believe it, then I thought, well, it's on the BBC so it must be true. I didn't know what to do. I wanted to tell someone, but both the kids were asleep and I didn't want to wake them, so I decided to run next door. My neighbour, Vi, worked the late shift on the buses and was always up till after midnight so I went round and banged on her door and when she opened it I shouted something like "He's dead, the old bugger's dead!" And she said, "What old bugger? Alfie?" Alfie was an old bloke who lived at the end of our road and really was a miserable old bugger, always shouting at the kids. So I said, "No, not Alfie, Adolf!"

'When the penny dropped Vi said, "Here, Else, you better come in" but I couldn't because I'd left the kids asleep, so she came back with me and brought a bottle of Guinness she'd been saving for a special occasion and we shared it.

Of course we didn't know any more than we'd heard, but Vi agreed with me that as it was on the BBC it must be true. She said, "Do you think it'll all be over soon now?" I think I nodded and I remember I suddenly started crying. I don't know why; I couldn't stop.'

It was shortly before 9 that evening when Radio Hamburg interrupted a concert of the works of Wagner and Weber to ask listeners to stand by for a 'government announcement' to be broadcast at nine o'clock.

Nine o'clock came and went without an announcement but at 9.30 the broadcast was interrupted again: '*Achtung! Achtung!* In a short time German Rundfunk will broadcast a grave and important announcement to the German people.' The German people could perhaps be forgiven for wondering what could be more grave or important than the fact that they were facing certain defeat after a senseless war lasting nearly six years and costing some five million German lives. They were to wait several minutes to find out.

At 9.42 another stand-by warning was repeated during a performance of Wagner's *Götterdaemmerung*. At 9.47 there was another warning, with the assurance that the announcement would be made 'in a few moments'. This was followed by the slow movement of Bruckner's Seventh Symphony, written to commemorate the death of Wagner.

Bruckner gave way to funereal dirges and a drum roll from a massed military band. At 10.25 an unknown announcer came to the microphone, his voice choking with emotion: 'It is reported from our Führer's headquarters that our Führer, Adolf Hitler, has fallen this afternoon at his command post in the Reich Chancellery, fighting to the last breath against Bolshevism and for Germany. On Monday the Führer appointed Grand Admiral Dönitz as his successor. Our new Führer will speak to the German people.'

Listeners were offered little time to ponder the mystery of Hitler's extraordinary prescience in appointing a surprise successor 24 hours before he fell in battle. For after another roll of drums Admiral Karl Dönitz, commander-in-chief of the German Navy, came on the air: 'German men and women, soldiers of the German Wehrmacht! Our Führer, Adolf Hitler, has fallen. The German people bow in deepest mourning and veneration. He recognized beforehand the terrible danger of Bolshevism and devoted his life to fighting it.

'At the end of this, his battle, and of his unswerving, straight path of life, stands his death, as a hero in the capital of the Reich. All his life meant service to the German people. His battle against the Bolshevik flood benefited not only Europe but the whole world.

'The Führer has appointed me as his successor. Fully conscious of the responsibility, I take over the leadership of the German people at this fateful hour.

'It is my first task to save the German people from destruction by the Bolsheviks and it is only to achieve this that the fight continues. As long as the Americans and the British hamper us from reaching this end we shall fight and defend ourselves against them as well. The British and Americans do not fight for the interests of their own people, but for the spreading of Bolshevism.

'What the German people have achieved and suffered is unique in history. In the coming times of distress of our people I shall do my utmost to make life bearable for our brave women, men and children … '

Immediately after his speech, an announcer read out Dönitz's mawkish Order of the Day to the German armed forces: 'German Wehrmacht, my comrades. The Führer has fallen. He fell faithful to his great ideal to save the people of Europe from Bolshevism. He staked his life and died the death of a hero. With his passing, one of the greatest heroes of German history has passed away. In proud reverence and sorrow we lower our flags before him … '

During the statement, some listeners heard a faint 'ghost voice' which had somehow managed to hi-jack the wavelength. As the announcer read the passage about Hitler falling as a hero, an unknown voice materialized out of the ether and said simply 'All lies!'

It was, indeed, uniquely appropriate that the German people should be fed a tissue of lies to mark the passing of the man who had caused them so much terrible sorrow. It was an act of extraordinary delusion to describe the Second World War as a struggle against Bolshevism in which Germany was the innocent and injured party, bravely battling to 'save the peoples of Europe'. Neither did Hitler fall heroically at the head of his troops, fighting to the last breath against Bolshevism. On the contrary, he took the coward's way out, locked himself in his quarters in the bunker under the Chancellery in Berlin, put the barrel of a revolver in his mouth and pulled the trigger.

The Führer had made his last public appearance on 20 April 1945, his 56th birthday. Wrapped in a greatcoat, smiling grimly, he inspected a pathetic little parade of SS troops and Hitler Jugend in the Chancellery garden. In the far distance could be heard the boom-boom of heavy artillery as Soviet troops breached the defence perimeter around the outer suburbs of the city. Hitler walked up and down the line of troops, stopped briefly to talk to a small, solemn boy in the black uniform of the Hitler Jugend, then disappeared through the steel door leading into the bunker and the fantasy world from which he now conducted the war.

On the following day, the Red Army's 6th Tank Corps overran the German High Command's abandoned headquarters at Zossen, south of Berlin. Increasingly deranged, Hitler seemed incapable of understanding the catastrophe inexorably engulfing him and from the bunker he continued to issue a stream of orders to generals of armies that no longer existed. General Karl Koller, chief of staff of the Luftwaffe, spent the entire day fielding calls from the Führer: 'In the evening between 8.30 and 9 he is again on the telephone. [He says] "The Reich Marshal [Göring] is maintaining a private army in Karinhall. Dissolve it at once and place it under SS Obergruppenführer Steiner" and he hangs up. I am still considering what this is supposed to mean when Hitler calls again: "Every available air force

man in the area between Berlin and the coast as far as Stettin and Hamburg is to
be thrown into the attack I have ordered in the north-east of Berlin". There is
no answer to my question of where the attack is supposed to take place—he has
already hung up.'[2]

Forty-eight hours after the Führer's birthday, Berlin was cut off on three sides
and Soviet tanks had been seen to the west of the shattered city. For Berliners the
situation was desperate: after the Allies' massive bombing raids, there was no water
or electricity, food supplies were almost exhausted and public order was breaking
down. Looters ransacked the huge Karstadt department store in the centre of
the city, undeterred by SS troops with orders to shoot on sight anyone suspected
of looting.

A young Berliner, a clerk by the name of Claus Fuhrmann, wrote a graphic
account of life in the beleaguered city:

'Panic had reached its peak in the city. Hordes of soldiers stationed in Berlin
deserted and were shot on the spot or hanged on the nearest tree. A few clad only
in underclothes were dangling on a tree quite near our house. On their chests
they had placards reading: "We betrayed the Führer."

'The SS men went into underground stations, picked out among the sheltering
crowds a few men whose faces they did not like, and shot them there and then.
The scourge of our district was a small one-legged *Hauptscharführer* of the SS who
stumped through the streets on crutches, a machine-pistol at the ready, followed
by his men. Anyone he didn't like the look of he instantly shot. The gang went
down cellars at random and dragged all the men outside, giving them rifles and
ordered them straight to the front. Anyone who hesitated was shot. The front was
only a few streets away.

'Everything had run out. The only water was in the cellar of a house several
streets away. To get bread one had to join a queue of hundreds, grotesquely adorned
with steel helmets, outside the baker's shop at 3 a.m. At 5 a.m. the Russian [artil-
lery] started and continued uninterruptedly until nine or ten. The crowded mass
outside the baker's shop pressed closely against the walls, but no one moved from
his place. Often hours of queueing had been spent in vain; the bread was sold
out before one reached the shop. Russian low-flying wooden biplanes machine-
gunned people as they stood apathetically in their queues and took a terrible
toll of the waiting crowds. In every street dead bodies were left lying where they
had fallen.

'At the last moment the shopkeepers who had been jealously hoarding
their stocks, not knowing how much longer they would be allowed to, now
began to sell them. A salvo of heavy calibre shells tore to pieces hundreds of
women who were waiting in the market hall. Dead and wounded alike were
flung onto wheelbarrows and carted away. The surviving women continued to wait, patient, resigned, sullen, until they had finished their miserable
shopping.

'We left the cellar at longer and longer intervals and often we could not tell whether it was night or day. The Russians drew nearer; they advanced through the underground railway tunnels, armed with flamethrowers; their advance snipers had taken up positions quite near us; and their shots ricocheted off the houses opposite. Exhausted German soldiers would stumble in and beg for water—they were practically children. I remember one with a pale, quivering face who said "We shall do it all right; we'll make our way to the north-west yet". But his eyes belied his words and he looked at me despairingly. What he wanted to say was: "Hide me, give me shelter. I've had enough of it." I should have liked to help him, but neither of us dared speak; each might have shot the other as a "defeatist".'[3]

On the afternoon of 25 April at Torgau, on the river Elbe, 75 miles from Berlin, a patrol from the US 69th Infantry Division, advancing from the west, ran into a patrol from the Russian 58th Guards Rifle Division, advancing from the east. By then Berlin was completely encircled by eight Soviet armies, which were smashing through the city's feeble defences towards the Chancellery.

The diary of an anonymous German staff officer records the last days:

'April 26. The night sky is fiery red. Heavy shelling. Otherwise a terrible silence. We are sniped at from many houses ... About 5.30 a.m. another grinding artillery barrage. The Russians attack. We have to retreat again, fighting for street after street ... New command post in the subway tunnels under Anhalt railway station. The station looks like an armed camp. Women and children huddling in niches and corners and listening for the sounds of battle.

'Shells hit the roofs, cement is crumbling from the ceiling ... People are fighting round the ladders that ran through air shafts up to the street. Water comes rushing through the tunnels. The crowds get panicky, stumble and fall over rails and sleepers. Children and wounded are deserted, people are trampled to death ...

'April 27. Continuous attack throughout the night. Increasing signs of dissolution. In the Chancellery, they say, everybody is more certain of final victory than ever before. Hardly any communications among troops, excepting a few regular battalions equipped with radio posts. Telephone cables are shot to pieces. Physical conditions are indescribable. No rest, no relief. No regular food, hardly any bread. We get water from the tunnels and filter it. The whole large expanse of Potsdamer Platz is a waste of ruins. Masses of damaged vehicles, half-smashed trailers of the ambulances with the wounded still in them. Dead people everywhere, many of them frightfully cut up by tanks and trucks ... We cannot hold our present position. At four o'clock in the morning we retreat through the underground railway tunnels. In the tunnels next to ours, the Russians march in the opposite direction to the positions we have just lost ... '[4]

Hitler was already preparing for the end. In the early hours of 29 April, in a maudlin little ceremony conducted by an official of the Propaganda Ministry, he married his mistress, Eva Braun. Some time during the morning the latest news from the outside world was brought in. It was bad: the German forces in

Italy were in full retreat and Mussolini, his partner in crime, had been captured and summarily executed by partisans. The Führer was probably not told that Mussolini and his mistress, Clara Petacci, had been suspended by their heels from the roof of a garage in Milan to be mutilated and spat on by a jeering crowd, but in any case he had already made certain that no such fate should befall him and Eva Braun. His instructions were that their bodies were to be destroyed 'so that nothing remains', adding, as if anticipating the fate of his friend the Duce, 'I will not fall into the hands of an enemy who requires a new spectacle to divert his hysterical masses.'

In the afternoon, Hitler summoned his personal surgeon to the bunker. The doctor was busy treating the many civilians wounded by shellfire but he could not, of course, ignore a summons from the Führer. When he arrived, Hitler ordered the doctor to administer poison to his favourite Alsatian, Blondi.

Later in the afternoon the Führer dictated his final messages, which included a last, bitter plea for his persecution of the Jews to continue: 'I charge the leaders of the nation and those under them to scrupulous observance of the laws of race and to merciless opposition to the universal poisoner of all peoples, international Jewry.' For his generals, whom he blamed for the defeat, he had stinging words: 'The people and the Wehrmacht have given their all in this long and hard struggle. The sacrifice has been enormous. But my trust has been misused by many people. Disloyalty and betrayal have undermined resistance throughout the war. It was therefore not granted to me to lead the people to victory. The Army General Staff cannot be compared with the General Staff of the First World War. Its achievements were far behind those of the fighting front.'

Hitler thanked his two secretaries, praised their courage and added, characteristically, that he wished his generals had been as reliable as they were. He then gave them each a poison capsule for use, *in extremis*, and apologized that he could not offer a better parting gift.

SS guards had warned all the Führer's personal staff that they were not to go to bed that night until orders had been received that they could do so. At half past two in the morning of 30 April, the staff were instructed to assemble in the bunker's dining room so that the Führer could say goodbye. Some 20 officers and women staff were lined up along the wall when Hitler entered from his private quarters, accompanied by Martin Bormann. The Führer seemed distracted, his eyes were glazed over and some who saw him assumed he was drugged. He walked down the line shaking each person by the hand, sometimes mumbling inaudibly but generally saying nothing.

Later that morning, Hitler received reports without emotion that the Russians were closing in on the Chancellery. After lunch, there was another brief farewell ceremony with those senior officers still remaining in the bunker and their wives. Hitler and Eva Braun shook hands with each of them and then returned to their own suite. Shortly before 3.30, a single shot was heard. After an interval of a few minutes, an aide entered the suite and discovered the bodies of Hitler and Eva Braun lying side by side on a blood-soaked sofa. Hitler had shot himself through the mouth with a revolver; Eva Braun had apparently taken poison.

In accordance with the Führer's orders, SS guards carried the bodies out of the bunker and laid them in the garden. With the fearsome cacophony of battle all around, the bodies were splashed with petrol from a jerry can, watched by mourners sheltering from the Russian bombardment under a porch. A petrol-soaked rag was lit and flung onto the corpses, which were instantly enveloped in flames.

On the evening of the following day, 1 May, with the fall of the city imminent, the bunker itself was set on fire and its 500 occupants dispersed as best they could through burning streets littered with rubble and bodies as the Third Reich neared its inglorious end.

'We are in the Aquarium,' the unknown German staff officer wrote in his diary. 'Shell crater on shell crater every way I look. The streets are steaming. The smell of the dead is at times unbearable ... Afternoon. We have to retreat. We put the wounded in the last armoured car we have left. All told, the division now have five tanks and four field guns. Late in the afternoon, new rumours that Hitler is dead, that surrender is being discussed. That is all. The civilians want to know whether we will break out of Berlin. If we do, they want to join us ... The Russians continue to advance underground and then come up from the tunnels somewhere behind our lines. In the intervals between the firing, we can hear the screaming of the civilians in the tunnels. Pressure is getting too heavy ... We have to retreat again ... No more anaesthetics. Every so often, women burst out of a cellar, their fists pressed over their tears, because they cannot stand the screaming of the wounded.'[5]

That afternoon, William Joyce, the notorious 'Lord Haw-Haw' whose 'Germany Calling' broadcasts had provoked such fury in Britain, recorded his last talk, apparently roaring drunk. 'We are nearing the end of one phase in Europe's history,' he said, his voice noticeably slurred, 'but the next will be no happier. It will be grimmer, harder and perhaps bloodier. And now, I ask you earnestly, can Britain survive? I am profoundly convinced that without German help she cannot ... ' There was a long pause, then he seemed to admit that it was all over. 'You may not hear from me again for a few months ... Germany is, if you will, not any more a chief factor in Europe.' After another long pause, he made a final gesture of defiance, booming: '*Es lebe Deutschland ... Heil Hitler.* And farewell.'[6]

Vladimir Rubinstein was an Estonian working for the BBC monitoring service at Evesham in Worcestershire: 'Towards the end of the war we were all so anxious to see what was going to happen that everybody was just sitting and waiting in the listening room for any kind of indication. In the last ten days of April, the whole enemy-controlled radio network in Europe began to disintegrate and split up into regional services with their own programmes.

'On 30 April, there was an announcement suddenly by two of the radio services, the south-western and the south-eastern services, I think, saying a very, very
important statement was going to be broadcast tonight. There was terrific excitement and all the staff began to come in from other departments and collect in the
listening room. The whole listening room was full and extremely noisy and we
repeatedly had to say to them, "Shut up, for God's sake!" because nobody could
hear anything. We had no idea what it was going to be about, just that it was
extremely important.

'People were milling around, all waiting, and nothing happened! We sat and
sat and absolutely nothing occurred. There was supposed to be something by
11 o'clock in the evening and still nothing happened. So the whole thing was a
flop. Nothing happened, so everybody dispersed.

'Then the next day one of the people working in the monitoring service was
Sir Ernst Gombrich, the famous art historian. It was towards evening and he
suddenly realized that the radio had started playing a Bruckner symphony, very
solemn music. He said, "That seems very strange" and started to prepare himself. In those days, when you monitored a broadcast, if you had something very
urgent, to avoid leaving the set unattended, you would write it down on a bit of
paper and give it to the next person to run off to either the news bureau or information bureau, from where it was teleprinted or telephoned straight through to
No 10 Downing St or the War Office.

'So Gombrich prepared two or three notes for himself, alternative things that
he thought might happen: Hitler dead, Hitler taken prisoner, or Hitler escapes.
Then there came the announcement, and while everybody held their breath
Gombrich picked up the "Hitler dead" note.'

Harold Nicolson MP was dining at his club, Prat's. 'Lionel Berry [son of Lord
Kemsley] was there,' he wrote in a letter to his son, Nigel. 'He told us that the
German wireless had been putting out *Achtungs* about an *ernste wichtige Meldung*,
and playing dirges in between. So we tried and failed to get the German wireless
stations with the horrible little set which is all that Prat's can produce. Having
failed to do this, we asked Lionel to go upstairs to telephone one of his numerous
newspapers, and he came running down again (it was 10.40) to say that Hitler was
dead and Dönitz had been appointed his successor. Then ... I returned to King's
Bench Walk and listened to the German midnight news. It was all too true.' *Unser
Führer, Adolf Hitler, ist* ... and then a long digression about heroism and the ruin
of Berlin ... *gefallen.*' So that was Mussolini and Hitler within two days. Not bad
as bags go.'[7]

Inevitably, the news of Hitler's death made banner headlines in all the morning
newspapers the following day, along with encouraging reports from the front of
the Allies' progress. Russians troops were said to be at the Brandenburg Gate in
the centre of Berlin, having taken 14,000 prisoners in the previous day's fighting. The British Second Army was only 18 miles from Lübeck and poised to cut

off the enemy's only escape route from the advancing Russians. The American Seventh Army had cleared Munich and was pushing into the Austrian Alpine passes while the US Third Army had reached the Czech frontier.

Such was the mood of confidence in the country, that all the newspapers also reported the progress of the arrangements for VE Day, in particular a circular letter issued by the Home Office expressing the government's sober views on the form that national celebrations should take. It was a poignant reflection of the austerity that still went hand in hand with victory:

'His Majesty's Government have had under consideration the way in which the defeat of the enemy in Europe should be celebrated. The end of the war in Europe will not be the end of the struggle and there should be no relaxation of the national effort until the war in the Far East has been won. It will, however, be the general desire of the nation to celebrate the victorious end of the European campaigns before turning with renewed energy to the completion of the tasks before it.

'Accordingly, as already announced, the day on which the cessation of organized resistance is announced, which will generally be known as VE Day and the day following, will be public holidays … The cessation of hostilities in Europe will be announced by the Prime Minister over the wireless and His Majesty the King will address his people throughout the world at nine pm the same day. It is the wish of his Majesty the King that the Sunday following VE Day should be observed as a day of thanksgiving and prayer.

'In view of the shortage of fuel, materials and labour, it is still necessary to observe economy in the consumption of fuel and light and the government regret that they will not be able, even on VE Day, to agree to the restoration of full street lighting.

'Except in the coastal areas in which dim-out or black-out restrictions are still maintained, they will, however, raise no objection to the use on the VE night or the succeeding night by local authorities and public bodies of such flood-lighting facilities as exist and can be brought into use. In addition, the Armed Forces will make available for illumination purposes such lighting as can be spared.

'Bonfires will be allowed, but the government trust that the paramount necessity of ensuring that only material with no salvage value is used and the desirability of proper arrangements with the National Fire Service to guard against any possible spread of fire will be borne in mind by those arranging bonfires.

'In view of the pressure on public transport generally throughout the country it seems to the government desirable that facilities for indoor entertainment should be available as widely as possible. They would not suggest that theatres, music halls and cinemas should remain open later than the hours prevailing before VE Day, but, provided that adequate staffs can be made available, they hope that the managements of theatres, music halls and cinemas will keep their premises open until the usual hour.

'As regards premises licensed for public dancing, the government think that these might be allowed to remain open later than the normal closing hour … '

Pub landlords throughout the country were obviously anticipating big business on VE Day, since the circular letter continued: 'Licensing authorities for the sale of intoxicating liquors are already receiving applications from licence holders for special orders of exemption, or special permission in respect of VE Day, from the requirements as to permitted hours. His Majesty's government suggest that advance individual applications for special orders of exemption or special permission for an extension of the evening permitted hours on VE Day should receive sympathetic consideration in the light of local circumstances … '

However, such aberrant behaviour as drinking in the afternoon was certainly not to be countenanced in a country which considered such Gallic habits to be especially sinful, and neither would any relaxation in the licensing laws extend beyond VE Day. 'No exemptions should be granted in respect of the afternoon "break", nor should applications be entertained in general for any special order of exemption or special permission on the day following VE Day.

'So that the essential requirements of the public be met, the government recommend that businesses selling and distributing food should remain open for a few hours on VE Day to enable the public to get supplies and, subject to maintaining the sale or delivery of essential commodities such as bread, milk and rations, close on the following day. They appreciate this will mean some inconvenience to those engaged in these essential services, though it is understood holidays in lieu will be granted under trade agreements.

'On Thanksgiving Sunday His Majesty's government think it appropriate that local authorities should organize victory parades either with the local service of thanksgiving or later in the day.

'In addition to such representation of the Armed Forces as can be arranged with the local commander, the local authorities will no doubt wish to include all those associated with the wide range of the Civil Defence Services, the National Fire Service, the Fire Guard, the Police, the Women's Land Army, war workers of all categories, and members of various youth organizations and voluntary societies.' [8]

No such preparations were, it seemed, being made in the United States. On the same day the disbelieving British were being told that the pubs could stay open to midnight on VE Day, that the London County Council was organizing floodlit dancing in no less than eight different parks and that hundreds of London policemen had been put on stand-by for extra duty on the great day, in Washington President Truman expressed the hope that there would be no celebrations in the United States, only a 'national understanding of the importance of the job which remains'. The White House issued a statement promising that the President would address the nation over the radio 'in the event of the end of the war in Europe', but emphasized that the statement was not intended to suggest that the end was imminent.

It was a curious reversal of the commonly accepted characteristics of each nation. The Americans had become unusually guarded and cautious; the British had become infected with the kind of heady optimism frequently found across the Atlantic.

For most people, the death of Hitler was another nail driven firmly in the coffin of the Reich, although considerable scepticism remained. It was understandable enough: in the previous six months there had been frequent rumours that the Führer was dead, only to be scotched by his strutting appearance at a Nazi rally or some other public function where those present could attest that he was all too alive. One in four of the people questioned by Mass Observation stated simply that they did not believe Hitler was dead. Many of them ventured the view that it was part of some dastardly plot to help him escape:

'Saying Hitler's dead and playing a funeral march over the radio, I don't believe that tale, do you? The papers talk as if he was, but I think it's more likely a lie while he gets away. The more you think it over the more it sounds all wrong.'

'What again? I'm fed up with hearing that bloke's dead.'

'I don't believe he's dead at all. He's hidden away in the mountains, and he'll come out again in a few years' time, and start another war … He'll find a way, he's cunning. We haven't heard the last of him, you'll see.'

Even those inclined to believe that the Führer had departed this life, suspected that there was probably some chicanery involved:

'I think if he *is* dead, he died when there was that attempt on his life. But he's got five doubles, you see, so that you can't quite tell.'

'I don't believe he died fighting. They just said that to make it seem more, you know, the way he'd have wanted people to think he died. But I think personally he's been out of the way for a long time now. The last time he spoke he didn't sound the same man at all. He sounded very ill. I think he's been dead for a long time now, or at at least too ill to count for anything.'

A considerable number of respondents offered the opinion that death was 'far too good' for someone like Adolf and described in lurid detail what they would like to have done to him had they had the opportunity to get their hands on him. Many of the most bloodthirsty accounts came from women:

'It's too good a death for him, that's all I can say. If I'd had my hands on him he wouldn't have died that easy. I wouldn't have finished him off quickly like that, I'd have cut off little bits of him, one at a time, until he was dead.'

What most of the sceptics wanted was evidence:

'They say Hitler's dying. What I want to know is, who says so? How do we know it's Hitler? Whose word can we trust? They said weeks ago that he was going to fly to South America. I won't believe that man's dead until I see his dead body on the pictures.'

'Ooh, the rumours! Hitler's dead. Hitler's not dead but he's dying. Hitler's only having his face lifted. Some people say Churchill will announce peace on the nine o'clock news tonight. Oh, they're saying *everything*! My ears are dropping off with the rumours I've heard. The one thing you can take for certain is that Mussolini's dead.'[9]

That was undeniably true, because the newspapers on the morning of Tuesday 1 May were full of grisly pictures of his body, and that of his mistress, hanging upside down in Milan for the ghoulish entertainment of passers-by.

Harold Nicolson was among many who found the pictures thoroughly distasteful: 'We had really dreadful photographs of his [Mussolini's] corpse and that of his mistress hanging upside down and side by side. They looked like turkeys hanging outside a poulterer's: the slim legs of his mistress and the huge stomach of Mussolini could both be detected. It was a most unpleasant picture and caused a grave reaction in his favour. It was truly ignominious—but Mrs Groves [Nicolson's housekeeper] said that he deserved it thoroughly, "a married man like that driving about in a car with his mistress".' [10]

Clara Petacci was a curious focus of people's interest, although there was precious little sympathy either for her or her lover:

'There was a wonderful account in the *Daily Worker* of Mussolini's death, how he was shot in the head and his brain spattered out, and he looked awful, but his mistress was hanged beside him in a new white blouse and looked lovely.'

'Some woman in the office looked at a picture of Mussolini's death and all she said was "Nice legs, hasn't she?"'

Those who professed to be shocked were not so much disgusted by the deaths as by the reaction of the Italians:

'I was absolutely horrified about the Italians, the way they took revenge on Mussolini. I can't imagine what we're fighting for, if that's the way the anti-Fascists behave. I was just reading in the paper that they hung them up in the most lewd, indecent positions, and spat at them, and threw stones. *And* laughed. The Italian people don't seem to feel any horror at this either. I think it is just too ghastly for words.' [11]

Briefly among the crowd jeering and spitting at the bodies was a 19-year-old captain in the Devonshire Regiment by the name of Alan Whicker, who would later make a considerable name for himself as a television personality. In May 1945, Whicker was attached to an Army Film and Photo Section in Italy and he remembers the day of Mussolini's death as pretty hectic:

'I had a marvellous big Italian car that I had liberated after the capture of Rome and myself and a couple of sergeants drove across the Apennines into Verona and Milan. I think we were the first people into Milan and we got a reasonably enthusiastic reception as we drove into the cathedral square, although there weren't a lot of people about because they thought there was going to be a lot of fighting.

'The first thing that happened in the square in front of the Duomo was some partisans came up in a great state of excitement. All these chaps emerge from the long grass as soon as the fuss is over and they said there was a hotel full of

Germans just round the corner. They were the last Germans in Milan and they were refusing to surrender to the partisans, not unreasonably I suppose. They were insisting on surrendering to an Allied officer, and as I was the only one around I thought I better go there.

'I followed the partisans down a road, not too far from La Scala, and there was this bloody great hotel surrounded by barbed wire and armed SS guards. The general in command who was insisting he would only surrender to an Allied officer was rather disappointed when he saw my lowly rank. Nevertheless, he presented me with his Walther revolver and surrendered the hotel full of SS men. He could speak good English and said he didn't want to surrender to "this rabble", indicating the partisans who were shouting and getting very excited on the other side of the barbed wire. I must say I had a sneaking sympathy for him. I didn't bother to disarm them, I mean for them the war was over and I could see they were finished, but they were very anxious to show me things and made a lot of fuss about handing over a tin box, which didn't interest me very much because I had other worries on my mind. But when we opened the box we found it was full of money, every known banknote you can imagine. I thought, my God I could be a mega millionaire. I don't know where the money came from and I never did discover what happened to it.

'I knew there were some American troops arriving soon because we had overtaken them as we were driving in, so I just accepted the surrender and waited. After two or three hours some American tanks arrived and I handed my hotel full of SS men over to them.

'Afterwards I went to a radio station and asked them to put out a call for John Amery. Amery was the son of Leopold Amery, the secretary of state for India, and was the Lord Haw Haw of Italy. During war he had been the traitorous voice of Fascism. A message went out and within half an hour I got a call from a chap in charge of a jail who said that Amery had been arrested and was in his prison. I went over there. He was with his very pretty Italian girl friend and was very grateful I arrived because he thought he was going to be killed by the partisans. Before I arranged to hand him over to the military police I had a talk with him. He said, "I've never been anti-British, you can read the scripts of my broadcasts over years and you'll never find anything anti-British; I am just very anti-Communist. At the moment maybe I've been proved wrong, but in the future you may think I was right." He was a pleasant, intelligent man. After he was repatriated to Britain, he stood trial at the Old Bailey for treason, was convicted and hanged.

'Later that day we discovered Mussolini had been shot and hung up in a garage with his girl friend. We went over there and took pictures of them. A Milanese mob was baying, spitting and screaming at the bodies. I still have a terrible picture of Mussolini hanging upside down in that garage.

'Although the war was virtually at an end in Italy, everything was all falling to pieces and they were all giving up everywhere. I don't remember celebrating at all.

There was a very exhilarating spirit because one was alive after having been through some very hairy times, but one was too busy to celebrate. I just remember having a hell of a day and driving back to Verona to get all my pictures away. It was quite a crowded day for a 19-year-old.'

It was the pictures that convinced the world that Mussolini was dead and the lack of pictures that created such scepticism about the death of Hitler, at least in Britain. In Germany, people were eager to accept the news as an indication that their suffering would soon be over. Only a few die-hard Nazis would grieve over the passing of the Führer; most Germans experienced more relief than grief.

This was certainly the case for the British-born writer Christabel Bielenberg, who was living with her German husband, Peter, and their three sons in Rohrbach, an isolated village in the Black Forest. Peter Bielenberg had been in hiding, having been arrested after the failure of the bomb plot against Hitler in July 1944. He spent seven months in Ravensbrück and was then assigned to a punishment squad in the army, from which he had escaped to join his wife and family in Rohrbach.

By 1 May the area around Rohrbach was occupied by the Allies. Christabel described their reaction to Hitler's death like this: 'The news reached us as we sat around the stove in the *gute Stube* of the Gasthaus Adler listening to the wireless which was our only remaining link with the outside world. Since the arrival of the French in our little local town of Furtwangen, the Adler had recovered something of its pre-war repute and become once more a rallying point for many bewildered Rohrbach villagers, eager to pick up the latest rumour, eager if possible to hear the latest news, although Frau Muckle's ancient contraption gurgling and whistling away in the corner seemed sometimes as confused as we were as to quite which programmes we were listening to. Allied? German? To which side did all those voices at present belong? Which version were we supposed to believe, as day by day more German townships, further chunks of German land were overrun, changed hands and passed under the control of American, British, Russian and French armies?

'This time the wireless seemed certain of its message. (There had been plenty of rumours, but this was a certainty.) It gave no details as to where, how and when, but just crackled out something about Hitler (the Fuehrer), having first appointed Admiral Doenitz to be his successor, had made up his mind to die a hero's death and had done so.

'A sudden stillness came over the room as the message petered out along with the usual mechanical convulsions. Perhaps even the death of a devil casts a certain spell, for by force of habit some crossed themselves while others just stared at the stove, some took the odd sip from one of the lemonade bottles which Frau Muckle had managed to provide for our entertainment, others puffed on pipes filled with tobacco left behind by the departing German Wehrmacht. Only the measured clacking of the cuckoo clock on the wall behind us interrupted the silence …

'So that was it; he was dead. Although bombers still droned occasionally over-head, reminding us that some parts of Germany still had to pass through the final ordeal, he, Hitler, was gone. It could not be long now before the *coup de grâce*, the final knock-out-blow, was administered to his mad dream of creating a Thousand Year Reich, empty of all but pure-bred Germans; round blond heads, glowing blue eyes, Aryans one and all, oh dear.

'But we, Peter and I, and our three sons and the good friends around us were alive, we had outlived him. He had not managed to drag us off with him to some preposterous make-believe Valhalla. So perhaps it was for that reason the silence was suddenly broken and we found ourselves glancing at each other, pushing back our stools, starting to our feet and moving eagerly from one to another in order to hold hands, to embrace, to celebrate, one survivor with another.' [12]

On the other side of Germany, the reaction of a group of German prisoners of war was not dissimilar. Charles Wheeler, the distinguished BBC foreign cor-respondent, was then a young captain in the Royal Marines attached to 30 Assault Unit, a special naval intelligence commando unit charged with tracking down German equipment and inventions which might be of use to the Allies, and find-ing scientists and technicians who might have expertise that could be utilized after the war:

'For several weeks we had been driving through villages and towns with white bed linen hanging out of the windows, meaning white flags, to indicate that the fight was over. On whole, people were very anxious to surrender. I was heading for Hamburg, which I knew quite well because I had been brought up there—my father had a job there with a British shipping company.

'At that time it was very difficult to tell whether the war had ended or not; I don't think anybody knew. It ended at different times in different places. We weren't sure and I don't think the Germans were either. It was largely a matter of persuading them the war was over and there was no point in fighting on. Some anticipated the end of the war and surrendered early; others had to be persuaded.

'On the day Hitler's death was announced—I think I heard it on the BBC—I happened to be in a large PoW camp somewhere outside Hamburg. I could speak pretty good German and I asked the army officer in charge of the camp if anyone had told the prisoners. He said no and so I asked if I could. There must have been about 1,000 German prisoners standing there behind barbed wire in the rain. It was what they called a cage—basically just a gathering place enclosed by a couple of strands of barbed wire where prisoners could be held until they were properly sorted out.

'I got up on the roof of a truck, shouted for silence and then I told them, in German, that the Führer was dead. I'll never forget their reaction. First there was a long silence, probably about four seconds, then someone in the crowd started to clap slowly and rather uncertainly. Then someone else joined him, then more, and then the whole lot started clapping together and cheering wildly.

'At that time the German army was terribly demoralized, very much in retreat and surrendering in large numbers. Nevertheless the reaction was quite surprising. I think those prisoners were basically looking forward to the war ending and getting home.'

Wednesday 2 May

Before the Euphoria, the Horror

Early in the morning of Wednesday 2 May, workmen began erecting an exhibition in Trafalgar Square which had been sponsored by the *Daily Express*. On the outside of the hoarding were the words SEEING IS BELIEVING. Inside were blown-up images from photographs taken at Belsen, Buchenwald and Nordhausen.

That same day, newsreel cinemas throughout the country began screening stark black and white film of the terrible discoveries that had been made by the Allied troops advancing into Germany. Most people knew that concentration camps existed; few could possibly have imagined what went on within those camps. The truth was, indeed, unimaginable.

On 12 April a German emissary carrying a white flag was allowed through British 2nd Army lines just outside the little town of Bergen-Belsen in northern Germany, between Hanover and Hamburg. He explained that the whole area ahead was infected by a typhus epidemic and proposed that both sides should keep clear of it in order to prevent the disease from spreading. The Allies rejected the proposal. They knew there was a camp at Belsen and insisted on inspecting it. Eventually a local truce was arranged and 2nd Army sent a contingent of troops, including a Field Hygiene Section, forward to take charge of the camp. Close behind was BBC correspondent Richard Dimbleby, whose misfortune it was to be the first reporter into Belsen.

For the first time in his life, he broke down as he began to record this dispatch to send back to London: 'I passed through the barrier and found myself in the world of a nightmare. Dead bodies, some of them in decay, lay strewn about the road and along the rutted track. On each side of the road were brown wooden huts. There were faces at the windows, the bony emaciated faces of starving women too weak to come outside, propping themselves against the glass to see the light before they died. And they *were* dying, every hour, every minute. I *saw* a man, wandering dazedly along the road, stagger and fall. Someone else looked down at him, took him by the heels and dragged him to the side of the road to join the other bodies lying unburied there. No one else took the slightest notice—they didn't even trouble to turn their heads. Behind the huts two youths and two girls who had found a morsel of food were sitting together in the grass in picnic fashion, sharing it. They were not six feet from a pile of decomposing bodies.

'Inside the huts it was even worse. I have seen many terrible sights in the last five years, but *nothing, nothing*, approaching the dreadful interior of this hut at Belsen. The dead and dying lay close together. I picked my way over corpse after corpse in the gloom, until I heard one voice that rose above the undulating moaning. I found a girl—she was a living skeleton—impossible to gauge her age, for she had practically no hair left on her head and her face was only a yellow parchment sheet with two holes in it for eyes. She was stretching out her stick of an arm and gasping for something. It was "Englisch—Englisch—medicine—medicine" and she was trying to cry, but had not enough strength. And beyond her, down the passage and in the hut, there were the convulsive movements of dying people too weak to raise themselves from the floor. They were crawling with lice and smeared with filth. They had had no food for days, for the Germans sent it into the camp en bloc and only those strong enough to come out of the huts could get it. The rest of them lay there in the shadows growing weaker and weaker. There was no one to take out the bodies when they died and I had to look hard to see who was alive and who was dead. It was the same outside, in the compounds and between the huts. Men and women lying about the ground with the rest of the procession of ghosts aimlessly around them.

'In the shade of some trees lay a great collection of bodies. I walked round them, trying to count—there were perhaps 150, flung down on each other. All naked, all so thin that their yellow skins glistened like stretched rubber on their bones. Some of the poor, starved creatures whose bodies were there looked so utterly unreal and inhuman that I could have imagined they had never lived. They were like polished skeletons—the skeletons that medical students like to play practical jokes with. At one end of the pile a cluster of men and women were gathered round a fire. They were using rags and old shoes taken from the bodies to keep it alight and were heating soup on it. Close by was the enclosure where 500 children between the ages of five and twelve had been kept. They were not so hungry as the rest, for the women had sacrificed themselves to keep them alive.

'Babies were born at Belsen—some of them shrunken wizened little things that could not live because their mothers could not feed them. One woman, distraught to the point of madness, flung herself at a British soldier who was on guard in the camp on the night it was reached by the 11th Amoured Division. She begged for him to give her some milk for the tiny baby she held in her arms. She laid the mite on the ground, threw herself at the sentry's feet and kissed his boots. When in his distress, he asked her to get up, she put the baby in his arms and ran off crying that she would find milk for it because there was no milk in her breasts. When the soldier opened the bundle of rags to look at the child he found it had been dead for days ...

'As we went deeper into the camp, further from the main gate, we saw more and more of the horrors of the place, and I realised that what is so ghastly is not so much the individual acts of barbarism that take place in SS camps, but the gradual breakdown of civilisation that happens when humans are herded like animals behind barbed wire. Here in Belsen we were seeing people, many of them lawyers, doctors, chemists, musicians, authors, who had long since ceased to care about the conventions or the customs of normal life. There had been no privacy of any kind. Women stood naked at the side of the truck washing in cupfuls of water taken from British Army water trucks—others squatted while they searched themselves for lice and examined each other's hair. Sufferers from dysentery leaned against the huts, straining helplessly and all around and about them was this awful drifting tide of exhausted people, neither caring nor watching. Just a few held out their withered hands to us as we passed by and blessed the doctor whom they knew had become the camp commander in the place of the brutal Kramer.

'We were on our way down to the crematorium where the Germans burned alive thousands of men and women in a single fire. The furnace was in a hut, about the size of a single garage, and the hut was surrounded by a small stockade. A little Pole, whose prison number was tattooed on the inside of his forearm as it was on all the others, told me how they burned the people. They brought them into the stockade, walked them in. Then a SS guard hit them on the back of the neck with a club and stunned them. Then they were fed straight into the fire, three at a time—two men and one woman; the opening was not big enough for three men ... They burned ten thousand people in this fire in reprisal for the murder of two SS guards.

'Back in the hut by the main gate of the camp, I questioned the sergeant who had been in charge of one SS squad. He was a fair-headed, gangling creature, with tiny, crooked ears—rather like Goebbels—and big hands. His SS uniform was undone and dirty. He was writing out his confession while a young north-country anti-tank gunner of the 11th Armoured Division kept watch on him with a tommy gun that never moved. I asked him how many people *he* had killed. He looked vacant for a moment—and then replied "Oh, I don't remember".

'I have set down these facts at length because in common with all of us who have been in the camp, I feel that you should be told without reserve exactly what has been happening there. Every fact I have so far given you has been verified, but there is one more awful than the others, that I have kept to the end. Far away in the corner of Belsen camp there is a pit the size of a tennis court. It is fifteen feet deep and it is piled to the very top with naked bodies that have been tumbled in one on top of the other. Like this must have been the plague pits in England three hundred years ago, only nowadays we can help by digging them quicker with bulldozers and already there's a bulldozer at work in Belsen. Our Army doctors, examining some of the bodies, found in their sides a long slit, apparently made by someone with surgical knowledge. They made inquiries established beyond doubt that in the frenzy of their starvation, the people of Belsen have taken the wasted bodies of their fellow prisoners and removed from them the only remaining flesh—the liver and kidneys—to eat.

'May I add to this story only the assurance that everything that an army can do to save these men and women and children is being done and that those officers and men who have seen these things have gone back to the Second Army moved to an anger such as I have never seen in them before.'[1]

When Dimbleby's report was received in London, BBC editors, unable to believe what they had heard, refused to broadcast it until it had been verified by the newspapers. Outraged, Dimbleby telephoned Broadcasting House and swore he would never make another broadcast unless it was transmitted at once.

Newspapers in Britain gave massive coverage to the discovery of the camp at Belsen and those at Buchenwald and Dachau, where American soldiers, unhinged by what they had witnessed, machine-gunned 120 SS guards. Such was the nature of the pictures which came out of the camps that many editors felt the need to justify, in the leader columns, their publication.

The *Daily Mirror* was typically pugnacious. 'We are glad those horrifying pictures which show some of the abominations practised in German concentration camps have been published. We hope that any more of a similar character will be given even more prominence ... There are still too many people who fail to appreciate what has been going on all these years; people who find the truth "difficult to believe". Perhaps they will be less sceptical now ... When the stupid soft-hearts attempt to draw a distinction between the Nazi war-makers and torturers and the German people as a whole, we must remember that the hundreds of thousands, nay millions, of fanatics and sadists who have committed or ordered these crimes are all Teutons. Germany bred them. A race that can produce so much foulness must itself be foul. To cleanse this stable of its moral filth will be a tremendous task. Revenge we do not seek. Cruelty is alien to our creed. But purge the world of this evil growth we must and shall!'[2]

Despite all this, the newsreels still came as a terrible shock. No still photograph could convey the ghastly bestiality of the camps in the way that the newsreels could. This was the reaction of a 21-year-old woman emerging from the New Gallery Cinema in Chelsea: 'Of course I expected it to be terrible, but it's much *more* terrible, not because of the piles of corpses—after all, they're dead—but because of the survivors. They just aren't human any more. They don't talk together—they just go about with their eyes on the ground. I think the worst moment of all was when one of these skeletons tried to smile at an American soldier—you know, his face simply couldn't express a smile any more. The audience were deathly quiet; not a whisper. Some of it's shown without commentary and I've never heard such a hush as there was all over the cinema.'[3]

She was among many in the audience most affected by the pathetic survivors, or at least by those who were still clinging to life when the film was shot. As another woman explained: 'The ones who are still alive just aren't human any more, they're dead already as human beings. I think that's the most terrible part of all. I hear that some of the most hopeless cases are just being quietly put to sleep—there's nothing else to be done with the poor wretches.'[4]

It was hardly surprising that it was all too much for many people, as Mass Observation reported:

'Investigator went to see the film at the Newsreel Cinema in Victoria. She arrived at the end of a Donald Duck film, saw the news first and the atrocity film at the end. The audience was intensely still throughout the latter film. No words were spoken. There were occasional sniffs, as of people restraining tears but blowing their noses, and several sounds of sharp in-breathing, particularly as the skeleton-like bodies of those still just alive were shown. A very large number of the audience got up and went out at the end of the film, and from over-heard comments ("Don't let's stay for this, I don't want to see it"; "Let's go now.") Investigator formed the impression that many found it distasteful to see a Donald Duck film immediately after the horror film. They filed down the staircase fairly silently; in the case of five couples, the men were holding the women by the arm or half supporting them; one woman of about 35 was covering her eyes with her hands; several others were dabbing their eyes or using their handkerchiefs. Several men blew their noses violently. One man aged about 45 murmured "Ghastly, really ghastly" to his female companion, whose hand was pressed to her forehead in an anguished way. Another man was heard to say "And they've not shown the worst by a long way".'

This was a theme taken up in a discussion by some of the audience on a bus back to Chelsea. One woman was indignant that the film had been censored: 'I know several people who have seen the whole thing and I think it's ridiculous, handling the public in this kid-glove way. They should show the whole thing, and nothing else, in special programmes in all the newsreel cinemas, and they shouldn't mix it up with Donald Duck or any light relief at all. The majority of people are neither squeamish nor sadistic, and they can stand the full truth. And the deeper the impression it makes the better. People *must* stop saying about horrors "It's just propaganda". I used to get excited and worked up about the government white papers on the subject, and I kept telling people about them, but they wouldn't listen: I heard that parrot cry "Mere propaganda" over and over again.'[5]

The incongruous pairing of Disney cartoons ('some damn silly film called *The Three Stooges*, or something') with documentaries of such stunning barbarity was crass. The idea was to offer audiences some light relief, but it backfired: 'I went with an American friend to see the atrocity film at that little newsreel cinema near Trafalgar Square and I thought it was very badly arranged indeed. For one thing, though the film's terrible, it's very short—too short to be properly convincing, and of course you know quite well that the worst shots have been cut out. And then it's followed up by a Walt Disney, and that sort of removes any impression it made—people are laughing again within a minute. And it's all mixed up with a propaganda film about "Noble London" and how wonderful Londoners were in the blitz. Being with an American, well, I can only say I felt thoroughly ashamed of the whole thing.'[6]

The journalist and MP, Tom Driberg, had been a member of the parliamentary delegation sent out to inspect Belsen and Buchenwald and was not unnaturally infuriated when he heard a report from Bournemouth that some people were reluctant to believe the newsreels.

Driberg, never a man to mince words, had a weekly column in *Reynolds News* and he gave Bournemouth both barrels:

'Last week I tried to convey what those of us who were members of the Parliamentary Delegation had seen and heard and felt during our visit to Buchenwald camp.

'Since then many of you may have seen the newsreels of the visit. Fragmentary as they are, I think they indicate something of the atmosphere of the place. I hear from Bournemouth, however, that when the film was shown there "not a few came out saying it was all a fake and they did not believe a word of it".

'Bournemouth is a less starkly uncomfortable place to live in than Buchenwald, but even at Bournemouth there must be many people less deaf, blind and mulish than this.

'Such incredulity is really itself mere credulousness: people who would believe that those pictures—of the dead and of the living dead—could be faked, and the MPs induced to connive at the imposture, would believe anything.'[7]

Almost the first person in Britain to view any of the cine footage from the camps was 24-year-old Private Peter Ustinov of the Royal Army Ordnance Corps. Private Ustinov had spent most of his service making propaganda films for the Army, which suited him very well since he had dual German and British nationality and since at that time under German law, it was not possible for him to renounce his German nationality, had he fallen into enemy hands he would almost certainly have been executed as a traitor:

'At the end of the war I was engaged by SHAEF to record the English commentaries on the official film of the War in the West, which was made up of documentaries coming in from the front. It was very convenient as I was living in Knightsbridge and the head of censorship had an office in a street near Claridges. I had to go in every morning and watch the films as they came in, so I was aware of the concentration camps almost before anybody. I saw the horrifying results from Army cameramen going into Belsen and other places, including a lot of stuff that was obviously cut out later. We saw it all without sound of course, which made it even more dramatic.

'The film from the concentration camps was absolutely awful, awful because it was not over-stated. One saw a sergeant coming out from Belsen and ordering his troops to fall out and have a smoke. He was obviously playing for time but one didn't realise why yet and then he called them back to order and had them enter Belsen at a sort of slow march, as though it was a parade, and one after another fell out and vomited. One saw an old German, he must have been a private in his 50s, sitting there with the flaps of his cap down—he looked really like a very old gundog—and suddenly a British private ran over, picked him up and kicked him and punched him and kicked him until he was pulled off by other soldiers the sergeant had called to his assistance. So one saw very dramatically the automatic effect it had on people. The inmates were just watching glumly, they had no energy to do anything else. It revolted me that human beings could be treated that way, although one knew that they were very inhuman, the Nazis.

'People had heard rumours about the existence of the concentration camps, of course. It is now assumed that everybody knew about them all the time, that there were no Germans who didn't know, but I think that is absolutely wrong. They forget that news travelled very much more slowly in those days and was never confirmed. There was no television. Since there were very few survivors and since from the beginning of the war very few people who went into a camp came out again, I think very few people did know. The notion that everyone knew is extremely exaggerated and very unfortunate because it makes a consciousness of war crimes almost co-evil with their occurrence and I don't think that's true.'

Even after the war, many Germans found it hard to believe what had been happening in their country. Renate Heinsohn was a 14-year-old schoolgirl when the war broke out and a few years later got a job as a secretary in a regional administration office of the Nazi party. She did not know anything about the concentration camps and when she was told about them she simply didn't believe it. 'I didn't know about Belsen until well after the war. Some time later in 1945, because I had worked for the Nazi party I was forced to go and see the documentary film about the camps. My mother volunteered to come with me. I don't remember it too clearly, except I know when I came out I said I thought it was a load of lies; it couldn't have been true. I thought it was more propaganda, but this time by the Allies. The thing was, we were so accustomed to the propaganda machine, to being told lies throughout the war, that I thought it was more lies. My mother told me to be quiet, but I never could keep my mouth shut so I just told everyone that I definitely didn't believe it.'

Hannelore Hoffmeister was a *Mischling*, a child of mixed parentage; her mother was Aryan but her father was a Jew. In 1945 she was 26 years old and working in an office in Hamburg: 'We were not supposed to discuss the war, but I was lucky because I worked in a firm where people discussed the war very openly, the different incidents, what had happened, the huge lies they were telling us.

'There was a lot of talk about the camps. We knew that these weren't simply work camps, that they were camps where people were murdered because no one who was sent there ever came back. You couldn't talk freely about this, but in certain close circles we would discuss it. I think a great many people were wondering about these places and what went on there.'

'The only thing I ever heard about camps,' said Dr Hans Dietrich, then the 26-year-old commanding officer of an E-boat, 'was that the mentally disturbed were being killed by euthanasia. I heard it from my Number One on the E-boat and he said he had heard it in 1941 from his father. Otherwise I knew nothing about the concentration camps, although, of course, I know many people say this now.'

Dietrich's E-boat had struck a mine shortly after midnight on 7 June 1944. Clinging to a raft at daybreak he saw hundreds of Allied aircraft droning overhead to support the Normandy invasion. He was picked up around noon by a British minesweeper, transferred to an American tank-landing craft off one of the American beaches and eventually sent to a prisoner-of-war camp in the United States. When war ended, just under a year later, he was in a camp in Dermott, Arkansas.

'On the ship on the way over to America, we had a choice of the meals we were served, it was amazing. We thought this was being done to make us write home and say that life in America was marvellous, that you should all give up and become prisoners of war. There seemed no other explanation. It was unbelievable.

'Once in a prison camp in America, I accepted that the war was now over for me and that there was no chance of escape. In our camp, there were no efforts to escape and I believe that only few escapes were attempted in any of the camps. I think someone made it as far as Mexico.

'We listened to the American radio and read newspapers. We had free access to them and so were quite well informed as far as American sources were concerned. We realized gradually what was happening in Germany because more and more German officer prisoners were coming to this camp and bringing information.

'Right after the end of the war, when we were still in the camp in Arkansas, they sent us into the cinema, all of us, and we had to see this film, about Belsen, about the hundreds of dead. More than half the people in the cinema laughed and called out that this was not believable, that this was simply war propaganda.

'When the film was over, they let us out one by one and asked us how we felt about it and from our responses, they must have realized we didn't believe it, that they couldn't convince the people this way.'

The war correspondent Alan Moorehead, with the advanced Allied forces in Germany, made a point of asking every German he could what they knew about the camps and always got the same reply—no one knew anything. 'A German newspaper editor in Hamburg raised the subject himself. "I have been wanting to meet someone who can tell me, are these stories coming out on the radio about Belsen and Nordhausen really true? Everyone here thinks they must be Allied propaganda."

'At Schneverdingen I said to a garage proprietor: "How do you explain these fifty Russian bodies in the open grave outside the town?" "Oh I know about that," he replied. "It was a train-load of foreigners going through three days ago. It stopped here and the guards dumped off these bodies. I refused to let my wife look. No, I didn't know what it was all about and it was not wise to inquire."'[8]

Understandably, the liberators of the camps found ignorance hard to believe. How could people living nearby not know what was going on? Corporal Howard Katzander, a staff correspondent for *Yank*, the US Army's weekly newspaper, came away from a nightmarish visit to Buchenwald, near Weimar, highly distressed and convinced of the complicity of ordinary people. 'I have no further sympathy for the Germans as a nation or race. Some people talk about differentiating between Hitlerites and the people of Germany. There is no difference.

'Besides, although this place was well guarded to keep the towns people away, many of the prisoners worked in the Weimar factories. They collapsed of hunger at their benches and no one asked why. They died along the road on the long walk back to the camp and no one expressed surprise. The people of Weimar shut their eyes and their ears and their nostrils to the sights and sounds and smells that came from this place.'[9]

At Stalag III in Ohrdruf, the American colonel in command of the troops who first discovered the camp made it his business to ensure that the local people knew, at least in retrospect, what had been happening there. Colonel Hayden Sears, officer commanding Combat Command A of the 4 Armoured Division, US Army, assembled all the leading citizens of Ohrdruf to view the piles of bodies that had been beaten to death or shot. Sergeant Saul Levitt was there:

'Ohrdruf is a neat, well-to-do suburban town with hedges around some of its brick houses and concrete walks leading to their main entrances. The richest man in Ohrdruf is a painting contractor who made a lot of money in the last few years on war work for the German Army and now owns a castle on a hill near the town. You can see the castle on the way to the concentration camp.

'Colonel Sears, a big, tough-looking man, ordered the leading citizens of Ohrdruf out from behind the smug privacy of their hedges and housefronts and had them driven in Army trucks to the concentration camp to let them see the killing that is sprawled on the bare ground and piled in a shack.

'The crowd of the best people in Ohrdruf stood around the dead and looked at the bodies sullenly. One of them said at last. "This is the work of only one per cent of the German Army; you should not blame the rest."

'Then the colonel spoke briefly and impersonally through an interpreter. "Tell them," he said, "that they have been brought here to see with their own eyes what is reprehensible from any human standard and that we hold the entire German nation responsible by their support and toleration of the Nazi government."

'The crowd stared at the dead and not at the colonel. Then the people of Ohrdruf went back to their houses. The colonel and his solders went back to their tanks, and we went out of this place and through Ohrdruf and Gotha, where the names of Beethoven, Mozart and Brahms are set in shining, gold letters across the front of the opera house.'[10]

It was probably inevitable that the discovery of the camps should result in the wholesale demonization of the entire German nation, at least in some quarters. 'I thought those pictures in the paper were just too terrible,' a fireman told the *Daily Mail*. 'Do you know, I keep seeing them in my sleep and dreaming about them. I don't know what you do with a nation like that, they ought to be wiped clean off the map, they're not human, they're devils. Some people talk about teaching them different. But I don't see how you can teach devils any different.'

Others were of a more practical bent. Kathleen Barnett was a volunteer worker with the Red Cross and the Women's Institute: 'When they began to find the camps, we had an SOS through the WI to get together as many second-hand clothes as we could find for the concentration camps. We sent about five or six sack-fulls from our village and we had to do it within 24 hours. I always remember one old gentleman, he used to have his shoes made for him because he had a club foot and he gave us six pairs of these boots. It was amazing. We were doing make-do-and-mend to get by, yet people still looked in their cupboards to find something wearable they could give. We took the clothes down to High Wycombe station, with special labels, and they were sent off to London.'

Sir George Pinker, the eminent gynaecologist, was then a student at Harefield Hospital and volunteered to join the medical team going out to Germany to help clear up the camps. 'People like Lord Haw Haw had pooh-poohed the existence of the camps and so one was keen to find out how things were, but I was not lucky—or unlucky—enough to be selected.

'My reaction to the discovery of the camps was one of disbelief and sympathy for the families involved. One had heard for some time that there were concentration camps and ghettoes, but one could hardly believe it was true. You could never be sure in that situation that what you are being told is true and what everybody else is being told on the other side is false. So in a way it was something of a relief to know that your side was not fabricating the story. It was easier to back up what our government was doing when one knew it was true.'

While the institutionalized atrocity of the camps overwhelmed the individual atrocity stories that had been circulating for months, some, particularly those concerning the prisoner of war camps, were still being regularly aired in pubs up and down the country. One favourite was the Christmas bonfire story: 'A nephew of mine's just come home—been a prisoner of war for three years. He told us that last Christmas Eve their guards came to them and said, "We've got a nice bonfire outside, a lovely bonfire, come and have a look and warm yourselves at it." They were a bit suspicious at first, but in the end they went out. The guard asked them if they hadn't made them a lovely bonfire, and they agreed. The guards started roaring with laughter. "That's your Christmas mail and all your Christmas parcels—*that's* what made your lovely bonfire."'[11]

In the main, Allied prisoners of war in Germany were spared the worst excesses of the concentration camps. Alan Moorehead described the day the first British prisoners of war were released:

'The big one [PoW camp] was at a pleasant watering-place called Fallingbostel just beyond the river Aller. As the first of the British army came up they found their comrades, the prisoners, drawn up in ranks in the compound before the Union Jack, their gaiters and belts whitewashed, their badges shining. Many of these men had spent four or five years in Germany and now on this great day they stood to the salute. To those who came to deliver them it was a moving thing to see this parade which was also a gesture, a determination to show that as prisoners they had not been beaten by imprisonment.

'It seemed too many of the prisoners who had been taken years before at Dunkirk and in the desert that an immense gulf divided them from this new army which had rescued them. They felt that their imprisonment was time out of life and that they would never catch up. That was the first reaction. Perhaps the most revealing remark of all was this: "So that's what a jeep looks like." The man who made it had been captured before the days of jeeps, before Alamein and Stalingrad, before England seemed to have a ghost of a chance in the war.

'Another day we drove into Hanover which was still a lovely town despite its ruins, and the car broke down in front of the Rathaus. Two British prisoners of war came up and helped me change the wheel. As they worked they talked. They said "The Jerries were all right at first, when they were winning. We had last-war guards and there was an inspection every Saturday morning; your kit and all that. They looked inside the collar of your tunic for lice and you got hell if you were dirty. That camp was a real credit. Then in the last year they began to change. We were marched back here from Poland. When anyone went sick he was beaten by the German sergeant. He beat us up a lot and killed some. German women used to come out to us while we were on the march with buckets of water, but the guards turned them off. He was a bastard, that German sergeant.

'I asked what had happened to him.

'"We told the Yanks about him when they released us and they started to beat him up. When our own sergeant-major, who was one of the prisoners, heard about it he sent out word to the Yanks to stop it. But the Yank sergeant just answered that he was in charge and went on with the beating up."'[12]

Private Thomas Park, a signaller in the Argyll and Sutherland Highlanders, was taken prisoner south of Abbeville in France in 1940 and spent the war in a succession of different work camps: 'We sensed that things were coming to a head with the war because in the last camp we were in, in a place called Erfurt, we saw the troops in the nearby barracks digging foxholes and putting up machine gun posts and so we knew the Allies must be getting close.

'We were marched out of there pretty quickly. We used to march twenty, thirty kilometres a day and at night shack up in a barn, in a village somewhere. They marched us during the day until our air force more or less took control of the skies and would shoot up anything that moved, then they moved us at night. We felt that anything could happen to us.

'We reached Czechoslovakia and as usual, were shacked up in a barn in a small village. One day we woke up and discovered that the Czechs in the village had disarmed our guards. We were free except we were in a sort of no man's land with nowhere to go, with Germans in front and behind.

'Next morning, two German officers with machine guns slung round their necks came towards us across the fields and we thought, well, this is it! My friend Ernie and I dodged behind one those concrete cylindrical pillars used for bill posting and we thought, What now? What a bloody irony that this should happen after five years as a prisoner of war.

'As they didn't look too aggressive, we decided to face them because it was obvious they knew we were there. I don't know if they knew what had happened to the guards, but it turned out that all they wanted was to find someone who could speak German to go with them to the Yank lines to talk terms. I could speak German, so I went with them. We found the Americans in a small town that we had marched through a couple of nights earlier. I had never seen so many tanks in my life. They loaded me up with some American cigarettes, Camel and Chesterfield, and delegated a big lorry to take me back to the village where my pals were waiting. Of course, when I got there, I was standing on this lorry and saying "Right, in an hour's time, you'll be free." Not a titter, they wouldn't believe it. Then I remembered the cigarettes I'd got from this tank sergeant and started throwing packets of fags all over the place and the penny dropped.

'The war ended very soon after that, but you couldn't adjust really to a life outside the prison camp. Even after we got back and they paid us in British money, if I went shopping I always gave a note if I bought anything. I didn't have a clue about British prices. It was a long time before I recovered from the after effects of being a prisoner. I dreamt about it every night.'

After most of the prisoner-of-war camps had been overrun, one group remained in captivity. The Prominente were well connected prisoners originally held at Colditz Castle whom the Germans hoped to use as hostages. By mid-April they were being shunted around southern Germany. At a stop near Berchtesgaden they were told by the general in charge of PoW affairs that he had received direct orders from Hitler that they were all to be shot. The general had, however, generously decided to defy orders and the party was loaded into two lorries and set off eastwards towards Austria. Michael Alexander, nephew of the future Field

Marshal, takes up the story: 'We drove across the bridge and towards the widening Inn valley. In a meadow to the left was an old wooden barn. Creeping towards the barn were two figures carrying rifles. They were Americans. We cheered. Round the next corner was a troop of three American tanks. A dusty, steel helmeted figure was peering out of the turret of the leading one. A raised hand and a slowly swivelling gun signalled us to stop. The American soldiers gave us chocolate and bottles of wine taken out of their tanks. They were the spearhead of the 53rd Division, whose headquarters were in Innsbruck about 30 miles down the valley … They said, laconically, that they were way ahead of their main body because the officer in charge was anxious to get a name for himself.

'Innsbruck was all gold in the morning sun. At the cross-roads in the Maria Therese Strasse, American military police in snowdrop helmets and spacemen boots casually flipped the traffic by. Groups of GIs, heavily armed with Leicas, sauntered along the sidewalks in the style of Gary Cooper. The citizens, looking at the shops or sitting in the cafés, seemed already to have adapted themselves to the new climate of life. Next morning we travelled in an open truck to Augsburg, where, as we arrived, a British major said curtly: "You're very dirty". An American colonel, more intelligent and more practical, indicated the washroom.'[13]

All prisoners of war liberated by the advancing Allies had only one ambition—to get home as soon as possible. The writer Henry Treece, then serving in the RAF, recorded in his diary the day he went to Brussels in a flight of twelve Lancaster bombers to bring back British prisoners of war. Each plane was to carry 24 PoWs and the captains were warned at their briefing not to carry out any fancy manoeuvres on the way back as some of the 'boys' may still be 'a little sick'. Actually, they turned out to be in fine shape.

'[At the airfield outside Brussels] we learn that no PoWs have yet arrived, owing to a slight hitch, and that some aircraft have been waiting over two hours for them, so we go off to the next tent, marked Canteen, where a very pretty Church Army girl gives us each a large mug of tea and two gigantic ginger biscuits, free of charge. We go outside and smoke a cigarette. All over the airfield groups of RAF personnel are standing about, waiting for their passengers. But nobody is grumbling for once!

'Then at last a fleet of lorries comes roaring up the perimeter track and out jump the PoWs dressed in khaki, blue, grey—a combination of all three. Here and there is a man carrying a guitar, wearing a German forage cap, and each one humping a new white kitbag. We are surprised to see that most of these boys are looking well and sun-tanned. And all are clean and shaven. They have been living on American rations for the last ten days, we hear.

'As we stand watching, the PoWs are formed up into batches of 24, and move off in the direction of the aircraft. There is no flap, and everything seems to be done with the maximum of good humour and the minimum of fussing.

'When we get back to the aircraft, we find our party of prisoners already wait-ing. They are talking quickly and smiling. We issue dehydrated rations, cushions and Mae Wests to each man. No one seems anxious about not being given a parachute—but one Army boy, who doesn't get an air-sickness bag, seems very fed up. Not that he is likely to need it, but he wants it as a souvenir. No one eats the dehydrated rations; they will be kept as souvenirs too.

'The PoWs climb the ladder into the aircraft in a perfectly orderly manner, and sit down where they're told, without any comment. They are not interested in the aircraft. They just want to get home …

'As we cross the English coast, the two soldiers who are positioned in the bomb aimer's compartment look at each other, stick up their thumbs and smile.

'I scribble on a piece of paper: "We are crossing the English coast now" and pass it back down the aircraft, as our passengers are not in inter-comm. The first man to get the paper reads it and stuffs it into his pocket. He smiles and shouts "Souvenir!" "Pass it back" I yell. He shakes he head, then turns round and tries to shout out the message above the roar of the engines. By the time he has made his companions understand, we are over north London.

'In 20 minutes we have landed at the deplaning airfield. As our passengers push their way down the aircraft they ask "Where are we?" "Are we near London?" "How long will they keep us here?"

'Some of them are wet-eyed. Some try to give us cap-badges and bits of equip-ment as souvenirs. It is hard to refuse their gifts. One of them scrambles out of the aircraft tightly clutching a German officer's gold-hilted sword—we hope he'll be allowed to keep it.

'As we roar off up the runway, we see batches of boys with their white kitbags. They wave and we wave back. We get back to Mess for a very late dinner. We had our last meal at breakfast time, but no one cares about that. It's been a grand day, and tomorrow we shall go again, and the next day, and the next, if we're wanted … In the bar they have a new barrel of Guinness on tap, and we get rather happy.'[14]

Another homecoming of a rather different kind was described by Janet Flanner, an American woman resident in Paris, who was present when 300 women pris-oners from Ravensbrück were exchanged for German women held in France: 'They arrived at the Gare de Lyon at eleven in the morning and were met by a nearly speechless crowd ready with welcoming bouquets of lilacs and other spring flowers, and by General de Gaulle, who wept. As he shook hands with some wretched woman leaning from a window of the train, she suddenly screamed "C'est lui!" and pointed to her husband, standing nearby, who had not recognised her. There was a general, anguished babble of search, of finding or not finding. There was almost no joy; the emotion penetrated beyond that, to something nearer pain. Too much suffering lay behind this homecoming, and it was the suf-fering that showed in the women's faces and bodies.

'Of the three hundred women who the Ravensbrück Kommandant had selected as being able to put up the best appearance, eleven had died on route. One woman, taken from the train unconscious and placed on a litter, by chance opened her eyes just as de Gaulle's colour guard marched past her with the French tricolour. She lifted an emaciated arm, pointed to the flag and swooned again. Another woman, who still had a strong voice and an air of authority, said she had been a camp nurse. Unable to find her daughter and son-in-law in the crowd, she began shouting "Monique! Pierre!" and crying out that her son and husband had been killed fighting in the resistance and now where were those two who were all she had left? Then she sobbed weakly. One matron, six years ago renowned in Paris for her elegance, had become a bent, dazed, shabby old woman. When her smartly attired brother, who met her, said, like an automaton, "Where is your luggage?", she silently handed him what looked like a dirty black sweater fastened with safety pins around whatever small belongings were rolled inside. In a way, all the women looked alike: their faces were grey-green, with reddish brown circles around their eyes, which seemed to see but not take in. They were dressed like scarecrows, in what had been given them at camp, clothes taken from the dead of all nationalities. As the lilacs fell from inert hands, the flowers made a purple carpet on the platform and the perfume of the trampled flowers mixed with the stench of illness and dirt.'[15]

If any good came out of the concentration camps, it was that their existence alone justified the war. No one among the Allies could have had any doubt, after Belsen and Dachau and Buchenwald and Ravensbrück and all the other terrible names that had been engraved in the history of infamy, that they were fighting on the right side.

Thursday 3 May

Collapse of the Reich

At 11.30 a.m. on Thursday 3 May, a four-man delegation of German officers escorted by British armoured cars arrived on the windswept Lüneburg Heath, where Field Marshal Montgomery had set up the advanced headquarters of 21st Army Group in a cluster of caravans, trucks and tents, to discuss surrender terms.

Dönitz, now controlling what was left of the German armed forces from a naval base at Flensburg, near the Danish border, had accepted the war was lost. Field Marshal Ernst Busch had appealed for him to display 'Hitler spirit' and order a counter-attack on the British divisions advancing on Hamburg, but he had already been warned that the Buergermeister of Hamburg had threatened to call on civilians to rise up against the army if the city was not handed over without further fighting. Dönitz recognized that the German people could take no more. He ordered the remaining troops to be deployed to keep open escape routes for refugees and authorized Field Marshal Wilhelm Keitel to open negotiations for a surrender.

The delegation to Lüneburg Heath was made up of General-Admiral Hans von Friedeburg, General Kinzel, Rear-Admiral Wagner and a Major Freidel, a staff officer who had been one of Hitler's aides. They had simply driven into the Allied lines outside Hamburg and reported to the senior officer present, who had promptly provided an armoured-car escort front and back to take them to Montgomery's windswept headquarters on Lüneburg Heath. Astounded British soldiers, watching them arrive, were reassured to note that they looked like caricature Nazis in their jackboots and long coats—one even sported a monocle.

Field Marshal the Viscount Montgomery of Alamein left a detailed account of what happened next in his memoirs: 'They were brought to my caravan site and were drawn up under the Union Jack, which was flying proudly in the breeze. I kept them waiting for a few minutes and then came out of my caravan and walked towards them. They all saluted under the Union Jack. It was a great moment; I knew the Germans had come to surrender and that the war was over. Few of those in the signals and operations caravans at my Tac headquarters will forget the thrill experienced when they heard the faint "tapping" of the Germans trying to pick us up on the wireless command link—to receive the surrender instructions from their delegation.

'I then said to my interpreter: "Who are these men?" He told me.

'I then said: "What do they want?"

'Admiral Friedeburg then read me a letter from Field Marshal Keitel offering to surrender to me the three German armies withdrawing in front of the Russians between Berlin and Rostock. I refused to consider this, saying that these armies should surrender to the Russians. I added that, of course, if any Germans came towards my front with their hands up they would automatically be taken prisoner. Von Friedeburg said it was unthinkable to surrender to the Russians as they were savages, and the German soldiers would be sent straight off to work in Russia.

'I said the Germans should have thought of all these things before they began the war, and particularly before they attacked the Russians in June 1941.

'Von Friedeburg next said that they were anxious about the civilian population in Mecklenburg who were being over-run by the Russians and they would like to discuss how these could be saved. I replied that Mecklenburg was not in my area and that any problems connected with it must be discussed with the Russians. I said they must understand I refused to discuss any matter connected with the situation on my eastern flank between Wismar and Domitz; they must approach the Russians on such matters. I then asked if they wanted to discuss the surrender of their forces on my western flank. They said they did not. They said they were anxious about the civilian population in those areas and would like to arrange with me some scheme by which their troops could withdraw slowly as my troops advanced. I refused.

'I then decided to spring something on them quickly. I said to von Friedeburg: "Will you surrender to me all German forces on my western and northern flanks, including all forces in Holland, Friesland with the Frisian Islands and Heligoland, Schleswig-Holstein and Denmark? If you will do this, I will accept it as a tactical battlefield surrender of the enemy forces immediately opposing me, and those in support in Denmark."

'He said he could not agree to this. But he was anxious to come to some agreement about the civilian population in those areas; I refused to discuss this. I then said that if the Germans refused to surrender unconditionally to the forces in the areas I had named, I would order the fighting to continue; many more German soldiers would then be killed, and possibly some civilians also from artillery fire and air attack. I next showed them on a map the actual battle situation on the whole western front; they had no idea what this situation was and were very upset. By this time I reckoned that I would not have much more difficulty in getting them to accept my demands. But I thought that an interval for lunch might be desirable so that they could reflect on what I had said. I sent them away to have lunch in a tent by themselves, with nobody else present except one of my officers. Von Friedeburg wept during lunch and the others did not say much.

'After lunch I sent for them again and this time the meeting was in my conference tent with the map of the battle situation on the table. I began this meeting by delivering an ultimatum. They must surrender unconditionally all their forces in the areas I had named; once they had done this I would discuss with them the best way of occupying the areas and looking after the civilians; if they refused, I would go on with the battle.

'They saw at once that I meant what I said. They were convinced of the hopelessness of their cause but they said they had no power to agree to my demands. They were, however, now prepared to recommend to Field Marshal Keitel the unconditional surrender of all the forces on the western and northern flanks of 21 Army Group. Two of them would go back to OKW [German High Command] to see Keitel, and bring back his agreement.'[1]

Friedeburg and Freidel were escorted back through Hamburg to the German lines with orders to return with an answer by six o'clock the following evening.

Montgomery was confident that an unconditional surrender was imminent. None of the troops who had fought with him across Germany would have disagreed. They had crossed a country utterly ravaged by war, its great cities reduced to rubble and its people living no better than animals in the ruins. Those houses that still stood draped white sheets from their windows to indicate surrender. Every road was swarming with refugees bolstered by retreating soldiers who had exchanged their uniforms for any civilian clothes they could scavenge and were forced to beg for food whilst struggling to find their way back to whatever remained of their homes.

Private John Frost, in Lübeck with the 11th Armoured Division, wrote a moving letter to his mother describing the conditions in Germany: 'Chaos is sweeping Germany today. All business in the towns, apart from coffin-making is at a standstill and civilians must conform to all the rigid regulations and laws set up by the local AMGOV (Allied Military Government). We shun all Germans, and they usually turn their heads away from us. In the larger towns, destruction is complete, though in outlying districts the damage is negligible. Trudging along the busy highways are freed Allied prisoners, they are mostly Russians but there are also many Poles, French and Yugoslavs. This is their first breath of freedom for four years or more. Their clothes are in tatters, they are half-starved, they are human wrecks. In their craving for food, they loot and pillage from wayside houses. They just smash their way into German homes and take whatever they can find. To help them get away from the war zones they 'borrow' horses, cars, bicycles or anything else on wheels. They smile and wave to British troops and beg for cigarettes and a bite to eat. The scenes are fantastic and horrible. I never thought man could fall so low.'

At home, BBC correspondents kept the impatient British public in touch with what was going on in Germany as best they could, since reports still had to be cleared through the censor. Chester Wilmot was in the Press team on Lüneburg Heath: 'the general surrender of the German forces opposing the Second British Army may now come at any hour; except in the pocket west of Bremen there is no longer any real opposition on General Dempsey's front, and pilots today reported that there are white flags flying from the houses 50 miles behind the nominal enemy line.

'It's been a day of surrender and negotiation for surrender by German officers ranging from commanders of regiments to commanders of armies. Last night, two German divisions surrendered intact. Early this morning the commander of the Hamburg garrison, General Wolz, agreed not only to hand over unconditionally Germany's greatest port, but also personally to lead the 7th British Armoured Division into the city this evening. During the morning the 11th Armoured Division received word that the garrison of Neumuenster, 35 miles north of Hamburg and only 30 miles from the great naval base of Kiel, was ready to give in. The Neumuenster garrison also said that other troops on the Kiel Canal itself were anxious to surrender.

'But the biggest news of the day was the complete break-up and the attempted surrender of two of the German armies in Army Group Vistula, the group defending the area north of Berlin. These armies had retreated about 150 miles since the Russian breakthrough on the Oder last month, and yesterday our columns cut right through the area where they were vainly trying to reorganize. Their fighting spirit was already broken, and they disintegrated at once.

'Today, their commanders, General Manteuffel of the 3rd Panzer Army and General Tippelskirch of the 1st Panzer Army, offered to surrender their completes forces to Field Marshal Montgomery. This was refused, though we have accepted the personal capitulation of the two generals and many senior officers of Army Group Vistula.

'The official British attitude is that as these two armies are still engaged in fighting the Russians, we can't accept their surrender, and in any case their commanders are in no position to hand over the armies to us. And so tonight in the woods and villages between the Baltic and the Elbe there are tens of thousands of Germans from Army Group Vistula vainly trying to find someone who will accept them as prisoners. Their commanders have surrendered, their staffs have disintegrated; only those units still in direct contact with the Russians continue fighting—fighting rather than yield to the Red Army.

'The fact is that at all costs the Germans want to avoid surrendering to the Soviet troops. They know how great are Germany's crimes against Russia, and they know the Russians won't forget.'[2]

Later that day Wynford Vaughan Thomas reported on the dispirited departure of German soldiers from Hamburg, which officially surrendered at 6.25 p.m.:

'Since two o'clock this morning this endless stream of transport has been pouring through this town, under the white flags hung over the shattered houses by the inhabitants who are standing in the streets looking dumbfounded at this wreckage of the Wehrmacht that's going past us. For, make no mistake about it, this army we see going by us is the most curious collection of wreckage you ever saw— improvised cars with people riding on the bumpers, half-track vehicles, thousands of them, going through in a steady stream, and to make matters even more fantas- tic they've got their own traffic policemen directing them, under British orders, standing on the corner waving listlessly on, as the thing goes steadily by us.

'These people are defeated soldiers—you can see it in their eyes. In the middle of them there comes a much more joyous note. We see a charabanc full of RAF released prisoners, cheering as they go by, and the Germans on the half-trucks looking glumly on.'[3]

Although the news was all good, events were moving so quickly it was hard for the people at home to fully comprehend what was happening. The confusion created a breeding ground for rumours; everyone seemed to have different, but always authoritative, information about when victory was to be declared.

The fact was that most people had ceased to be interested in lines and flags on maps indicating the progress of the war. Everyone now believed that the end was very near, but there had been so many disappointments, hopes had been raised and dashed so often, that all they wanted was final confirmation that yes, it was over. The delays and rumours caused considerable resentment:

'The mess they're making of it! First they've surrendered, then they haven't. Then peace will be declared in a few hours, then it won't. It's tearing people's nerves to shreds.'

'What strikes me is that the war's ending in just the same phoney way as it began. It's peace. It isn't peace. They've surrendered. They haven't surrendered. It does bring back those first months where there was, and there wasn't, a war.'

'V Day? God alone knows when. I think everyone's got to such a pitch of saying "You can't believe this", or "You can't believe that", that when peace is declared they won't be able to take it in. Ooh, I do think it's a muddle. Good thing we can keep our heads. Not like those Americans. They say they've finished all their peace night stocks of liquor already, and it was all a rumour.'

'Oh, it's coming all right. It'll come along presently. Only it's getting people disappointed, all this thinking it's peace when it's not. It's all because they won't surrender to the Russians, that's what's holding it up.'

'Know what they're doing? You can see what they're doing with all their false alarms, they're taking all the thrill out of it, so that nobody'll be excited when V Day does come. Oh, it's a mean trick. It's making people properly fed up. I know I don't care whether they ever have a V Day or not. I'm just disgusted with it all.'

Despite this last speaker, most people had some vague plans to celebrate, even if it was only to get drunk:

A soldier, aged 25: 'They tell us that on V Day we will be confined to camp for 48 hours. Most of us know plenty of ways out. Myself, I'm going to get tight and stay that way as long as the money lasts. I came out of Dunkirk with bad gastric trouble, so I feel that at last I can let myself go and damn the consequences.'

A window cleaner, aged 40: 'For some time now I've been putting a bit by every week, so that on V Day I can get really blind drunk, what with getting bombed out in Balham, and business worries, I want to forget it all for a bit.'

A Dorking publican expresses doubt about whether the necessary tipple would be available: 'I can't imagine why they are fussing about people getting drunk on the night. They will have a hard job to do it on draught beer, and that is about all I've got left.'

A WAAF, aged 20: 'If V Day comes within the next three days I will be home on leave. I suppose I will have to go to church, just to keep the family quiet. After that I'm going out just to see what other people are doing. I expect I will have a drink or two, but I won't get drunk—it's not worth it. Of course, if I am back at Harwell, I will be supposed to stay on at the camp, the Group [Captain] has said that he will lock the gates; still, there will be organized "amusements" and an issue of one bottle of beer each. Be funny to see what some of the lads do with one bottle.'[4]

Ever since the early days of April people had been buying flags and red, white and blue bunting in anticipation of the big day and by the beginning of May many of the stores in London's West End had sold out, although endless victory souvenirs were still available. At Woolworths, victory bows, victory rosettes and victory hairslides were a shilling each, victory scarves were 6s 6d, plus one coupon, and red, white and blue ribbon was fourpence ha'penny a yard. Bourne and Hollingsworth did a roaring trade in victory scarves with 'There'll always be an England' embroidered on one side, 12s 5d each. Selfridges, said to have the best flag department in London, sold thousands of 'Welcome Home' union jack flags at 4s each and 'God Save the King' posters. Churchill, too, featured in many of the souvenirs and was said to be very popular.

Back in Germany, on the late evening of 3 May Norman Ford, then a 21-year-old private in the Devonshire Regiment, had the dubious honour of fighting off one of the last German counter-attacks in north-west Europe:

'We were in Vahrendorff, a wooded area close to Hamburg. No one expected a counter-attack when we took up our positions in and around the hamlet. We had been advancing without opposition for some time, not even bothering to dig in when we halted. The end of the war seemed close, though no one guessed it was only days away. Oddly enough, we did dig trenches that night, but only because heavy Allied bombing was expected in the area. We had no supporting armour, except a tank-mounted SP gun, whose presence was to prove vital in the action that followed. One platoon commander, I remember, declared the position he was allocated indefensible. He was right, in the event.

'Company headquarters was a farmhouse commanding the junction of three country lanes. With a sloping bank opposite, farm buildings on one side, and two lanes curving away on the left, it gave a limited field of fire. However, I felt safe enough to take my boots off when I came off duty—an unusual practice for front-line infantry.

'The most chilling words I have ever heard woke me from my slumbers that night. "Jerry's in the village!" Since the "village" was just a handful of houses, this could mean only one thing, that the enemy were in amongst us! The noise, the confusion, the voices, German ones among them, confirmed our fears.

'I took up a position at the left window, but it was too dark to fire at anything effectively. We could hear German orders being given and grenades rattling against the walls before exploding. Flashes lit up grey clad figures running in our direction. Our Bren gun created a deafening din firing in the tiled entrance hail.

'For some reason the expected assault on the house, which we had little hope of stopping, never came, but I, for one, thought we had no chance of survival.

'The confusion, if anything, increased as the night went on. Running feet on the lane outside proved to belong to men of two of our three platoons forced out of their positions. There was talk, inside the house, of surrender, a prospect which, for some reason, filled me with more dread than the alternative.

'Then tank tracks were heard. We knew that they were not ours and our second-in-command yelled "Get that bloody SP out on the road". Just in time! In the light of dawn a Tiger tank appeared round the bend in the lane. It was immediately stopped by an armour piercing shell, then set on fire, its unfortunate crew still trapped inside.

'Another incident in that pale, early light sticks in my memory. A lone German soldier simply strolled into my field of fire, only about 20 or 30 yards away but still in semi-darkness. I opened fire but assumed I had missed and that he was adopting a firing position.

'It was the only time in the whole campaign from Normandy that I recall seeing an enemy that close, aiming at me personally! The Bren gun, having no other target at this point, added a few bursts to my fire and no other movement was seen.

'With daylight came the realization that the counter-attack had failed. Germans began coming in from all directions with their hands on their heads. A supporting armoured vehicle reached us, sweeping through the area and forcing out pockets of resistance.

'As we were able to emerge and take stock, the position of the German dead, right amongst the buildings and trenches we had used, confirmed the fears of the night that it had been a "damned close run thing". But we soon realized why it had failed. Though led by tough SS officers, our attackers included boys of 14 as well as the Home Guard veterans. My personal assailant was a boy of nineteen, only three months in the army. It was clear that most of them had been even more frightened and confused than we were.'

IV

Friday 4 May

Ceasefire in the West

Muriel Green and her sister Jenny worked in a hostel for war workers in Somerset. On Friday 4 May, like everyone else in the country, she was speculating on which day would be VE Day and what she would do on that day. This is what she wrote in her diary:

'Mrs C says Sunday is to be the great day and that seems to be the general opinion chiefly because it began on a Sunday. It all seems wonderful to think we have really and truly whacked the Nazis. I thought it would be impossible for us to smash them in their own land. They deserve to have it at their heart after the way other countries have suffered. I wonder if the world has learned the lesson of war this time. Will my unborn children know the horrors that my generation has known in the same way that our parents knew before us?

'Tonight, Jenny, A and E (workmates) and myself discussed whether we should get drunk on V Day. As none of us have ever done so before we thought it a suitable opportunity to "try anything once". We have decided we shan't worry a snap of the fingers as to what our bosses and the residents think then and we have as much right on that day to be [as] uncivilised as anyone else. We have always kept up appearances to "keep the hostel running for the war workers" and living on the spot there has never been any absenteeism of hostel staff. I don't really think we shall get drunk but we have told the management not to rely on us to do anything that day or the following days as we have for once as much right to experience "hangovers" as any of the residents.' [1]

What Muriel did not know, as she chatted with her friends that night about their right to mark the end of the war with a hangover, was that at long last the final act was being played out on Lüneburg Heath.

Shortly after five o'clock, Montgomery called all the war correspondents to his tent to give them a briefing on what he hoped was going to happen within the next hour. One of them described the scene: 'Calmly, almost breezily,

Montgomery began to tell us of the events leading up to the armistice. The field marshal as a rule did not have the knack of giving good press conferences. But on this day he presented a masterpiece of simplification and condensation. Halfway through his talk Colonel Ewart came in to say that the German delegates had arrived back with their answer, the answer that was to mean whether or not nearly six years of bitterness and death in Europe was at last to end.

"'Tell them to wait," Montgomery said, and he went on addressing us for the next half-hour. During this period he did not attempt to learn either by word or sign or message what answer the Germans had brought back. Montgomery was finishing his war exactly as he had begun it—absolutely convinced that he was right and that things were going his way.

"'And now," he said at last, "we will attend the last act. These German officers have arrived back. We will go and see what their answer is." He led the way to his caravans on the hill-top.'[2]

Montgomery, the leading player, continues the narrative: 'The German delegation was paraded again under the Union Jack outside my caravan. I took von Friedeburg into my caravan, to see him alone. I asked him if he would sign the full surrender terms as I had demanded; he said he would do so. He was very dejected and I told him to rejoin the others outside. It was now nearly 6 p.m. I gave orders for the ceremony to take place at once in a tent pitched for the purpose, which had been wired for the recording instruments. The German delegation went across to the tent, watched by groups of soldiers, war correspondents, photographers and others—all very excited. They knew it was the end of the war.

'I had the surrender document all ready. The arrangements in the tent were very simple—a trestle table covered with an army blanket, an inkpot, an ordinary army pen that you could buy in a shop for two pence. There were two BBC microphones on the table. The Germans stood up as I entered; then we all sat down round the table. The Germans were clearly nervous and one of them took out a cigarette; he wanted to smoke to calm his nerves. I looked at him, and he put the cigarette away.

'In that tent on Lüneburg Heath, publicly in the presence of the Press and other spectators, I read out in English the Instrument of Surrender. I said that unless the German delegation signed this document immediately, and without argument on what would follow their capitulation, I would order the fighting to continue. I then called on each member of the German delegation by name to sign the document, which they did without any discussion. I then signed on behalf of General Eisenhower.'[3]

In an uncharacteristic moment of carelessness, Montgomery dated the document 5 May. He tried to change the five to a four, then crossed it out and wrote the correct date alongside, initialling the alteration. Someone pinched the pen as a souvenir but Montgomery managed to hold on to the original surrender document, typed on an ordinary sheet of army foolscap, even though he had been asked to forward it to Supreme Headquarters in Versailles: he only sent photostats.

At SHAEF's forward headquarters, in a red-brick college in Rheims, northern France, staff paced the floor, anxiously waiting for news from 21 Army Group. Kay Summersby, an Englishwoman who was General Eisenhower's driver, secretary and (it later transpired) lover, recalled the suspense: 'All afternoon we waited tensely for Monty's call. Air Chief Marshal Tedder [the Deputy Supreme Commander] joined the General in his tiny office; Butch (Eisenhower's naval aide, Captain Harry Butcher), up from Paris, joined me in my office. We waited and waited. Finally, General Ike declared he was going home and could be reached there. Afraid of missing the big surrender, I succeeded in urging him to wait just another five minutes.

'The phone rang exactly five minutes later, about 7 p.m. I answered it. It was Monty.

'Butch and I eavesdropped shamelessly through the open door. The ceremony had gone through ... Although dead tired, the General sat down and dictated a special message to the Prime Minister praising the courage and determination of the British people ... Then he and Butch went off for dinner.'[4]

In his caravan on Lüneburg Heath, Montgomery, too, was drafting a final message to his troops. It was heroic stuff, typically Monty:

'On this day of victory in Europe I feel I would like to speak to all who have served and fought with me during the last few years. What I have to say is very simple and quite short.

'I would ask you all to remember those of our comrades who fell in the struggle. They gave their lives that others might have freedom, and no man can do more than that. I believe that He would say to each one of them: "Well done, thou good and faithful servant."

'And we who remain have seen the thing through to the end; we all have a feeling of great joy and thankfulness that we have been preserved to see this day. We must remember to give the praise and thankfulness where it is due: "This is the Lord's doing, and it is marvellous in our eyes."

'In the early days of this war the British Empire stood alone against the combined might of the Axis powers. And during those days we suffered some great disasters; but we stood firm; on the defensive, but striking where we could. Later we were joined by Russia and America; and from then onwards the end was in no doubt. Let us never forget what we owe to our Russian and American allies; this great allied team has achieved much in war; may it achieve even more in peace.

'Without doubt, great problems lie ahead; the world will not recover quickly from the upheaval that has taken place; there is much work for each of us. I would say that we must face up to that work with the same fortitude that we faced up to the worst days of this war. It may be that some difficult times lie ahead for our country, and for each one of us personally. If it happens thus, then our discipline will pull us through; but we must remember that the best discipline implies the subordination of self for the benefit of the community.

'It has been a privilege and an honour to command this great British Empire team in western Europe. Few commanders can have had such loyal service as you have given me. I thank each one of you from the bottom of my heart.

'And so let us embark on what lies ahead full of joy and optimism. We have won the German war. Let us now win the peace. Good luck to you all, wherever you may be.'[5]

Warrant Officer Arnold Johnson was on duty that night in the 2nd Army cipher headquarters, which had been established in a large suburban house commandeered in Lüneburg. 'When a top priority Emergency Ops cipher message came in I handed it to my best machine operator to have it deciphered as quickly as possible. He began to type out the five figure groups and the message in clear began to emerge from the side of the machine. Just as I became aware of its importance, there was a power failure and all the lights went out.

'I hurriedly lit a candle and held it over the keyboard of the machine so the operator could continue. I was flabbergasted when I saw what it said. "THIS IS IT!" I shouted to the other men on the shift and read out "... all troops to cease fire 0800 hours tomorrow, Saturday, 5 May".'

The message, originated from HQ 21 Army at 2050 hours, read: 'SECRET. All offensive ops will cease from receipt of this signal. Orders will be given to all troops to cease fire 0800 hrs tomorrow Saturday May. Full terms of local GERMAN surrender arranged today for 21 Army Group front follow. Emphasise these provisions apply solely to 21 Army Group fronts and are for the moment exclusive of Dunkirk. Ack.'

'We knew that Montgomery and the Germans were meeting on Lüneburg Heath and that a cease fire was in the offing, but to have the confirmation in my hand, well, it was a wonderful, marvellous moment. I rushed it to the signals office because I knew the sooner the message got out to all formations, the sooner the fighting would stop and the quicker lives would be saved.

'Later that day we had a mail distribution, the first for three weeks. I got three letters. Three letters and the end of the war! It was almost unbelievable.'

No one received the news in a less dignified situation than Lieutenant General Sir Brian Horrocks, commander of 30 Corps:

'On May 3 I was told confidentially that the Germans were negotiating for surrender, but this was not to be communicated to anyone else. I was particularly anxious to avoid even a single casualty with the war practically over, so instead of urging on the divisional commanders I went round inventing excuses to slow them down. I could see them looking at me with astonishment and they were no doubt saying to themselves "The old man has lost his nerve at last".

'I had often wondered how the war would end. When it came, it could hardly have been more of an anti-climax. I happened to be sitting in the military equivalent of the smallest room when I heard a voice on the wireless saying "All hostilities will cease at 0800 tomorrow morning, 5th May." It was a wonderful moment—the sense of relief was extraordinary; for the first time for five years I would no longer be responsible for other men's lives.'[6]

Lord Deedes, then an officer in the King's Royal Rifle Corps, had just finished dinner with the 13th/18th Hussars, the armoured regiment to which his rifle company was attached, when the cease fire signal arrived. He recalls distinctly mixed feelings: 'There was a supply of Krug non-vintage in the mess and this was opened. My first thought was: well, this at least will ditch "Operation Curling", in which most of us were due to play a part at 0730 next morning ... it was never fulfilled, and just as well. It had a hazardous air about it.

'Even that thought, and the Krug, did not lift my spirits very high. This today must seem absurd, attributable to depressive tendencies ... Depression is sometimes the companion of exhaustion, but there were other considerations. We had suffered casualties only days before, when the battle was ending. What a pity, I thought, this surrender didn't come a little sooner; what a difference it would have made to those families.

'I also felt dimly aware, with recollections of keeping a company together in England, how much the perils of battle impose their own disciplines. I tried not to think about the likely state of the men's billets next morning, danger departed. They would be unimaginable. We would be back to those awful days off the battlefield, when the Adjutant would call me in for a little talk with the Colonel. "Bill, I have to tell you that I am not at all happy about the way things are going in your company."

'We'd be back to all that. Worse, military discipline would have to be restored amid a colossal shambles. We had laid waste a great part of the neighbourhood. Hundreds of thousands of displaced persons were drifting around. All the railways were cut and canals filled with bridge wreckage. All important roads were cratered. A great many Germans were starving, and the famine was aggravated by the disappearance of officials who had been prominent Nazis. A whole country had been battered to a stop. The Germans immediately around us now had lain in the path of our advancing army, of which we were the leading elements, so the damage was freshest and the agony deepest just where we were.

'To be honest and selfish, one must enter another depressing consideration which circled my mind—and the minds of many more—on this night and on the days that were to follow. This ceasefire threatened not only one's professional occupation but what had become the framework of one's life.

'Army life in battle can be dirty and dangerous and uncomfortable, but the system is supportive. The Corps or the Brigade might issue unreasonable orders; but they looked after you, body and soul. The quartermaster saw to the first, the padre to the second. The system had for five years protected us from almost all the irritants and anxieties which bedevil our lives in peacetime. Further more, after five years' soldiering, some of us (even as sons of the Territorial Army), felt more confidence in our military professionalism than in any other prospective occupation. The ceasefire had made us redundant.'[7]

No such ruminations bothered Harry Hardwick, a sapper with 52nd Scottish Division, who was busy helping to rebuild a bridge over a small canal outside Bremen. 'I had crossed over the bridge and was standing on the road, when one of the lads high up on the bank with the guns, watching the countryside, said "Hey up, lads, hey up, what's this?"

'I looked up quickly and there was this Mercedes staff car coming down the road flying a bit of a white sheet from somewhere, and a staff officer sitting inside, wearing a monocle. I thought about looking for some shelter pretty quick, but then I realized it was flying a white flag.

'The car came over the bridge and carried on to our HQ and I stood there and watched it go by. We just thought it was some German soldiers packing it in, we didn't realize until we were back at the billet, a big army place in Bremen, that it was the official surrender, that it had come through that the whole German nation had surrendered, so we went wild with what drinks we could get.

'Me and my friend Joe Edgar went across to a large block of flats where a lot of DPs were drinking wine and getting drunk as little monkeys. Getting to the top of a flight of stairs on our way back, my friend Joe suddenly lets out a shout "It's all over, Harold. We can go home!", flings his arms in the air and knocks us both head over heels down the stairs.

'Back at the billet, some of what we called "the heavy gang"—they used to have the bulldozers and everything, the heavy stuff, tank transporters—had acquired a couple of big barrels of beer from somewhere and were so drunk that they left the taps running. The place was swimming in beer. Next morning, some joker called parade—not a pretty sight.

'My mother was still alive then and anxious about me, the way mothers are. My father had died in the First World War, when I was only 18 months old and here I was, aged 25, as old as my father had been, fighting the same enemy going over the same routes, past all the monuments and cemeteries of the First World War. So she was glad it was over.'

That same night a young German officer by the name of Breuninger wrote a disconsolate letter home from the eastern front:

'Dear Father,

'Now everything is coming to an end … Until yesterday we still hoped that all of us would be shipped back to Germany and would keep on fighting the Russians from there. Three days ago, we received a secret oral message from our commander, General Hilpert. It said that Admiral Dönitz had made contact with the Western powers and would make peace in the west. In the east, the war would go on. Army Group Courland would be moved across the Baltic Sea and would go back into action on the Elbe front … Some officers claimed to know that the British would send ships to pick us up. It was even said that English troops would land here and attack the Russian flank together with us.

'We had all expected a turn in our fortunes because of the new weapons. Then we received the news of the heroic death of our Führer—it was a terrible, bitter disappointment. But then came the secret orders about the withdrawal, and all of us took new hope. We have fought here with all we have against one enemy: Bolshevism. If we fought English and Americans, it was only because they did not want to understand the meaning of our fight in the east. So our hopes were high when we heard about a separate peace in the west—our years of war would have a purpose, even though a whole nation would have been sacrificed.

'You can imagine how disappointed we are, now that we have been told that all our forces have surrendered, and that Army Group Courland has joined in the surrender. Russian commissars are expected every day now. They say the English prevented the sailing of the ships that were to come for us. But no one knows for sure who has stabbed us in the back ...

'Many of the men still do not believe in the surrender. They think they will march from Kiel against the Russians. The port is cordoned by military police, to keep unauthorised personnel from entering the ships. But everything has come off in perfect order, without any panic. Just as the Army has fought. We have done our part as German soldiers, if necessary to the bitter end.

'We do not know how our Fuehrer died. We did not know what weakness and treason took place back home during the last few weeks. We only know that to this day we have fought Bolshevism, the enemy not of us alone but of all Europe. We have seen Bolshevism in action as no one else has. We have seen the Bolshevist paradise. We knew what we fought for. And if it is true that the English have kept our ships from leaving port, they will remember it one day when they see and go through what we have seen and gone through ... '[8]

In London, the BBC broadcast a brief news flash announcing the surrender at 8.40 in the evening, then followed with a longer report from Chester Wilmot describing the surrender ceremony. Later, Wynford Vaughan Thomas, whose first report from Germany had been made in a bomber over Berlin in 1942, sent a final triumphant dispatch from William Joyce's studio in Hamburg:

'This is Germany calling. Calling for the last time from Station Hamburg, and tonight you will not hear views on the news by William Joyce, for Mr Joyce—Lord Haw-Haw to most of us in Britain—has been most unfortunately interrupted in his broadcasting career, and at present has left rather hurriedly for a vacation, an extremely short vacation if the Second British Army has anything to do with it ... [Joyce was arrested a few weeks later and subsequently hanged as a traitor.] And in his place this is the BBC calling all the long-suffering listeners in Britain who for six years have had to put up with the acid tones of Mr Joyce speaking over the same wavelength that I'm using to talk to you now.

'I'm seated in front of Lord Haw-Haw's own microphone, or rather the microphone he used in the last three weeks of his somewhat chequered career; and I wonder what Lord Haw-Haw's views on the news are now? For Hamburg, the city he made notorious, is this evening under the control of the British Forces, and we found a completely and utterly bomb-ruined city.

'We thought Bremen was bad, but Hamburg is devastated. Whole quarters have disintegrated under air attacks. There are miles upon miles of blackened walls and utterly burnt-out streets, and in the ruins there are still nearly a million people and 50,000 foreign workers living in the cellars and air raid shelters. Today you don't see a single civilian on the streets; as soon as we came in we imposed a 48-hour curfew, and there's a Sunday quiet over the whole city; all that stirs in the streets is a British jeep or an armoured car, or a patrol of British Tommies watching that the curfew is strictly enforced.

'The docks are even more devastated than the town, the great shipyards of Bloem and Voss are a wilderness of tangled girders, and in the middle of this chaos fourteen unfinished U-boats still stand rusting on the slipways. Work on them finally stopped two months ago; after that Hamburg was a dead city.

'Rummaging through Lord Haw-Haw's desk we found a revealing timetable he drew up for his work for April 10 1945, and at the end of it is the glorious item: "1450—1510 hours, a pause to collect my wits." Well, he and the citizens of Hamburg have now got plenty of time to collect their wits, for tonight the sturdy soldiers of the Devons, the famous Desert Rats, are on guard over Haw-Haw's studios, the Allied military authorities are now running his programme, and instead of "Germany Calling", the colonel in charge gives you now the new call-sign of "Station Hamburg". This is Radio Hamburg, a station of the Allied Military Government. And from Hamburg we take you back to London.'[9]

In London that night, the Tory MP Sir Henry 'Chips' Channon, filled in his diary as usual: 'I had dinner with Mrs Keppel who, in spite of her years, looked magnificent. We discussed the war, and I really wondered, as we talked, which war we were on to, the Boer War or the Crimean War, so eternally charming is she. After dinner I went along the corridor of the Ritz, being, like everyone else, in a restless mood (all London has been on edge these last few days, waiting for the final announcement) and went to read the latest news on the tape machine. There I read that at 9.13 a communiqué had been issued at SHAEF that the Germans had capitulated in Holland, Western Germany and Denmark and that the cease fire will begin tomorrow at 6.0 a.m. We were all immensely moved and celebrated in Kümmel, the Linlithgows especially as it means that their prisoner-of-war son, Charles Hopetoun, whom they had not seen since Dunkirk, will soon be home.'[10]

At his country house in Wiltshire, Cecil Beaton was ambivalent about the news as he completed his diary entry for 4 May: 'During these long years of war the one o'clock news has so often brought disappointment or dread, that we have learned to brace ourselves for almost any kind of shock. Yesterday we were caught off guard, and could hardly grasp what had happened when we learned of the utter and complete collapse of Germany.

'Perhaps we are too exhausted to retain any strong emotions. We can just manage to give a hungry gasp of relief from perpetual queasiness in the pit of the stomach—and a sigh of gratitude.

'The winter this year seemed bleaker, colder and grimmer than ever before. Then, prematurely and all of a sudden, spring arrived and was immediately followed by a freak fortnight of summer heat. Out came—all at once—the lilac, the tulips and honeysuckle. It's been almost too much to believe in. Now, with the avalanche of summer, good news, like the blossom and flowers, is pouring from every source. "Berlin falling!" "Göbbels dead." "Germans surrender to Montgomery." Now, any moment, we expect the full, unconditional surrender. The worst of the nightmare is past: the terrible casualty lists, the ghastly deaths of so many unquestioning young people fighting in all the elements, the gassing of Jews, the torturing of prisoners, the butcheries in German-occupied territories, the children soaked in petrol and set alight, the rows of naked women hung upside down from windows ... Yet one is conscious of so much continued suffering throughout the world that it is hard to celebrate ... '[11]

In Cheltenham, Private Norman Wisdom was doing a 12-minute spot in a concert for the troops at the Town Hall. Norman had joined the army in 1931 as a 14-year-old boy soldier. He was sent to India, learned to play the clarinet in the band and taught himself tap-dancing in the wash-house in Lucknow. In 1938 he was discharged, got a job as a telephone operator then re-enlisted in the Royal Signals at the outbreak of war.

'At the end of the war I was working the switchboard at a telecommunications centre in Cheltenham, but in the evenings I used to do this spot with an amateur dance band. It was nothing special, just a bit of tap-dancing, singing, comedy and falling over. But people seemed to like it.

'That night at Cheltenham Town Hall everyone laughed like mad and at the end of the show I was sitting in the dressing room at the back when this very nice fellow came round and said "Are you a professional?" I said, "No." So he said, "Well, if you don't try and become a professional when you leave the Army you must be bloody mad." That gentleman's name was Rex Harrison.'

In Liverpool, 24-year-old Vi Bottomley listened intently to the ten o'clock news that night as she did every night. 'When I heard they'd surrendered I just started to cry and I couldn't stop. I don't know what was the matter with me, I should have been happy, but I was crying my eyes out.

'I kept thinking of Jack [her husband]. He was killed on D Day. I never knew quite what happened to him, only that he was dead. And I kept thinking, what a waste, what a waste. He was such a lovely man, always laughing and joking. He worked in the docks and needn't have gone in the Army at all, but no, he had to go and do his bit. And for what? He'd never even seen the baby, his baby, sleeping upstairs.'

V

Saturday 5 May

Is It the End?

Although the surrender on Lüneburg Heath prompted huge headlines in the newspapers on 5 May, no announcement was forthcoming from the government about VE Day. Uncertain whether the war in Europe was over or not, celebrations in Britain were muted.

'I don't think anyone wanted to jump the gun,' said Sydney Woodhouse, then a 26-year-old fireman in East London. 'Obviously everyone was pleased that the Germans have given in to Monty, but no one knew what was happening on the eastern front with the Russians. All the papers were full of what was being arranged for VE Day, parades, parties, boozers staying open all hours and what have you, but what everyone wanted to know was when it was going to be—and no one was saying.

'As far as I can remember me and some of the lads at the station had a pint or two to celebrate the cease fire, but I can't say there was dancing in the streets, least not where we were. We were still bloody glad not to be out every night fighting fires from them V2 rockets.'

Telephone operator Christine Metcalf recalls a livelier night in Blackpool, where she was attending her first Union of Postal Workers conference at the Winter Gardens. 'We followed the war very closely, everyone did. Everybody was hopeful that the end of the war was close and when we heard the news of the surrender everyone hugged and cried and cheered. It was unforgettable. The chairman adjourned business and we all took to the streets. Everybody was running around, all the troops were dancing and there were loads of Americans there.

'A small group of some of the girls that I was in the hotel with had booked to see Vivien Leigh in *Skin of Your Teeth* at the theatre. There was no particular excitement in the theatre, it just seemed as though things were the same. We went because we had bought the tickets, but I don't remember a single word of it. I don't think I even did the next day, as it was impossible to concentrate.

'When we left the theatre we went to the sea-front, everyone was there linking arms, singing and dancing. All the public houses had signs "Sorry, no beer" but who needed it, anyway? We were all high on relief, excitement and joy that the war was nearly over.

'At midnight we were on the sands, still linking arms and singing, splashing in and out of the water, wet through but no one cared. I don't remember going back to the hotel, though I am sure we did. It must have been terribly late and we were terribly exhausted.'

For Phyllis Bailey, the 26-year-old mother of two small children living on the outskirts of Leeds, the day had a different meaning: it was her birthday. 'I would have loved to have gone into the services, I really liked the idea of doing something of national importance, being away from home, having fun with the other girls. Looking after two children under five made you yearn for a bit of reckless, selfish fun, even in those days.

'Bob, my husband, was in the RAF doing fighter maintenance at an airfield somewhere way up in the north Scotland and I was working part-time as a book-keeper for a company which made military textiles, stuff like straps and webbing. We had my mother-in-law move in with us—she was a Londoner—and she did knitting for the WI and looked after the kiddies when I was at work, or nights when I did fire watching.

'Bob always told me to listen to the radio and read whatever newspapers we could get our hands on to see what was happening with our boys in Europe. I don't think I would have bothered if he hadn't insisted. He said it was very important not to lose faith with them, or forget what they were doing for those of us at home. But to be honest, often you were just too busy to sit down and read a paper. If you weren't at work or minding the children, you were in the allotment digging vegetables or at home trying to scrape a decent meal together out of your rations.

'Anyway, I read enough to know that the Allies were pushing up through Germany and that it probably wouldn't be too much longer before they surrendered. That's what we thought. I mean, we'd heard Hitler was dead and whether you believed it or not—he'd definitely been quiet for a time—and it looked as if the Germans were finished.

'It was funny how I heard about it. My birthday is on 5 May and on the day before, there was a knock on the door about nine in the evening and there was an airman standing on the doorstep, rucksack on his back, hat over his eye, holding a package and grinning all over his face.

'He said he was a friend of Bob's and that Bob had asked him to drop off a package as he was on his way through Leeds. Then he said, right out of the blue, "You know the war's over, don't you?" Blimey, I'd heard so many people say the same thing in the past few days that I didn't take much notice. I asked him about Bob, how he was, when he was coming home, the way you do, gave him a cup of tea and a sandwich and sent him on his way.

'When I opened the package I found it was a lovely length of tweed with a card and a letter from Bob. Don't ask me how he got the material—in those days you didn't ask too many questions about things like that. In the letter he said that the place he was at was being scaled down and that he was expecting to be posted to out East. That was a shock, I can tell you.

'Next day when I went to get the paper from the corner shop the first thing I saw was this big headline SURRENDER and a picture of Monty being saluted by a row of German officers on Lüneburg Heath. I wondered why I hadn't believed the lad that had called the previous night.

'Of course I was glad, naturally I was. But I couldn't help thinking that it was so unfair that everybody else would be getting their husbands back soon and I would have to wait goodness knows how long before mine could come home. I wasn't even very sure where he was going, but it sounded a very long way away. 'Funnily enough, he never went because they dropped the atom bomb before he set off and he was home before Christmas. I made a lovely skirt out of the tweed and a pair of short trousers with a bib front for the boy. It ended its life as a draught-excluder years later. It was strange, I could never look at it without thinking about that bloke who came to the door and said "You know the war's over, don't you?" I never saw him again. I don't think I even knew what his name was.'

Twenty-one-year old Winifred Maryon, a civilian clerk working in the Royal Navy victualling yard at Deptford, was far too involved with her wedding plans to worry about what was happening with the war: 'There was no hesitation about having a proper church wedding, even though it was war time. I borrowed a white dress in figured velvet, beautiful material, from one of the girls in the office whose sister had just married and another girl who had also recently married lent me a long, trailing veil with embroidery.

'My sister-in-law, who was about 17 at the time, was the bridesmaid and I bought her dress with extra coupons which I had begged from someone and my cousin, who had been in West Africa, came home just before the wedding and brought back some bouclé material which I used for a going-away dress.

'Was it the wedding I dreamed of? Oh no! First the buses were on strike and there was very little petrol so on the morning of my wedding I had to take a train from Greenwich to Deptford to pick up the bouquet and the flowers. The bus strike also meant it was difficult for our guests to get to the church, so my boss at the victualling yard commandeered this Naval lorry and all the guests climbed on the back of it in all their wedding finery.

'To cap it all, we discovered when we arrived at the church that it had been bombed the previous Wednesday. It was badly damaged, certainly enough to let the rain in, so while we were standing at the altar the verger was behind me with a broom, sweeping the rainwater to keep it away from the hem of my dress. All the pew covers and kneeling pads had been taken away so we had to kneel on the bare stone. Afterwards Syd, my husband, said that when the vicar pronounced us man and wife, he nearly said "Thank God for that!"

'The reception was held in a room over a pub and we had the caterers in to do what they could with the food but most people also brought things to boost the buffet.

'I wasn't really aware that the war was nearly over, I don't recall it coming into my mind. I suppose I was too deeply immersed in getting the wedding organised. I just thought the war was carrying on as it had been. It wasn't until we were actually on the way to our honeymoon in Devon, a day later, that we met an RAF chap and his wife on the way to the hotel and he said that he thought the war was going to be over that week.'

June Barrow also has good reason to remember 5 May 1945—it was the day she got married. June was working in a shop in Norwich when the war broke out, but soon afterwards joined the Land Army. 'It was a lot dirtier and harder work than being in a shop, but I liked the outdoors and besides, I wanted to get out of the house and feel I was doing something for the war. My parents hadn't wanted me to join the forces because my brother was in the Army and one child on active duty was enough for them.

'I didn't want to join the forces either. From what I could gather, all you did was work in offices dishing out pay or billeting slips or likely as not, you'd be posted to some God-forsaken place miles away from home to plot the movement of V1s and V2s. I had a friend in the ATS who spent most of the war in a Nissen hut in the middle of a field with no toilets!

'Cliff, my fiancé was in the Army; he and my brother had volunteered together the day after war was declared. Cliff had been wounded in Belgium and was brought back home after being patched up in a field hospital near Antwerp. He got shot in both legs by tracer fire and it was ages before he could walk again.

'I went down to visit him at the Oxford military hospital as often as I could, but travel was difficult as you had to try and do the journey in daylight. Travelling at night was hopeless with the blackout, though I remember I had a very fetching illuminated flower to pin to my coat lapel. It was supposed to help people see you in the dark. What a laugh!

'We planned to get married as soon as my Cliff could walk comfortably and we named the day at the beginning of April. It was going to be at the register office in Norwich on Saturday 5 May, the day my parents got married. It left me only a few weeks to get organized. You don't really know where to begin, and it was even more difficult in those days. You didn't know who to invite because you were never really sure who was going to be available to come, what with so many people away in the services and war work and night shifts and everything. My Mum was worried stiff about the wedding breakfast.

'There was no question of a big church wedding in white with bridesmaids, which of course I had always dreamed about. First of all you couldn't buy the material for a wedding dress, there wasn't any around. You couldn't get any dresses at all—by 1945, you only got 45 coupons a year for your dress ration and a coat and a dress cost over 30.

'My Mum made me a blouse out of a silk tea gown of hers that she had hardly ever worn, and over it I wore a grey suit with a peplum and a plum-coloured felt hat, one of those saucy peek-a-boo hats with the dipping brim.

'By the time of the big day Cliff could walk quite well, although he had to use sticks. He looked very nice, even though he had to borrow a mate's uniform because his own was in tatters and we couldn't get another one in time for him to wear.

'The wedding breakfast, well, it was lunch actually, was smashing, my Mum had really put her back into it. They'd been saving a bottle of wine for years, for when the war ends, my Dad always said, and so we had that for the toast, really just a thimbleful in each glass, but it didn't matter because none of us much liked wine anyway. My Grandad used to call it "French muck". Dad got jugs of beer from the pub and we made shandy with Mum's homemade lemonade.

'All the neighbours had pooled their coupons, their egg and flour and butter rations and made a one-tier wedding cake, decorated with flowers, because you couldn't get food colouring. It was the sort of thing you did for your friends and your neighbours in those days.

'While I was getting ready for the wedding, I was still working and trying to do the arrangements at the weekends. I took no notice at all of what was happening in Germany, though people were talking more and more about the war ending. But it was nice to wake up on the morning of my wedding and read in the newspaper that Germany had surrendered. It made the day even more special.'

Nella Last, a WVS worker in Barrow, kept an extraordinarily detailed diary throughout the war, but made no mention of celebrations in her entry for 5 May: 'I think the changeable weather saps energy. It even makes Mrs Atkinson [her co-worker] say she is tired! All her talk and ideas lately seem to be about "how the Germans can be punished". She does not seem to see the horror that is Germany, millions of homeless ones adrift in the very essence of the word, no homes, no work, sanitation, water, light or cooking facilities, untold dead to bury, sick and mad people to care for. I said "Would you like to live in Barrow if every house downtown had gone in the blitz, the water, light and transport gone, and all the shipyard—with idle, desperate men beginning to seek food and shelter from *anywhere*, by *any means*?" Any safe corner or peaceful place with buildings or food of any kind—flocks, fields of growing food, orchards, cows and poultry—will be a target for the half-crazed, hungry people wandering round. She thinks it's "only right for what they did to Poland and Holland". I said, "There is no right and wrong in it. If a man has a gangrened wound, a malignant ulcer, he doesn't speak of right or wrong—he seeks cure or amputation before the poison has spread through the whole of his body."

'Tonight, before I came to bed, it had stopped raining and I went down the garden path to smell the grateful earth and the scent of damp greenery. At the bottom corner, I was conscious of an unpleasant smell and, as I thought, Murphy had left a very dead rat he had caught. As I got the spade, scolding him the while, and buried the loathsome thing in the soft earth, the thought of decay and death under the acres of fallen masonry in Europe set my mind again on "What *will* happen?"—till my head ticked so badly I could see the beat of a nerve in my throbbing temple when I looked in the glass. People say all round, "I'm glad the war is over before my son has to go"—not realising the problems of Europe or the Pacific War.' [1]

If the day was somewhat subdued in Britain, the same could not be said for Denmark and Holland, which were effectively liberated by the surrender. Holland, in particular, had suffered grievously under the rule of the hated Nazi Arthur Seyss-Inquart. Resistance in Holland had been ruthlessly crushed by the Gestapo with the enthusiastic assistance of the Dutch SS; it was less than a year since Anne Frank had been dragged from her attic in Amsterdam; transportation of Jews to the gas chambers had continued almost until the eve of the surrender; there were even reports that SS shot Dutch civilians pouring out of their houses to celebrate the news on the evening of 4 May. On top of all this, the population was virtually starving.

An official SHAEF report painted a terrible picture of conditions in the country: 'It is an empty country, inhabited by a hungry, and in the towns, a semi-starved population. It is no exaggeration to state that, had liberation been delayed for another ten days or so, many thousands of people would surely have died of hunger.

'The existing food supplies in the area are practically nil. A day's ration consists of a very small cup of nasty "ersatz" soup, a very small piece of an unappetising and sticky substance called bread, and a wafer of sugar beet. It is hardly surprising that a large proportion of the population, who were unable to buy on the black market, have lost on an average 45 pounds in weight.

'The people, especially those in the big towns, are exhausted both physically and mentally. Generally speaking, they suffer from great weakness and the men are quite unable to perform a full day's work. It is reliably estimated that certainly 50 per cent of the population are lousy. Figures were given to me by the Burgomaster of Amsterdam which showed that the death rate per week since January has been nearly double that of the corresponding week last year and in some cases three or four times as great. The relief teams sent in by the British Red Cross consider that the conditions in Rotterdam are even worse than those in Amsterdam. It is reliably estimated that more young children are dying per *month* now than per year in 1942 ...

'Out of 100 people taken at random from the streets (and these are the people that are seen walking about every day and does not include those that are so weak that they remain indoors) 15 per cent showed signs of bad malnutrition, 50 per cent were definitely undernourished and 35 per cent were more or less normal.

It is of interest to note that there were five times as many males suffering from starvation as females.

'The black market flourishes to an alarming degree. Alarming because many middle class workers, in order to live, sold practically all their worldly goods to obtain money to buy "black". There was also a considerable traffic in coupon books which were bought by the rich from the poor with obvious results. No one was allowed by the Germans to draw from the banks more than 80 guilders a month. As it was essential to obtain more in order to deal in the black market, naturally permanent belongings had to be sold.

'There is an absolute lack of necessities of life. There is no coal, consequently no light; no soap, and nobody has had any new clothes for five years. In many of the big towns there is no water pressure, which means that the sanitary arrangements are woefully deficient.'[2]

The Allies were quick to send supplies into Holland. On the afternoon of 5 May, war correspondents called to Wageningen to witness the German surrender reported passing a long convoy of Allied trucks loaded with food and fuel. They also passed Prince Bernhard, the heir to the Dutch throne, sitting in an open-top limousine recently owned by Seyss-Inquart and, perhaps understandably, 'looking very pleased with himself'.

J.L. Hodson was among the correspondents: 'At 4 p.m. we assembled in the empty bar and restaurant of a partly-destroyed hotel at Wageningen where the surrender terms were to be given to General Blasowitz, commanding the Germany army in Holland. The windows were out, brickwork near one window was precarious. Men were busy fixing up a BBC microphone and electric lamps for photographs. The room was dusty and dirty, and a litter of basket chairs strewn about ... General Ffoulkes [Canadian] and his men were fresh complexioned, ruddy, with rather plump faces, looking like businessmen who had put on soldiers' uniforms, men brisk but essentially human. Seated opposite across these shoddy tables was General Blasowitz, a short man about sixty, with a lean, hard-bitten face, hard grey eyes, slightly hooked nose, thin protuberant lips and sharp chin. Such hair as we saw was cropped close. Rechelt, his chief-of-staff, was almost as hungry-looking. Both personified war, men whose trade was war. They wore leather overcoats dyed grey, had red leaves on their jacket collars and iron crosses at their throats. The proceedings were brisk, and General Ffoulkes was blunt. But there was nothing grim, no attempt to humiliate, no stamping or clanking. Indeed, at times the atmosphere was rather akin to a business board meeting. The terms held many interesting points—that the Germans must accept further orders without argument or comment, that the Dutch SS must be disarmed and the Germans be responsible for their behaviour, that the Germans would be responsible for guarding all pumps at the dykes as we went in, and that the Germans must feed and maintain themselves until the enemy are moved out of Holland. Among Ffoulkes' admirably blunt remarks were: "I want to make it clear only one person will give orders and that's myself."'[3]

Despite the privations they had endured, the Dutch people came out in force later that day to celebrate their liberation. Mingling in the crowd in the little town of Deventer, about 20 miles north of Arnhem, was a young officer in the 22nd Dragoons called Ian Carmichael. 'I was a liaison officer at 3 Army Brigade headquarters, which was under canvas in a spruce little park in the centre of Deventer. On the night of May 4 I was duty officer and so I signed for the message from HQ 21 Army Group ordering the cessation of all offensive operations. We passed it on to all units under our command at 0115 the following morning.

'It is difficult to describe to anyone who has not lived through six years of total war the immediate feelings of euphoria that burst when the news arrived that the final whistle had been blown. For six long years the people of Europe had never seen a light of any sort or description in the streets after dusk unless it had been either a blue one, the slim pencil-light of a masked torch carried by pedestrians, or the narrow, extremely narrow, letterbox slits to which the lights on all vehicles had been reduced.

'The fact that the maiming and killing had stopped; the fact that one had come through unscathed; the fact that every light in the town could be put on and the curtains left wide open … it was magical, such a tremendous relief that it was all over. Deventer went mad that night. Lights were switched on everywhere and street after street was mobbed with people of all ages carrying bright orange lanterns illuminated by candles. It was a warm May night and windows and doors were thrown wide open. Music blared from radios placed on window sills and dancing in the streets was wild and abandoned. On one normally busy crossroads the traffic had stopped completely. The area had been floodlit with unmasked headlights and dancing was in full swing to music pouring out of a large amplifier that had been rigged up on the side of one of the houses. Then the processions started and every house as "open house".

'My chum and I went into a bar and got pretty plastered. That night everybody was everybody's friend and I remember talking to a local journalist, a very dour gentlemen, who told us to enjoy it all while we could because "Mark my words, in fewer years than you can imagine, you will have to go through the whole thing again with the Russians." We certainly didn't want to think about anything like that on that night. As far as I can recall, we ended up in the house of a family we visited quite often being tucked up on a camp bed and a sofa by the lady of the house with tears pouring down her cheeks.'[4]

Of all the occupied countries, Denmark had probably suffered least inasmuch as it was viewed as a model protectorate. Its liberation, however, was no less joyous. Alan Moorehead accompanied the Allied mission which flew in to Copenhagen on the morning of 5 May: 'Every house on that liberation morning flew the national flag on a pole, the white cross on the red background, and from the air the effect was as if one were looking down on endless fields strewn with poppies. Over the suburbs of Copenhagen there was at first not much movement in the streets; fearing just possibly this was the final air raid of the war the people ran indoors. But then as we came lower they gathered confidence and poured out into the open. A thickening procession of cars and bicycles and pedestrians came careering down the road to the airfield. One after another the Dakotas slid into a landing between the stationary German aircraft and drew up on line before the airport buildings. The airborne troops jumped down, and with their guns ready advanced upon the hangars. The scene did for a moment look slightly ominous, especially as none of us quite knew what to expect. Armed German guards were spaced along the runways. Two German officers stood stiffly in front of the central office and began to advance towards the landing aircraft. General Dewing, the leader of our mission, met them half-way and in two minutes it was clear: we would have no trouble in Denmark. Lindemann, the German commander, was waiting to receive the British and arrange the formal surrender. All German troops were confined to barracks and the Danish resistance movement had control.

'Cars were ready to drive us into the city. It seemed to us that we had never seen such pretty girls, such gay dresses, such glistening shops and gardens. The Danes had been celebrating the previous night, and now the streets—or such of them as you could see through the crowd—were strewn with bits of paper and bunting. Here and there one came on a building or a restaurant with the front smashed in and the furniture tumbled out on the roadway. "German headquarters" my driver explained briefly. The car was now festooned with ribbons and flowers and it was difficult to see. Each time the procession stopped the crowd closed in on us, and they had a strange manner of reaching out to touch our sleeves and tunics, apparently to make sure we were real.

'Dewing headed for the Hotel Angleterre, which he intended to make his headquarters, and once we were there the crowd swarmed forward, making it impossible to get in or out of the building. The scene in the lobby bordered on hysteria. One has a disconnected series of recollections, of corks coming out of champagne bottles, of tables laden with smoked salmon and caviare, of grilled steaks and strawberries, of singing and a receding and advancing wall of laughing faces, of bright flowers under the electric light and the sun streaming down on the people chanting in the street outside …

'In the midst of all this a German admiral roamed about the corridors of the hotel vainly trying to find someone—anyone—to whom he could surrender the cruisers *Nurnberg* and *Prinz Eugen*, their attendant destroyers and 600,000 tons of mercantile shipping then lying in the bay. It did not seem of much consequence to anyone at the time, and a good half-hour must have passed before the German tracked down our admiral in his suite.

'Those of us who had followed the armies across Africa and Europe knew pretty well the way a liberation went and what happened at the first moments of a city's rejoicing. But here there was a special flavour, a more simple and lighter spirit than usual; fewer shadows under the gaiety.'[5]

Saturday 5 May

Defeat

'The news came through that all fighting in NW Germany, Holland and Denmark was to stop at 0800 hours today,' Captain Joe Patterson, a medical officer with the 2nd Special Air Service, then just outside Kiel, wrote in his diary on 5 May. 'Almost at once we had a panic stand to, as one of our jeeps had just been shot up in the next village, and the four occupants wounded and taken prisoner by outposts of 400 militant SS in the immediate area. With armoured cars to support us, we went chasing up in the half light and found the jeep all shot up and full of blood. We swanned around a bit more, but only took a few prisoners, a few tough-looking SS among them, but mostly boys of 15 or 16, whom we let go.

'There were a lot of French PoWs in the village, thirsting for the blood of a German farmer who used to beat them up. We found that he had hidden weapons too, so we burned his farm and house. I took no part in these proceedings. Alistair MacGregor was explaining to the weeping wife how lucky she was that we were nice chivalrous English who didn't shoot people without trial, when there was a sharp burst from a tommy-gun behind the barn, and one of our tougher Poles, "Louis" for short, came round the corner with a happy grin and announced that he had just bumped the farmer off. The name of the British Raj took a bit of a set-back in the eyes of the widow after this.'[1]

Lieutenant General Sir Brian Horrocks, commander 30 Corps described the surrender: 'The surrender on our front took place at 1430 hours when the German general commanding the Corps Ems and his chief of staff arrived at our headquarters. Elaborate arrangements had been made for their reception. Our military police, looking very smart, escorted them to a table in the centre of the room; all round the outside was a ring of interested staff officers and other ranks of 30 Corps.

'When all was ready I came in and seated myself all alone opposite the two Germans. After issuing my orders for the surrender I finished with these words:

"These orders must be obeyed scrupulously. I warn you we shall have no mercy if they are not. Having seen one of your horror camps my whole attitude towards Germany has changed."

'The chief of staff jumped up and said:"The army had nothing to do with those camps!" "Sit down," I replied. "There were German soldiers on sentry duty outside and you cannot escape responsibility. The world will never forgive Germany for those camps."

'The German forces who were concentrated in the north-west corner of Cuxhaven peninsula were ordered to stack all their weapons at certain points. A couple of days later I drove round the area to see how the disarmament was proceeding and found the remnants of the parachute army concentrated on an aerodrome. When I saw the miserable equipment—just a few, old, patched up self-propelled guns and tanks—with which they had managed to delay our advance for so long, I turned to the divisional commander and said: "I must congratulate you on the fighting qualities of your division."' [2]

This was the text of Eisenhower's proclamation:

Proclamation No. 1

TO THE PEOPLE OF GERMANY

I, General Dwight D Eisenhower, Supreme Commander, Allied Expeditionary Force, do hereby proclaim as follows:

1 The Allied Forces serving under my command have now entered Germany. We come as conquerors, but not as oppressors. In the area of Germany occupied by the forces under my command, we shall obliterate Nazi-ism and German Militarism. We shall overthrow the Nazi rule, dissolve the Nazi Party and abolish the cruel, oppressive and discriminatory laws and institutions which the Party has created. We shall eradicate that German Militarism which has so often disrupted the peace of the world. Military and Party leaders, the Gestapo and others suspected of crimes and atrocities will be tried and, if guilty, punished as they deserve.

2 Supreme legislative, judicial and executive authority and powers within the occupied territory are vested in me as Supreme Commander of the Allied Forces and Military Governor, and the Military Government is established to exercise these powers under my direction. All persons in the occupied territory will obey immediately and without question all the enactments and orders of the Military Government. Military Government Courts will be established for the punishment offenders. Resistance to the Allied Forces will be ruthlessly stamped out. Other serious offences will be dealt with severely.

3 All German courts and educational institutions within the occupied territory are suspended. The Volksgerichtshof, the Sondergerichte, the SS Police Courts and other special courts are deprived of authority throughout the occupied territory. Re-opening of the criminal and civil courts and educational institutions will be authorised when conditions permit.

4 All officials are charged with the duty of remaining at their posts until further orders and obeying and enforcing all orders or directions of the Military Government or the Allied Authorities addressed to the German Government or the German people. This applies also to officials, employees and workers of all public undertakings and utilities and to all other persons engaged in essential work.

Dwight D Eisenhower, General

Supreme Commander

Allied Expeditionary Force

'We didn't really know what had happened on the Lüneburger Heide,' said Gunda Schwarz, who was then 22, working in a shipping broker's office in Lübeck. 'But even if we did know it was of no significance to me. We knew the war was over and that was that and now we had to get on with life as best we could. The first priority was survival.

'My sister had returned from the Land Army just before the end of the war and worked in an office which was set up to discharge and re-direct German soldiers in retreat, who filled Lübeck at that time and who, when the Allies arrived, were made PoWs. They brought with them the news that the war was pretty well over. The German troops were coming back from all sides, retreating from the Eastern front, from the West, and they were saying that it was all over. They knew.

'That the war would end, and that we would lose it, everybody knew months beforehand. In fact, a lot of people thought that we would lose the war when we went into Russia. I remember the day we went into Russia, it was a Sunday and the windows were open and the radios were blaring out the news that German soldiers had crossed the border into Russia and then everyone was saying, "Well, now we've lost the war." That was what broke the camel's back. Everybody knew it, the generals knew it, but Hitler was blinded and could not be told. I remember we felt defeated, everybody felt it was a lost cause, such gloom hung over the town that day.

'When we started to hear the rumours that we had surrendered, we started celebrating, any way we could, with anyone who had a squeezebox. We were singing, doing all kinds of stupid things but I remember my cousin being absolutely distraught because her husband went back to the front in the East just before the war ended and she never heard from him again. She never did know what happened to him.

'Although there was a great sense of anticipation that it would soon be over, it still came as a surprise when we suddenly heard that there were tanks at the top of our road. My best friend was an air force pilot and he'd been trained in the last few months on jets, but he had never been allowed to fly because there was no fuel. He was furious that he could not do anything to stop the tanks.

'Later, on the outskirts of the town, we saw a burning train and people from the housing estate were running across to the train, saying there were provisions on board and my sister, being very foolhardy, said we must go and get some. But I could see the tanks firing what looked like streams of light at the burning train. It looked quite harmless, even pretty.

'But we still went. You know, when you're young, you're not afraid, you think you're immortal. We found a whole suitcase full of macaroni on the train. I was more cautious than my sister and I kept looking out and I could see that the train had some wagons with fuel tanks on them and I could see the firing getting nearer to the fuel tanks. I said "Usch, it's going to explode any minute, we've got to get out of here" but Usch said "Oh just a minute" and grabbed a Mettwurst and God knows what else.

'It was quite a long way to walk back home, a few miles, and we thought, we can't carry this case all the way back, so we left it with a family on the housing estate and said if they would look after it for us they could have some of it. We thought we would never see it again, but much later, when we could move freely again, we went to pick it up and they had kept it. We ate macaroni for weeks afterwards!

'Survival was what mattered to everyone. There were no phones working, no trains running and hundreds of people coming from the East. I worked at the station quite often, handing out tea to the soldiers. It was terrible, the stories they told. They had nowhere to go, they just sat on the street, numbed. There were long, long queues for bread, for example and most people got scurvy because we couldn't get any soap. There was a great deal of helping one another, sharing things and also, you became an adventurer too, in a way. When I think of some of the things I did, well, nowadays, everything seems so tame compared with then.

'The main thing was to get firewood and my sister and I would set out with a handcart to the forest. The forests were patrolled by English MPs who were guarding the wood, but we took it anyway because it was all we had to cook with. We had no amenities at all.

'Even towards the end there were still many young soldiers, really Nazi-inclined young men. Downstairs in the flat in our house lived a young girl who had one of those as a boyfriend and she was telling us that he and his comrades had shot quite a few deserters. I can remember my mother urging me to come upstairs, to have nothing to do with him, because she thought he might have shot us if he had heard us saying the war was over.'

Guenter de Bruyn joined the army as a cadet at the age of 17 and was wounded not long after his 18th birthday. On 5 May 1945, he was lying in a hospital bed in Rakovnik, in a part of Czechoslovakia still occupied by Germany, waiting for the imminent arrival of the Allies: 'During the last ten days of April, words like turning point, retaliation and super-weapon (*Wunderwaffe*) were no longer heard. Nor was there much bragging about past acts of glory. Nobody, however, dared pronounce the words "the war is lost" out loud, though they all thought it was. This feeling was emphasized by the fact that discussion became more and more intense about who they would rather have arrive first in Rakovnik, the Russians or the Americans.

This theme, because of ever newer and more contradictory rumours, was inexhaust-ible. In the course of such discussion, the Americans were turned into guardian angels whose job it was to protect the remains of the German army from Soviet attack.

'The news of Hitler's death, which threatened to disappear in the welter of bad news, seemed to cause no noticeable mourning or shock. People were much more interested in how the composition of the front lines in the immediate prox-imity was developing and whether it was really true, as a rumour had it, that a jeep filled with US officers had already been seen in town. When, on the orders of the administration of the hospital, the SS ranks detailed on the medical charts were changed to those of army ranks, none of those involved protested, on the contrary all agreed with great relief to this protective measure ...

'With the radio transmission on the morning of 5 May, it was all over. The reason for this was not the Americans, whom wishful thinking had already placed at the railway station, but the Czechs, who had disarmed the garrison of invalided Germans in the city and who were now using the central public address system to announce in Slav-accented German that all weapons, including sticks, side arms and daggers, should be laid down in the yard before an inspection of the rooms. Failure to comply would most certainly result in death. After the morning rounds, during which the doctors attempted in vain to appear calm, the inspec-tion began. Even as we heard orders in foreign voices from the rooms on the first floor, all those who had treasures like tins of sardines, watches, rings, hid them behind the radiators or slipped them into their surgical dressings. I stuffed packets of cigarettes, Viktoria brand, under the mattress.

'I became scared during the inspection of my bed. The reason was that a German machine gun, rumoured to sometimes go off of its own accord, was more or less being held under my nose and the Czech who was holding it there seemed to be even less familiar with it than I was. He was no more than 17, wearing a confirmation suit that he had grown out of and over which he had lashed together a belt from which were suspended several ammunition pouches. He kept touching the trigger with the index finger of his right hand and with his left, pulled the cigarettes out from under the mattress and popped them into his pocket. "Nix Viktoria," he said, with a fierce expression.'[3]

Twenty-one-year-old Helga Zirkel came from a Swiss family that had emi-grated to Germany three generations earlier but had never given up its nationality. As theoretical foreigners, the family was victimized by the SS, subjected to spot searches, and Helga was barred from attending university. In the final months of the war, she and her mother joined the hordes of refugees fleeing from Koenigsberg in the path of the advancing Russians. They found rooms in a farm on the outskirts of a village in East Prussia.

'When the end of the war was formally announced, people received it very quietly. We were rather isolated, being on the farm, but in the village I think the talk was of "Let's hope my husband or son comes home soon" or "Will they be prisoners of war and for how long?" There was that sort of worry, but otherwise, everybody seemed to be waiting, they didn't know what was going to happen. I think they were all a little bit afraid of what would happen next. Would their houses be occupied, would their food be taken? People out on the farms had hidden food, you know, quietly killed a pig or something like that.

'I think we knew it wouldn't be very long before everything must collapse, because there wasn't much land left which wasn't conquered by the Allies or by the Russians and I think most people were practically waiting for it and longing for the finish of the war. The only way to find out how the war was going was to listen to the tales from the retreating soldiers who came our way. Radio broadcasts never told the facts as they were—retreat was a tactical withdrawal, for example.

'On the day the British arrived, the woman who owned the farm asked me to go into the village to collect something for her, some cotton or thread for needlework. It had been raining earlier and I had to jump over different puddles and because of that I wasn't looking ahead. I came round the corner and looked up and said "Oh my God". Right in front of me was a great big tank. I looked at it and I thought "Oh dear, it must have come over the fields where we had just planted the cabbages."

'And then I started to get a little bit scared because the gun barrel, very slowly, very gradually, moved from the side towards me. I thought "Surely they are not going to shoot me." It was a terrifying moment and I started to run away and then the top opened and out came a soldier and he just said "Stop". Of course I stopped and turned round and the soldier said "Put your hands on your head" so I did. He climbed out and he had a gun in his hand and with my poor school English—how I wished I learned a bit more—he explained he really only wanted to know where they were. He showed me the map and I showed them the village called Kiesdorf. I also told them that there were no soldiers there, that there wasn't any army anywhere near. Whether they believed me or not, I don't know; they might have thought I was trying to mislead them, but it was true. So, he just climbed back and the tank went off.

'I recognised it was an English tank from all the markings on it. You see, we had been taught to look out for tanks and planes already at school. We had had to learn the markings of different ones, so I recognised it straight away. I ran straight to the village and I went to see the Bürgermeister and I told him what I had seen and he straightaway went and told all the people in the houses to stay indoors because he thought that would be the best thing.

'At first, he didn't want me to go back to the farm but I said I had to go back because I had to tell the people there and particularly my mother, about what had happened. That was it.

'I think either that afternoon, or next morning, the English soldiers came in in open jeeps and motor cycles. They must have realised there wasn't any more fighting going on, people had laid down their arms. By then, a lot of people had already begun to desert and were hiding on farms and begging for civilian clothes. It was very demoralising.

'I don't think anybody tried to think very much about what would happen next. People were a little bit afraid of the English because they were the enemy. After all, even if the treatment was supposed to be all right, they were still the enemy. But I was very glad the war was over. I thought if it is now finished we can start to look for the rest of the family and maybe get back to Switzerland, or start again.'[4]

Major C.W. Kidwell of the 22nd Cheshires was the military government officer in Bentheim: 'We drove north through one devastated town after another, often with not one house standing. Both my driver and I were very silent. You can say "serves the Germans right" if you like, but you cannot be unaffected nor avoid a feeling of awe and depression. On arrival I sent for the Bürgomeister and told him "I want these two houses in 48 hours. The owners and occupants will be out by 1400 hours the day after tomorrow. They may take their personal belongings only, clothes, food, jewellery, but they will leave all the furniture and will leave the houses in a thoroughly habitable condition."

'At the stated time, two days later, I returned to find the houses stripped of everything, even carpets, and the owners had started on the flowers in the garden. I turned to my Dutch interpreter and said "Send for the Burgomeister! ... Tell him that I give him five minutes or he ceases to be Bürgomeister." In four and a half minutes he arrived, breathless, and I gave him my ultimatum. It was then 1430 hours. I would allow him until 1800 hours to get the houses back exactly as they were when I first saw them. Failure would mean that I would requisition all the houses on both sides of the street, but this time there would be no warning.

'In a matter of minutes, Germans arrived from every direction with furniture. It was rather like a Walt Disney film. Pictures were being put up, carpets laid, beds made and by 1800 I moved in, but not before I had a final word with the Bürgomeister. "Tell the people of the Kreis," I said, "they will find it much easier to obey my orders the first time. If they do not, this sort of thing will happen every time, except that as time goes on, and the more my orders are disobeyed, the shorter my temper will become."'[5]

Renate Heinsohn and her family had been bombed out of their house in Hannover and took refuge with friends in Hermagor, Austria. 'I was 21 and was working as a secretary at the Kreisleitung, the regional administration office for the Nazi Party. It was the only job I could get in that tiny town. There was only, in those days, the Landratsamt, the civilian administration, and they had no vacancies and then there was farming and a few shops and things. I'd grown up with the Nazis. I was eight when Hitler came to power, so I had grown up with the Hitler Youth and things and had no particular objection to working in the Nazi Party office, although I certainly felt it was useless pursuing the whole thing. We just wished it would finish sooner rather than later.

'We followed the progress of the war but of course we only got to know what we were supposed to know. If you live in a police state, a dictatorship, you just do not know anything that you are not supposed to know. We may have read that the war was going well, but it became clear that it was not, because the troops were withdrawing. We met all the soldiers as they came back from Russia and they told us what was really going on.

'I used to discuss the war with my mother and she even used to try to listen to foreign stations, which of course was expressly forbidden. She was quite cynical about the whole thing fairly early on and forecast gloom and doom. To begin with, I didn't think—right at the beginning—that things could go wrong and then go wrong as badly as she predicted, but bit by bit, I realized we would lose the war. You didn't somehow visualize things beyond that, you didn't even think about what might happen, you just took things one day at a time.

'I realized that the war was definitely over when, right at the end, the Kreisleiter—the local party chief who was actually a very nice man, by the way, but a completely mad idealist—said we had to make contingency plans and we started burning all the papers. There were only three or four of us females and we were issued with revolvers and taught to shoot. You see, we were right on the Yugoslav border and we expected Tito to come and that would certainly have meant goodbye for me, as a German, and, what is more, working in a Party office. I was frightened to death that the Yugoslavs might come because they had a fearful reputation.

'We went to work, burnt stuff, cleared up and sat around and waited. About a couple of weeks before the war actually finished, some time in April, the Kreisleiter decided we had better shut the shop down. He took to the hills and I don't know if he was ever found, but before he left he found us jobs. Another girl and I were sent to the local German military hospital, which was looking after the wounded soldiers retreating from the British Eighth Army. We worked there for a couple of weeks, in the office. I remember giving blood, vein to vein, to one soldier. It was very primitive then. He survived and came to thank me afterwards.

'I do remember walking to the office on the day the war ended for us. It was a beautiful morning, wonderful weather, and I was wearing a summer dress. I had never had to wear a uniform again after being in the Land Army in 1942. I walked down the high street of this little town and round the corner came tanks. My heart sank. I was absolutely terrified, because we had no idea who might be coming and you always fear the worst in a situation like that. We always thought it would be the Yugoslavs. In fact it was the British Army. The relief! I think they were East Surreys, standing in the tanks, and there was no waving or anything of course, not from them and not from me. They occupied the little town and, I think, the whole area. I was quite near the hospital at that point and just carried on and by that time they had arrived there, too. The soldiers didn't look at all intimidating, so I wasn't frightened of them. They didn't speak, nor were they threatening in any way.

'The British behaved impeccably, all of them, and I never had the sense of being a citizen of the defeated country, just very pleased it was all over. Six years is a long time, it was a miserable time. As far as thinking about the future was concerned, I think we still took it a day at a time.'

Wulfhard Wegner, the child of two doctors, was only ten when war broke out and by the time he was fifteen he was training to help 'defend the Fatherland'. It was, of course, too late. 'At the end of 1944, about November it started, I believe, every month we had to spend four days in a kind of camp, near the town where we lived in Schleswig Holstein, in order to be trained as *Volkssturm* (home guard). It was the law and we had to do as we were ordered; there was no possible way to avoid it. It was our duty to join this Hitler Youth organization.

'For four days every month, the schools closed and we had to go and learn how to use different types of weapons, we had to learn to fire an anti-tank weapon (grenade-launcher), all with the object of defending the Fatherland—at the age of 15!

'We knew that around this small town along the main roads they had dug sort of one-man trenches, deep holes, lined with concrete a bit like vertical pipes, and we were supposed, one of these days, to sit in these holes and man an anti-tank weapon and shoot at the advancing tanks. Even then we thought it was completely crazy.

'I have to say, I never really imagined that I would find myself in a fighting situation. We were being trained for that eventuality and every evening, some NCO from the Waffen SS would snarl "Who hasn't volunteered yet?" We wanted to be officers, naturally, but none of us wanted to join the Waffen SS and no one offered. It was simply too dangerous a possibility, everybody knew they were always posted to dangerous front-line stations.

'I wasn't exactly afraid, because nothing particularly definite lay ahead and it wasn't until March or April, when we were 16, that we were mustered for medical examination. We were sent to the next big city, about 10 kilometres away, I remember having to walk home afterwards. The military doctors there were reasonable men and they deferred our call up for three months at least, and in three months the war was over. You can imagine our relief.

'Of course, we didn't understand at that time that the war was nearly over, although we kept hearing that the Russian front, in particular, was drawing ever closer—first East Prussia, then Pomerania—and that the invasion forces were coming closer from the West. We found it all awfully exciting.

'On the day they finally did arrive, we sat there in our houses and said to one another, "Now they're coming". Then we saw, through the windows, moving slowly and deliberately down the road that ran past our house, this English armoured car. But nothing else, no one shooting or anything; it was all quiet. We concluded that the war in Europe was now over.

'My mother frequently listened to British radio, even though there was a death penalty for doing so. I remember going round the house to make sure that the sound of the radio couldn't be heard from outside.

'When I saw that tank, I knew it was over. I can't say I felt particularly "defeated". I suppose I was too young for that, but I remember my mother was relieved and happy when it was over—not that she had ever supported the war, as such. Mostly she, like so many other women, was anxious to see her husband home safely and quickly.'

Much to the embarrassment of her parents, Gisela Schröder, aged 17, was an enthusiastic member of the Hitler Youth movement. Towards the end of 1944 the special leadership school that she had been attending near Strasbourg was hastily evacuated as the Allies advanced. Gisela and her fellow pupils, wearing only the tracksuits they had been training in, embarked on a marathon journey across Germany to escape capture. She eventually returned home to Stargard in Pomerania in January 1945. 'My mother had sent me off like a proper lady with three suitcases of decent clothes—we were allowed to wear private clothes on certain days in my school, otherwise it was a green/black uniform and black ties. When I came home, all I had was an old margarine box and my tracksuit, which was in a thousand tatters. I had lived in it from 22 November to 4 January; it was revolting.

'Mother was delighted to see me safe and she and my father said "For God's sake, stay here now and help us, because we think Stargard will fall." [It was 35 miles east of Stettin.] My father said that they were fighting in Pomerania, but I didn't believe it. I believed not a word of my father's fears and told them they were nothing but negative pessimists. I always did know best.

'I discovered later that my parents used to listen secretly to the illegal BBC broadcasts. When I came home I wondered why my mother would shout such a lot. I suppose it was to warn my father that I was in the house, so that they did not inadvertently compromise me.

'We were all due to report to the Führer's headquarters in Fürstenwalde, where we were to be trained in Morse code and deciphering. I remember my father took me to the station and due to my status and my (replaced) uniform, I was allowed to travel on the Kourierzug, a special train only for high-ranking officers, the Hitler lot. And he was ashamed, as we stood on the platform, that his daughter was entering that train with that crowd. And I was proud and wanted him to be proud. And so we had an almighty row.

'Years later I went back with my cousin to that station. I wanted to find the pillar I leant against on the platform where I said goodbye to my father. I wanted to be able to say "Dear Father in heaven, will you forgive me?" Because I have never forgotten his words. How can a daughter be so grim, so utterly blinded to the truth? If I had been a stupid idiot, yes, but I wasn't. I was simply blinded to the truth, completely.

'Anyway, at the end of February we were all working in the bunker under the Führer's HQ, actually doing very little because everything was falling apart. We still weren't told what was going on. I remember being trained to listen to

Wagner's music and Furtwängler came with his orchestra into our bunker to give the top notchers the most wonderful concert. They knew what was going on, we didn't. I remember I used to love Wagner and today I hate Wagner. I cannot bear to hear a single note of Wagner because I connect it with this period of people being blinded by their ideology and rubbish.

'In February we were moved to a police school in Erfurt in Thuringen, which had been vacated so we could continue our training. While we were there a land-mine was dropped in the schoolyard. I was fed up with all these air raids and when the warning sounded I said "blow it" and stayed in my bedroom, which I shared with another leader. The moment the landmine hit, every thing just collapsed. The wardrobe fell on top of my mattress and I hit the ceiling, but I was unhurt. Meanwhile, the girls who had started going down the stairs to the cellars had masses of broken arms and all sorts of accidents. Having a bad conscience, I then worked like a Trojan for the next 24 hours, doing First Aid wherever I could. I never went to sleep, I just worked and worked.

'As a reward for that, I suppose, when I asked for special leave to attend a family golden wedding, it was granted. This was at the beginning of April. What I didn't know, and had never been told, was that the war was coming to an end. While I was away from Erfurt on this special four-day leave, all the girls were discharged and told to start heading for home. Some came from Vienna, some from Berlin, some from Hamburg, from the whole of Germany. They were just told to march and fight their way home as best they could, these girls. This is something I didn't find out until years later.

'After my leave I got onto a train to go back to Erfurt, but by the time I got to Weimar, there were no more trains. I got a lift in a Volkswagen staff car with some high-ranking officers who said they would take me to Erfurt. I was wearing my uniform and they said "Good God, haven't you got anything else in your suitcase?" I said that I had a pale grey ordinary suit and they told me to put that on. I thought there must be some reason, but they didn't tell me what it was. They were themselves still in uniform, but only in order to get through on the roads in their car.

'They took me as far as Erfurt and dropped me near the school and said they would go and do whatever business they had to do. (I thought they were going to an HQ of some kind as they were quite high-ranking officers, but I later discovered they were going off looting.) They said that if I wasn't back there within 20 minutes, on that corner, they would leave me there and I could find my own way back.

'When I realized the school was empty—somebody shouted out of a window "There's no one here any more, everyone has left"—I went straight back to the meeting place. The town was dead silent, it was as if everybody had stayed indoors. It was very frightening and creepy. I didn't know what was going on, I thought it was probably because there was going to be another air raid.

When these people came back in their car they were wearing civilian clothes—I had no idea where they got them. Of course, I was delighted and hopped in and they took me straight back to Weimar.

'It was getting late by then and they plonked me in some HQ in a hotel, where there were many other high-ranking officers, none of whom seemed to have a clue what to do next. On reflection, I realize it could have been dangerous for me, as they were all drinking heavily and thinking they were going to be killed and I was the only female there. Thank God, an older, rather fatherly officer there acted as my chaperon and put me in a tiny room and said "I'm going to lock you in. Don't argue, don't come out, shut up, nobody knows you're here." That's all I remember. But I am certain he saved my virginity, my pride and my dignity. Next morning, when he let me out, he gave me a piece of *Kommisbrot* with a scrape of marmalade and told me to go home to my mother, to forget the last 12 years and never think of them again. That really opened my eyes.

'He said I could get a train to Halle that morning. Sitting in the train at the station, there was suddenly an air raid warning. In my compartment there was a sailor without one leg and a soldier with an arm missing and the other one in a sling. These two said "We couldn't care less where we get killed, we've had enough, we're not going to leave this train."

'I, by this time, was so tired and so fed up and so cocky and I thought, well, if they don't go, then I'm not going either. We were the only ones left in this train.

'As I looked out of the window the sailor said, "Oh my God, it's us." There was a Christmas tree [the green marker light dropped by the RAF to light bombing targets] right above us. He said 'Come on, leg or no leg, we've got to get out of here." We got as far as the steps to the station subway when we we were knocked down into a heap in the corner by the blast.

'There I was with shaking knees, terrified, laughing my head off. I laughed and laughed and thought it was terrific. The world was shaking apart and I thought, any moment now we will be killed and all these two could do, one was a Hamburger, one a Berliner, was tell me jokes. They thought it was hilarious, but then they had seen the war and they couldn't care less any more. Suddenly, listening to that sailor and soldier tell jokes against the Nazis, the penny dropped and I realized it was all over for Germany.

'It wasn't a shock because you were so busy just trying to stay alive that you had no time to be shocked psychologically. At that moment the fear of dying was greater to me than the realization that I had wasted 12 years of my life.

'By the time we got to Halle, it had been bombed for about four days. I dragged my suitcase 12 kilometres from one side to the other, through the burning, burning town. It was the first time I had ever seen arms and legs torn from bodies and when I saw a head, that finished me.

'I was still only 17. But the drive for survival is enormous. I knew I had to get home intact. That night, I got to my mother's. The first thing she did was to burn everything. She dug my lovely black uniform suit into the compost heap, because for some reason it wouldn't burn.

'Three days later, the Americans arrived. We had had no news at all. We had no wireless, so we didn't even know in May that the war was over, not in my village anyway. The Americans told us it was all over, but we were occupied anyhow, so what does it matter whether the war is over or not?

'I grew up in Germany at a time of mob hysteria, which came between the ages 5 and 17. I was completely besotted with Nazi ideology. We worshipped Hitler until the last minute, what a load of balderdash. Unbelievable! When you think, I was an intelligent 17-year-old and I was still believing he was a great hero.

'When I realized at last I had been duped, for a while I was furious with my parents that they didn't tell me the truth. They did of course, but I just wouldn't listen.'

Edward Ward, a BBC correspondent recently released from a prisoner-of-war camp, agreed to act as interpreter when the unit he was with came across two SS officers and a woman in a smart Mercedes-Benz full of luggage at a checkpoint on a bridge over Kiel Canal.

'The senior SS officer told me he had given his word as an officer that he had no more pistols. With Buchenwald fresh in my mind I told the SS officer that word of honour or not we were going to carry out a routine search of some of his baggage. In the very first bag which we opened we found another automatic. After that the British troops went through those SS men's baggage in a way which would have done credit to the toughest customs officer. The SS showed signs of being somewhat restive in the course of this ordeal, but they soon quieted down when a heavy machine gun, manned by a very determined-looking Scotsman, was pointed at them. In the end four more automatics came to light. As well as this we found five brand new pairs of field-glasses, a radio, a number of bottles of schnapps and brandy and about 20,000 cigarettes. While the SS were grinding their teeth in silent and impotent rage, a large party of displaced persons came by, Frenchmen, Hollanders and Russians. Our troops handed over all the drinks and cigarettes to them and I confess I took considerable pleasure in explaining to the SS officers that this seemed only fair after the kind of things they have done to foreign workers when the boot was on the other foot.'[6]

Waldemar Hinrichs, a 21-year-old soldier in a tank regiment, was wounded on the Eastern front and evacuated to a military hospital in Goettingen, where he was still being treated when the Americans arrived.

'It is hard to say exactly when we noticed things were not going well for Germany in the war because we were all very young, optimistic and rather conservative. For example, after the attempt on Hitler's life in 1944, we were all suddenly supposed to salute with the Heil Hitler salute, but we carried on doing it the old way. We were also supposed to become an SS Division, but never did. We had such a good, strong comradeship in our unit that for three years I never willingly went on leave because I was afraid that if something happened while I was travelling, like an alarm, troops would be thrown out of the trains and rapidly sent off somewhere in a military transport to where no one had any names, no one knew each other and if anything happened, nobody would know. In my unit, I knew that if something did happen to me, my comrades would get me out of there and would see to it that I got back, or at least send my dog tags back.

'I was wounded in a big tank battle in Hungary in October or November of 1944 and shipped out of the area to Ipps on the Danube. In the military hospital, because I had had no leave for three years, I was sent on recuperative leave and got 14 days, so I went home to Göttingen but the garrison doctor there told me I had to go back to the hospital, even though I told him I thought my injury was sufficiently healed to rest up at home. He had enough foresight to realize that unless I was in the hospital I would be sent back to the front. So he insisted I get back to the hospital, where nothing could happen to me.

'Then the Americans came a few days later and I realized then that I was a prisoner of war as we stopped getting fed properly. Well, we got horrible thin soup cooked from vegetable parings. My father was also a prisoner of war, in Norway, but my mother lived in Goettingen and she used to sneak food to me by slipping past the American troops and coming to my ward in the lift that was used for transporting the cadavers.

'The end of the war meant, for me, no more bombs falling, no more alarms and bad food. The war was a lost time, what you learned from that was experience. When I became a soldier, my father said to me "Conduct yourself in whatever country you find yourself, like a tourist in a uniform. Apologize for your uniform." I always did that and I had the best relationships with the French, the Greeks, the Hungarians and even the Russians, who treated me very well indeed.

'Naturally one felt defeated, one had really been slapped down hard. But there were those who did not feel defeated because they had simply never believed victory was possible. Morale in some regiments was so low as to be non-existent.'

Grenadier Guards officer Nigel Nicolson was responsible for a PoW cage near Villach, Austria: 'With few exceptions they seemed to regard the capitulation as a mere transference of authority. In their dealings with the British they would venture thin jokes and offer limp cigarettes: there would be appeals to "honour among soldiers". In talking of the future they were most concerned about the date of their own demobilisation, as though the teams could disperse now that the game was ended … They would lie about all day, idling and sunbathing, their attitude to their British guards was one of servility more than of hostility or shame. Their officers would come for orders and advice on matters which were well within their own powers and capacities to solve.'[7]

Helga Schroer, aged 20, lived out the war in Rolandswert, a small town in the countryside close to Bonn, on the banks of the Rhine.

'When we heard the news that the war was finally over we breathed a deep sigh of relief. We heard it on the news and although almost everything in the area had been cut off—electricity, telephones etc—my parents had a connection to the local doctor and he telephoned my parents and said, "I believe we've made it through. I think it is only a matter of hours, now."

'My father said "Well, I think we can last out to the very end!" Then the Americans came here and our only fear was that there was still some resistance in the area and that there might still be some shooting which could endanger us. Fortunately, there was complete and absolute silence, nothing happened.

'The Americans were instantly loved by everyone as they rolled in on their tanks, throwing sweets and chocolate to the children and cigarettes for the adults. How the people cheered! My feelings were a little bit muted perhaps. I had been engaged at the time and my fiancé had fallen in the fighting and so one felt a bit strange. My heart was torn, but I was thrilled that the war was now over.'

Alexandra Pienkoh, now 83, moved with her daughter to Lower Saxony, to a village south of Hannover, in 1943 to get away from the air raids: 'After Stalingrad, we knew the war was hopeless, but had no idea how long it would take to end. We'd heard about the death of Hitler on the German radio and to be candid, hardly reacted at all to it.

'One thought only of looking after one's family and how one could continue to get through it all. Theoretically, now Hitler was dead and the head of the monster cut off, so to speak, the war would come to an end quickly but it was not until the first Americans came into our village in May 1945, that I knew for sure it was over.

'My sister was living with me at the time—my brother-in-law was a prisoner of war in America—and I was playing with the children in the garden when we heard the sound of gunfire. The Americans were coming along the main road, shooting into the mountains where they thought there were still some units of the German army setting up resistance.

'We rushed into the house and they came into the village, gathered in the market place and announced that no one was allowed to leave their houses that night. The first Americans we met had been perfectly friendly and polite, but had warned us that the troops following them might not be quite so agreeable.

'The following morning, the Americans came back and took over our house which was on the outskirts of the village, having decided to stay. The resistance in the mountains had proved rather stronger than they expected, so they dug in. Our house had a courtyard at the back and barns, so they drove their jeeps into the courtyard and turned our house into their main command post, using the kitchen as their centre of operations.

'We had to get out immediately, so I put the two children into their cot, which had rollers on, and pushed it down into the village and spent the night at the pharmacy with my friend; people looked out for each other during the war.

'We returned to the house next day. It looked as if it had been turned into a pigsty and they had taken simply everything with them—except the children's bed, which I had taken. They had taken all my nice English books. It looked as if the entire household had been bombed out, it was dreadful. The lavatories, you cannot imagine.

'Mostly I was treated politely by the Americans I worked for, but what spoiled it was those Americans who looted the village. We were still afraid of the occupation. For example, when the Americans said they wanted a chicken, they simply took one.

'We heard the official announcement that the war in Europe was over, but the Americans did not celebrate it in any way that we noticed and we certainly didn't, it was just another day for us.'

Nineteen-year-old Heinrich Scheunemann had volunteered as a pilot for the Luftwaffe, but by the time he started training in November 1944, the situation was already looking bleak: 'At this point, we started noticing that things were getting worse. We got no fuel, I myself never flew at all, we only did the ground training. At the end of the year, we were sent to the Ober-Pfalz where we waited a couple of weeks for fuel so that they could at least train us on actual aeroplanes. Nothing happened.

'Then we were transferred to a parachute regiment, without ever having flown or parachuted, simply because we were flyers and as we were going to be involved in fighting on the ground we were now parachutists. So, I was sent to Schwedt on the Oder front line. The Russians had reached the River Oder by then and so in the early days of 1945, we were lying on the other side of the river from the Russians—we could already hear them when we walked through the trenches in the evening. Our job was to defend the Oder.

'This lasted until about April 1945, by which time the Russians had established bridgeheads on the Oder, above and below our location and threatened to encircle us, so that we were forced to retreat in some disorder.

'I suppose this was when I realized the war was finally over. Until that point, we really believed that Hitler would still produce his big reprisal weapon. Virtually until the last moment, we simply could not conceive of defeat. We were told that if Hitler falls, then so will all of Germany. The signs were so aggravating that one simply didn't know what to believe.

'Yes, we were in retreat, undeniably. We knew we had been defeated, we knew that most cities in Germany had been devastatingly bombed and that most of the country was in Russian hands. We had been told of the second front as well but this was all cloaked in brave words—we were in strategic retreat, a victorious retreat, if you like.

'It was during our retreat from the Oder that I lost my unit. Suddenly, they were gone and I could hear Russians behind me. I ran into a companion, who had also become separated from his unit and we fled into the woods to lose ourselves as quickly as possible. In the woods, we found deserted camps, camps that had been set up by local farmers. Farmers had fled into the woods with horse-drawn carts full of provisions, to escape the approaching Russians. The Russians flushed them out of the woods and sent them back into their villages. They took the farmers' horses but the carts, still loaded with clothes, bedlinen, beds and groceries, were left in the woods.

'We crept around in those woods like red Indians, using the stars to find our direction, and searched for food more or less like animals, driven only by the rage to get home, to get out of there. I knew that I had to get out of my parachutist uniform and when I found civilian clothes I burned the uniform and my pay-book because I was afraid the Russians might think the parachutists were an SS regiment, which they weren't, but they had won the reputation through the war of being particularly strong invasion troops, plus had a distinctive camouflage which I was afraid the Russians might misunderstand. As it happens, the Russians, rather to my surprise, knew this; the SS people had their blood group tattooed under their arm and I, I am happy to say, did not.

'That night, we tried to make our way by the stars—it was a very clear night— towards the west, to Wittenberg. We were very isolated as we crept through the woods, no radios obviously, so we missed things like the news that Hitler was dead. I mean, we only found out the war was over from the Russians themselves.

'We had actually succeeded in getting quite close to the Elbe when we heard the Russians celebrating and we realized the war had ended. They had been celebrating victory and peace for several hours by then and were hopelessly drunk and all judgement gone. The Russians got drunk, danced around and made a fearful noise and whenever they met anyone, they shouted "*volna kaput*", which means "the war is over" and "everyone go home" and they meant themselves as well as us. They were jubilant at the victory, you couldn't help noticing it.

'When we ran into them in our civilian clothes, they were too drunk to realize we were anything other than civilians and didn't challenge us. We just kept saying to them "*volna kaput*". They said to us "everybody go home" which is just what we wanted to do.

'Once we had realized the war had ended, one's first reaction was not a sense of being defeated, but relief that one had survived it all. The only thing one wanted was to get home—that and survival, whatever the future held. One had been through so much already in the last few years. Basically you didn't give much of a hoot about anything. We were bone tired, broken down physically. You couldn't go on any longer, you didn't want to, you just wanted to get home and find out what was going to happen. We had no thoughts about the future, only where is my next meal coming from and what was going to happen next.'

Sunday 6 May &
Early Hours Monday 7 May

Unconditional Surrender

A curious element of farce characterized the end of the war in Europe. A delegation from Admiral Dönitz had been due to fly to SHAEF's forward headquarters at Rheims on 5 May to discuss the general surrender of all the German forces on all fronts, but the plane had run into bad weather and was forced to land at Brussels. General Admiral Hans von Friedeburg and Colonel Fritz Poleck from the German War Office continued their journey to Rheims by car, where they arrived at five o'clock in the afternoon. They were greeted by two British officers and escorted, to a toilet, where the Admiral hummed softly as he washed and changed his collar; Colonel Poleck appeared nervous.

Preliminary discussions were due to take place in the office of Lieutenant General Walter Bedell-Smith, Eisenhower's chief of staff and known throughout the headquarters as 'Beetle'. The discussions lasted only a matter of minutes since Admiral von Friedeburg was quickly obliged to admit that not only was he not authorized to sign any surrender agreement, but he had not brought with him the codes for communicating with Dönitz in Flensburg.

The surrender ceremony, due to take place in the War Room, was postponed until the following day, while a message was transmitted to the Allied headquarters nearest to Flensburg and thence by courier to Dönitz.

'The let-down was horrible,' Kay Summersby recalled. 'All staff sections closed their offices; everyone left in a grey mood. Press and brass hats filed despondently from the War Room, the room still rigged for a spectacular show postponed for at least 24 hours. I went on home to make the most of an opportunity for a good night's sleep … '[1]

The two German officers were accommodated for the night under guard at a small house on the Rue Godenot. They dined at eleven on tomato juice, pork chops with mashed potatoes, carrots and peas, fruit, coffee and red wine. Pfc Fred Stones, one of the American MPs guarding the house, disapproved. 'If I'd have been running the thing,' he said, 'I'd have thrown 'em a can of C Rations.'[2] The Admiral, apparently still quite relaxed and unaware of the enmity of the guards, commented on the fine quality of the table linen and offered, the view that the owner of the house must be rich. The two Germans listened to the radio in the sitting room until after midnight.

On the morning of 6 May, Captain Harry Butcher, Ike's naval aide, was frantically worrying what to do about the War Room. It had been set up the previous day to accommodate not just the major participants but the world's media. Butcher described it in his diary: 'The War Room, where Ike generally has met with his top commanders and staff each morning at nine, is now strewn with cables, camera equipment and batteries of klieg lights. The photographers generally take command wherever they go into action and they had pushed a huge table, normally in the centre of the room, into a far corner to permit more coverage for their lenses. The room is about thirty feet square and has pale blue walls covered with battle maps showing the disposition of the forces on all fronts. There are charts showing the current day's air operations, casualty lists, records of supplies landed, railway and communications systems, and today's, tomorrow's and the next day's weather—a series of charts that I have noticed always draws first attention of those entering the room. On one wall there was a thermom-eter, mounted on a background of swastikas, showing the mounting millions of German prisoners in Allied hands.'

Unfortunately for Butcher, on the morning of the 6th, Lieutenant General Bedell-Smith had taken a look in the War Room and decided he didn't like what he saw. 'Whoever's responsible for all that Hollywood equipment must get it out imme-diately,' he snapped. 'This isn't going to be a show. There's going to be a surrender.'

The man responsible was Butcher, but he had only been acting on instructions from Eisenhower, who had made it clear he wanted the widest possible coverage for the surrender ceremony. At one point, when it looked as if it might take place on a train, Ike had told his aide that he could 'lay them [war correspondents] in the aisles' if necessary.

Butcher attempted to get the Supreme Commander to solve the problem for him: 'During lunch at the house, I told Ike of my dilemma and he said that all he knew about it was that Beetle had come into his office during the forenoon and said that the War Room had been made into a Hollywood stage and that he didn't like it. Ike had merely said that it was Beetle's show and he could do as he liked. He had told the Chief of Staff to handle the negotiations and the sign-ing, if any, and the Chief of Staff said he didn't want any publicity and that was the answer. But so far as the Supreme Commander was concerned, he had no objec-tion but really desired that the public, through Press, radio and movies, should be given as much information as possible, since, after all, it was their war.

'General Ike was pretty well whipped down from the tension of waiting and interruptions to his sleep caused by the Prime Minister and others telephoning him [Churchill had been ringing from London at all hours of the day and night to get the latest news], so he decided to take a nap. I went back to the office to work out my problem.

'When I reached there I found that von Friedeburg had received a reply from Dönitz that the chief of staff of the German Army, General Gustav Jodl, who had succeeded General Guderian in the job, was flying to Rheims and would have authority to sign. Jodl was accompanied by his aide and the two were in the custody of Major General de Guignand, Monty's chief of staff.'[3]

General Francis ('Freddie') de Guignand: 'Jodl arrived at Tactical Headquarters and I was asked to fly him in my aircraft to Supreme Headquarters, which was then at Rheims. He looked very drawn and behaved perfectly correctly. It was a queer feeling to be in the same aircraft with the man who had for so long worked in the closest association with Hitler. We were met on the Rheims airfield by officers from Supreme Headquarters, who took charge of Jodl, and so my task was completed. Bedell-Smith had, however, asked me to stay the night, and in view of the great event that was soon to take place, I gladly accepted.'[4]

Butcher, meanwhile, had solved the problem of the War Room. A nap, he noted, had improved Beetle's disposition and he had agreed that all the equipment, except the battery of microphones, could stay. A single microphone was left on the table to provide a feed for those outside.

'Just as I was leaving the office, he [Beetle] said: "Ike asked me to make you superintendent of the fountain pens. Take these two and make sure they are used at the signing and that no one steals them." "Aye, aye, sir," I said as I examined the pens, one of which Beetle said was pure gold and the other gold-plated. I knew they had been sent to General Ike by an old friend he met in the Philippines many years ago, Kenneth Parker, who months ago had requested that when and if the peace was signed, these pens be used. However, he had made the stipulation that one be sent to him.

'About this time there was much scurrying around the corridors. Jodl and his aide were arriving. He strode arrogantly from the car into the headquarters building, expressionless. An MP saluted and the German chief of staff returned the salute and, like Friedeburg, did not give the Nazi gesture. He was taken to the same office previously used by Friedeburg, where the latter, with Colonel Poleck, was sitting. Pawley [an official correspondent], who practically had his ear to the keyhole, reported that when the Admiral opened the door to admit Jodl, there was no salute, but Jodl exclaimed "ah ha". The door closed, but soon the Admiral came out, asked for coffee and a map of Europe. Jodl could be seen inside marching up and down.'[5]

Agnes Pernazzo, one of three WACs assigned to serve tea and coffee during the negotiations, was married to a GI in a Third Army combat engineer unit. 'I felt terribly uneasy serving them coffee. It was an awful feeling, and I can't get over it. And then some officer made a wisecrack about my serving coffee to

Germans while my husband was shooting them. He thought that was funny. And that General Jodl! I'd liked to have spilled hot coffee down his neck.'[6]

Soon after six o'clock, Jodl and von Friedeburg were escorted to Bedell-Smith's office, where they continued negotiations behind closed doors for more than an hour. The sticking point was that Eisenhower was insisting that all German troops remained where they were at the moment of surrender and the German High Command could not guarantee that those of its soldiers facing the Russians would abide by this condition. Jodl suggested a two-stage surrender: an immediate cease fire and a halt to troop movements two days later.

Bedell-Smith left the room to submit this proposal to Eisenhower, who took no direct part in the negotiations. Jodl could have had no doubt about Eisenhower's response, because Bedell-Smith was back almost immediately. Eisenhower, he reported, demanded the immediate signing of the surrender document and gave Jodl half an hour to think it over. 'If you decline,' said Bedell-Smith, 'the discussions will be considered closed. You will have to deal with the Russians alone. Our Air Force will resume operations. Our lines will be closed, even to individual German soldiers and civilians.'

Jodl, pale as death, rose to his feet and left the room. A few minutes later he sent a brief signal to Dönitz: 'I see no alternative—chaos or signature. I ask you to confirm to me immediately by wireless that I have full powers to sign capitulation.'[7]

By this time the WAC officers at the headquarters were hosting a cocktail party. 'It was a very cheerful affair,' General de Guignand recalled, 'and the excellent dry Martinis coupled with the impending end of the war, produced a distinctly friendly atmosphere.'[8]

Kay Summersby remembered it rather differently. 'Actually, the party wasn't very abandoned or gay, for no one was able to ignore the event about to take place in the schoolhouse. The Rheims champagne disappeared surprisingly slowly, although one of the Russian officers, attempting to drink American rye as though it were vodka, got so drunk that he and his colleagues had to leave. General Eisenhower stayed only a few minutes, his thoughts far away from casual cocktail chatter. "Keep in touch with the office," he told me. "Let me know what's happening."'[9]

At 1.30 on the morning of 7 May, Harry Butcher was woken by the telephone ringing in his room. It was a secretary from the headquarters calling to say that the 'big party was on', that the Germans were about to sign and that he should hurry over with the fountain pens.

'At the front door there was a hornet's nest of correspondents waiting to get into the school building. If I had good sense, or had seen them first, I would have driven around the schoolhouse into the courtyard and sneaked into the offices the back way. They had driven up from Paris on the chance that they would be permitted to cover the ceremony, despite the fact that a pool of seventeen already was on hand for the job. I respected their enterprise, but from the standpoint of scores of correspondents who had stayed in Paris and not driven to Rheims on the understanding that they would not be allowed into the ceremony, there wasn't much that could be done for them ...

'I was about to miss the big show myself, so I hurried around to the War Room ... Beetle arrived, looked over the seating arrangements, spoke briefly as to procedure. He didn't seem to notice the one lonely microphone upon which the whole world was now dependent. He blinked in the floodlights, but I felt that now with the proper pool of 17 correspondents assembled quietly but attentively in the rear, he would not call off the proceedings.

'General Jodl and Admiral Friedeburg, the two principals, arrived, escorted by General Strong and Brigadier Foord. General Strong placed the documents for signature in front of General Bedell-Smith, before whom I laid the solid gold fountain pen. Beetle spoke briefly to the Germans, which was interpreted for them by Strong. It was merely that the surrender documents awaited signature. Were they ready and prepared to sign? Jodl indicated assent with a slight nod. I already had before him the gold-plated pen ...

'At the conclusion of the signing, General Jodl stood at attention, addressed Lieutenant General Bedell-Smith and said, in English, "I want to say a word." Then he lapsed into German, later interpreted as: "General! With this signature the German people and the German armed forces are for better or worse delivered into the victor's hands. In this war, which has lasted more than five years, both have achieved and suffered more than perhaps any other people in the world. In this hour I can only express the hope that the victor will treat them with generosity."

'The official time of the signature on the surrender document was 2.41 a.m. British double summer time.'[10]

Jodl and von Friedeburg were then escorted to Eisenhower's office, where Kay Summersby had returned to duty, rather disappointed at missing the surrender ceremony. 'At the sound of heavy boots nearing our door, I rose from my desk in the same respectful attention I showed to any high-ranking officers. They marched straight by without as much as a glance, exact prototypes of filmland Nazis, sour-faced, glum, erect and despicable. The whole thing seemed unreal.

'In the inner office, they came to a parade ground halt, clicked their heels and saluted smartly, with no hint of the Nazi salute. General Eisenhower stood stock still, more military than I had ever seen him. Any human curiosity at this first meeting with his enemy [it was the first and only time he was to see the German chiefs] was completely submerged in an icy West Point formality. I bent over my diary to take his words down. His voice was brittle. "Do you understand the terms of the documents of surrender you have just signed" I heard a "Ja, ja," following General Strong's interpretation.

'General Eisenhower concluded this historic meeting with two more coldly undramatic sentences: "You will get detailed instructions at a later date. And you will be expected to carry them out faithfully." I nodded. General Eisenhower stared silently in dismissal. The Germans half-bowed, saluted, did an about turn and marched back past my desk and out of the office.

'Afterwards, General Ike's face stretched into the broadest grin of his career. As the photographers milled around, he said, "Come on, let's all have a picture!" Everyone gathered near the boss as he held up two of the signature pens in a V-sign.

'Almost as if it was expected of him—and without the slightest sign of exuberance—General Eisenhower remarked that the occasion called for a bottle of champagne. We repaired to his house. The next two hours or so bore more resemblance to a group sitting around discussing a just-ended bridge game than to people who had just seen the end of a war. There was no gaiety, no joking, no laughing. The Supreme Commander spent most of the time listing those to whom true credit belonged for the successful conclusion of the war; there was no gloating, no personal pride, absolutely no buoyancy. Everyone simply seemed weary, indescribably weary. We broke it up as dawn came through the chateau windows.'[11]

In recent months staff at SHAEF had often joked about the exact form of words that would be used to inform the combined chiefs that the war had been won. Many colourful versions were on offer. In the end, Eisenhower chose the greatest possible understatement: 'The mission of this Allied force was fulfilled at 0241 local time, May 7, 1945.'

Monday 7 May

Why Are We Waiting?

If anything convinced the nation, on Monday 7 May, that the war in Europe was finally over it was a terse little announcement from the Board of Trade: 'Until the end of May you may buy cotton bunting without coupons, as long as it is red, white or blue, and does not cost more than one shilling and three pence per square yard.'

'When I heard that on the news,' said Mabel Foreman, the wife of a policeman in Cardiff, 'I said to my husband "That's it. It must be over. The Board of Trade wouldn't give nothing away unless it had to."'

It was a strange way to end a war, but it was the strangest of days, with not a word from the government about the war being won, even though the news was transmitted to London in the early hours. Eisenhower had telephoned General Sir Hastings Ismay, Churchill's chief of staff, who rejoiced in the nickname of Pug, as much from his doggedness as his dogged looks. 'At about three o'clock in the morning,' Sir Hastings wrote later, 'I was awakened by my telephone bell and told that the Supreme Commander was on the line. These nocturnal calls had never brought good news and I was afraid that something had gone wrong. But my mind was soon put at rest. "Is that you, Pug?" "Yes, Ike. What has happened?" "They have signed on the dotted line. It's all over." My wife heard what had been said and her eyes filled with tears. I, too, felt a lump in my throat and could scarcely voice my congratulations.'[1]

Churchill wanted to broadcast the news to the people as soon as possible, but it had been agreed that the announcement would be made simultaneously in London, Washington and Moscow and the Russians were insisting that the news should not be made public until the surrender had been formally ratified in Berlin. Despite being on the telephone most of the morning to Washington and Moscow, Churchill was unable to get his own way. He was obliged to cancel a broadcast scheduled at noon, then one at four o'clock, then another at six.

The mood of uncertainty which was to characterize the day had been set by the headlines in the morning newspapers. 'It May Be Today' the *Daily Mail* ventured; 'Germany's Surrender Imminent' said the *Daily Telegraph*; 'End Of the War At Hand' offered *The Times*. The *Daily Express*, which had distinguished itself in 1939 with the collectors' headline 'No War This Year', played it safe with 'The Last Hours'.

'A definite atmosphere today,' a City worker noted. 'Travelling to business a person remarked that it was hardly worth making the journey as work would finish this afternoon. Exactly the same feeling in the office, most people expect peace today. I travelled to the City about 10.30 and made a point of being near a wireless at 11 o'clock. Nothing happened. I made half a dozen business calls but found most people disinclined to settle down to work. I feel the same.'

'Oh, I hope it's not tonight,' said a 25-year-old girl interviewed on her way to work. 'I don't know what to wear. I'm going out with my boy friend and I want to wear my best costume, but I don't want to be caught in it if it's VE night. I thought it was going to be announced in the morning. It'll be awfully unfair if they announce it in the evening and then only give us one day's holiday.'

The Germans, paradoxically, were considerably better informed. Shortly after two o'clock, Count Schwerin von Krosigk, the newly appointed Reich Foreign Minister, broadcasting from Flensburg, broke the news of Germany's defeat in a heavy and sombre voice: 'German men and women, the German High Command has today, on the order of Grand Admiral Dönitz, announced the unconditional surrender of all fighting troops. After almost six years of heroic struggle of unequalled severity, the strength of Germany has succumbed to the overwhelming might of our enemies. The continuation of the war would mean only senseless bloodshed and useless devastation.

'No one should be deceived as to the severity of the conditions which our enemies will impose on the German people. We must face them squarely and soberly, without questioning. No one can doubt that the coming period will be hard for each one of us and will demand sacrifices in all walks of life ... We can only hope that the atmosphere of hatred which today surrounds Germany in the eyes of the world will make way for a spirit of conciliation among the nations, without which the recovery of the world is impossible ... '

Susan Temple, a 23-year-old English-educated Viennese, was working for the BBC monitoring service at Caversham, listening in to all German broadcasts: 'By that time everybody was waiting with bated breath for the end of the war. I worked in H Section, the *Heilschreiber* [a German system of transmitting and receiving electric impulses, converting them into signals, which are then decoded and come out on a long paper tape]. So we were able to pick up anything that was teleprinted in Germany via the *Hellschreiber*, including their dispatches to their newspapers from the Front.

'It was towards lunch time when the wavelength that I was watching suddenly came up. You know when a station is coming up, there is a sort of humming sound. It was Schwerin von Krosigk, and as far as I can remember he said, "*Ich habe allen deutschen Truppen befohlen die Waffen niederzulegen* (I have ordered all German troops to lay down their arms)." I let out a yell to say that my station had come up and then other monitors also listened. Reception was very poor, you see. Then I went off and translated the first sentence and somebody went off and translated the second sentence. We recorded it on dictaphone belts.

'I went off duty before the whole thing was over and I had a friend in London I was just longing to get to, so I shot out and stopped a car, which you could do in those days, and said "If you're going to the station, could I have a lift? And the war is over!" And he said "I've heard that so many times, I don't believe it".'

At three o'clock the BBC reported von Krosigk's statement. Harold Nicolson heard it at Sissinghurst. '3 p.m. and the news,' he wrote in his diary. 'It says that an hour ago Schwerin von Krosigk had spoken on the wireless from Flensburg. He has said that Germany was obliged to surrender unconditionally, crushed by the overwhelming might of her enemies. Ben and I dash off to tell Vita [Sackville-West] who is in the courtyard. The three of us climb the turret stairs, tie the flag on to the ropes, and hoist it in the soft south-west breeze. It looks very proud and gay after five years of confinement.'[2]

In fact, flags were going up everywhere, in every town and village across the land. Fighter planes appearing over London took to executing spectacular victory rolls. Expectant crowds gathered outside Downing Street and Buckingham Palace … yet still there was no word of VE Day from the Prime Minister. It was hardly surprising that people were mystified and confused by his uncharacteristic reticence at such a moment.

'Still we wait,' a woman working in an insurance office in the City wrote in her diary. 'Everyone was convinced peace would be declared at three o'clock. Now it will be four o'clock. Everyone is tensed up and waiting, almost in the same state of nervous anticipation as during the bombing.'

'Rumours are flying about the factory,' the storekeeper at a Hertfordshire chemical factory noted. 'Every hour a crowd gathers round the little portable radio in our engineer's shop … A few minutes ago they said the German radio had already announced that Dönitz had signed the surrender terms … A stream of flags draped across the main factory roof will shoot up any hour now. I'm expecting a rush for my stocks of beakers when the beer-drinking orgy commences.'[3]

King George VI seemed as muddled as his frustrated subjects. 'Monday morning came the news that the Unconditional Surrender document had been signed in the early hours of this morning,' he wrote in his diary. 'Preparations for the announcement of VE Day today were going on apace, outside Buckingham Palace & other places. Placing of loud speakers & flood lighting lamps etc. The Press has worked everybody up that VE Day would be today as the news was already known. The P.M. wanted to announce it but Prest. Truman and Ml. Stalin want it to be announced tomorrow at 3 p.m. as arranged. The time fixed for Unconditional Surrender is Midnight May 8th. This came to me as a terrible anti-climax, having made my broadcast speech for record purposes with cinema photography & with no broadcast at 9 p.m. today!!'[4]

Kay Summersby reported similar confusion at SHAEF. 'I found VE Day [not unnaturally, Summersby assumed May 7 *was* VE Day] to be the worst day I ever put in at the Supreme Commander's office. One glance at the messages awaiting the General indicated that there would be no parties that day. Everything was in a muddle. One message stated the Germans in Czechoslovakia refused to surrender to the Russians opposite their lines, instead Nazis were flooding our front. A second message noted that, even while Jodl signed the formal papers at Rheims, the German radio announced the Nazis had made a separate peace with the Western allies, not with the Russians. The latter not only complained bitterly at this report, but advised SHAEF they no longer felt General Susloparov had been an acceptable Soviet representative at the Rheims ceremony. The anti-climax was complete with a new demand from the Russians: the formal surrender must be signed in Berlin.

'General Eisenhower sent a message to Moscow saying that he would be delighted to go to Berlin for a formal surrender ceremony. Then the Prime Minister began calling [he called no less than eight times that day], Beetle was in and out a dozen times, other staff members added to the pressure …

'Around 3 p.m. the final blow fell. Beetle roared into the office like a madman: Ed Kennedy of Associated Press had smuggled into America a story of the Rheims surrender. The "scoop" already hummed over AP wires into the United States, leaving a pack of angry correspondents in France, a group of very upset gentlemen in the Kremlin, 10 Downing Street and the White House—and a very irate Supreme Commander at Rheims … '[5]

All seventeen correspondents invited to witness the surrender ceremony in the schoolhouse at Rheims had been silenced by a strict embargo. A SHAEF press officer warned them not to file their stories until the surrender had first been announced by the respective heads of governments: 'I pledge each of you on his honour as a correspondent and as an assimilated officer of the United States Army not to communicate [the news] until it is released on the order of the Public Relations Director of SHAEF.' The correspondents had protested, but were told that the decision had been made at a 'high political level' and could not be changed.[6]

Edward Kennedy of the Associated Press was an experienced war correspondent and was convinced the embargo would not hold for more than a few hours. He had returned to Paris from Rheims, written his story and lodged it with SHAEF to await clearance. When he learned that Count von Krosigk had broadcast news of the surrender in Germany he argued there was no possible justification for a continuing embargo and warned the chief American censor that he was going to send his story out. Since the censor controlled communications with the United States he was unconcerned by Kennedy's threat, but the enterprising correspondent managed to establish a telephone link with AP's office in London. 'This is Ed Kennedy,' he snapped. 'Germany has surrendered unconditionally. That's official.' He then began dictating his story: 'Rheims, France, May 7—Germany surrendered unconditionally to the Western Allies and the Soviet Union at 2.41 a.m. French time today … 'Within a few minutes, teleprinters in New York were clattering madly.

Kennedy's colleagues would later write to Eisenhower deploring 'the most disgraceful, deliberate and unethical double-cross in the history of journalism' but why should Kennedy care? He had pulled off the scoop of a lifetime.[7] SHAEF tried to limit the damage with a snooty statement pointing out that no official announcement had been made and no story about a surrender had been authorized. It was too late, at least as far as New York was concerned.

It was shortly after 9.30 in the morning in New York when Associated Press put Kennedy's sensational story on the wire. 'It swept the city with gale velocity,' the *New York Times* reported next day. 'Men and women, utter strangers, shouted it to one another … housewives screamed it from the windows. Clerks and typists shrilled it from the skyscrapers. River craft east and west took it up and fed the din with sirens and whistle blasts. Cabbies pounded it out on their horns. Women ran down 23rd Street and Eighth Avenue excitedly shouting "It's over! The war's over!"

'Then the great paper and cloth throwing orgy began. Paper in every possible form and description cascaded from a hundred thousand windows—scrap paper, ledgers, playing cards, torn telephone books, fragments, stationery, streamers, ticker-tape … [garment trade workers] threw bale upon bale of textiles into the street: rayon, silk, woollens, prints, foulards, every conceivable remnant in every possible shade and hue turned and squirmed in the thin morning sunlight … Within the hour, Sixth, Seventh and Eighth Avenues and Broadway were eight to ten inches deep in multi coloured fabrics. Thrifty passers-by forgot their delirium long enough to salvage some of the larger remnants. Passing trucks, pleasure cars and cabs were draped in the material. It clung to ledges, sills and cornices and the wind played with it and tore at it. Men and women in the streets tore it from their hats and shoulders … Opposite Macy's women hung from windows waving bottles of liquor and screaming "Hey soldiers, hey sailors, come on up and get a drink!" A Times Square jeweller, seized with the common fever, ran up to a passing news photographer shouting "I have two sons overseas. They'll come home to me now?," dashed into his shop, came out with a handsome wrist watch and pressed it on the photographer. "Keep it," he cried, "I want you to have it." The bewildered photographer had not quite absorbed this welcome shock when a few yards down the street a stationer charged up to him with a carton of cigarettes and thrust them at him. The stationer was in much the same state of hysteria as the jeweller. "Take that, keep that," he insisted … '

The *New York Times* estimated that between ten o'clock in morning and five o'clock in the afternoon, a million or more New Yorkers danced in the streets earning a rebuke from Mayor La Guardia 'I want all the people of the city of New York who have thoughtlessly left their jobs to go return and I want to beg of them not to do it again. Maybe there's still some fighting going on. You don't know and I don't know. Let's be patient for just a few hours more.'

John Sampson, the *Daily Mirror's* New York correspondent, wrote: 'In Times Square thousands of people, yelling ceaselessly, packed the streets, stopping all traffic as far as the eye could see. Milling crowds blocked all thoroughfares. Press photographers climbed onto window ledges to snap the fantastic scenes of men and women going wild in the mid-morning sunshine … Outside one Broadway hotel a group of Allied servicemen, Americans, British and Canadians, formed a grinning line while an endless queue of girls marched past to give them congratulatory kisses.'

All this was happening while official sources continued to deny that there was any news. At noon, New York time, CBS sarcastically announced: 'It's obviously a fact. But not official. Official is official is official. And there, for all the purpose of absolute definition, goes the day we thought might be called VE Day. If the objective of supernatural powers had been to snafu (situation normal, all fouled up) the actual end of the war in Europe, so as to save all the waste of climactic hysteria, nothing could have worked out better.'

David Walker, the *Daily Mirror's* man at SHAEF, echoed the sentiments in this bitter report: 'Through no fault of the censorship, which must obey higher orders, I cannot even tell you whether the war is over or not—and coming from Supreme Headquarters tonight, I suppose that's funny.

'This must be the greatest single Press fiasco of all time. While the peace news has been broadcast all over the world, British and American newspapermen's copy still lies here pending the permission of officialdom.

'Even in their defeat, the Germans can laugh at us for our confusion, and for those who have been abroad since 1938 and 1939 this is the final humiliation.

'It is a pity that SHAEF lacks the courage of Lord Nelson, who put his telescope to his blind eye; the only advantage they seemed to have over Nelson is that they are more at sea.'

By late afternoon in London, news vendors were shouting the war was over, the billboards and headlines said the war was over and toilet rolls were streaming out of office windows. Jean Cawkwell was a 21-year-old clerk working in the Air Ministry: 'My office was on the sixth floor of a building in Woburn Place opposite the Royal Hotel, which was always full of GIs on leave. They were always shouting out of the windows and whooping it up. I didn't seem to have read in the papers that victory was imminent—we had had so many false alarms after the invasion we tended to disbelieve anything until we heard it officially—so the first intimation of the great news was a joyous hullabulloo from the GIs leaning out of the hotel windows.

'We looked out of the window at our end of the building to see what the noise was and saw the typists throwing all this ticker-tape stuff out of the window. We realized it was something exceptional and the news soon spread to our office. We didn't throw anything from our windows and the typists were reprimanded for their unseemly behaviour. Their streamers hung untidily from the trees below us for ages.'

In the City people were milling about, perhaps in the hope that they might stumble across some news: 'About 4 o'clock walk down to the Mansion House— already a crowd there—newspaper men, photographers, etc. Most of the flags are being unfurled, planes overhead, a press van has a notice "All over". Waited here till 5 o'clock—still no announcement.'[8]

'At last I am beginning to feel fluttery inside,' a 23-year-old ATS clerk confided in her diary. 'There is an atmosphere of exhilaration in the office, with everyone cracking feeble jokes and laughing enormously at each other's efforts. I have just bought a couple of yards of red, white and blue ribbon, a paper Union Jack and a tawdry Stars and Stripes on a stick—the latter price 3s 9d from Harrods!

'The war is over—that's obvious—but when is Churchill going to say so? Everyone gives his opinion—"At nine", "Not till tomorrow", "At midnight". Normally, the office is clear by 5.55 but tonight every single member of the staff stays to hear the 6 p.m. news—and still it is the same … '[9]

Susan Woolfitt, a young mother working on a canal barge in the Midlands was hoping that VE Day would be announced so that she did not have to go back to work: 'Not that I didn't want to go back to the boats; merely that I could think of nothing worse than having to spend two days' holiday, and such a holiday, down the Newdigate arm, which is scarcely more than a ditch, narrow and malodorous, with coal and cinders on the one hand, and rats in the muddy bank on the other …

'Although the evening papers were full of headlines there was still nothing definite by the time I was due at Euston for the 4.24 and I trailed miserably through the station to find my train. Suddenly the loudspeaker said in imperious accents: "Here is an important announcement!" Everybody in the whole station stopped dead as if instantaneously petrified. The voice went on: "The 4.9 for Northampton will leave from Platform 6 and *not* from Platform 9 as stated on the indicator."

'There was—or it felt as if there was—a sort of howl of fury from everyone on the station, including myself; deliverance had really seemed to be at hand and now there was nothing for it but to go back to Coventry, which I duly did. When I got back to where I had left the boats there wasn't a sign of them, but an obliging boater next door said they had moved round to Hawkesbury, "loaded you this morning, they did". This meant a walk of half a mile down the towpath carrying my bag and wearing a very uncomfortable pair of heavy boots that my husband had had in the Home Guard. It was also boiling hot.

'When I got to Hawkesbury, passing a bean field in full bloom on the way which partially restored me, the others took one look at my bedraggled form and said in chorus: "Whatever have you come back for? Don't you know the war's nearly over and it will be V Day tomorrow … "'[10]

The official announcement of VE Day finally came at 7.40 p.m. when the BBC interrupted a piano recital to read a bald statement issued by the Ministry of Information. Heroic prose might have been appropriate for the occasion, but was clearly eschewed by the civil service. 'It is understood that, in accordance with arrangements between the three great powers, an official announcement will be broadcast by the Prime Minister at three o'clock tomorrow, Tuesday afternoon, 8 May.

'In view of this fact, tomorrow, Tuesday, will be treated as Victory in Europe Day, and will be regarded as a holiday. The day following, Wednesday May 9, will also be a holiday. His Majesty the King will broadcast to the people of the British Empire and Commonwealth, tomorrow, Tuesday, at 9 p.m.'

Reactions ranged from relief to joy to a curiously flat sense of disappointment, possibly prompted by the almost unbearable tension of the day, or perhaps by the Ministry's stilted language, or perhaps by an increased awareness that the war would be continuing in the Far East.

'I merely cried when I heard the news. I can't grasp the fact that it's all over. We've been bombed out twice, and we've got no roof over our heads, only a tarpaulin. My boy's home on leave, after being away for nearly five years, but for tonight I don't care what happens. I'm going to be really happy. I'm glad of the opportunity to relieve my pent-up feelings. And after this I'll be ready to get on with the second part of the job.'

'Well, I'm sick and tired, browned off with them I am. The way they've behaved … why, it was an insult to the British people. Stood up to all what we've stood up to, and then afraid to tell us it was peace, just as if we was a lot of kids. Just as if we couldn't be trusted to behave ourselves.'

'I was cleaning my mother's pantry when I heard the news. I put down my whitewash brush and we opened the bottle of sherry we had been saving for that moment. Just two women—my father had died during the war—and a sleeping baby girl. The ones who suffer most from man's folly.'

'Evening paper says "Surrender". Came through Piccadilly Circus, Trafalgar Square, Whitehall—crowds everywhere—perhaps we shall hear something at 6 o'clock. Still no news, went home. Wireless announcement—official proclamation at 3 o'clock tomorrow. Can't see the point of this, disappointed.'[11]

'I was at home with my parents. We had not long finished dinner, the table was still set, my father was reading in the armchair, my stepmother was busy about the house, I was in the garden, mending a puncture on my bicycle. The announcer on the radio gave the news that tomorrow would be V Day. Quietly, my father said, "It's over." Personally, I was unmoved.'

'Well, it's only the bombing that's stopped that I'm thankful for. It often seems a miracle we're still here. We'll have to forget what we've been through. And of course, there's the other war yet. I've just got my son home … he's gone a bit queer in the head through being in the Navy. I don't know if they'll take him back for the Jap war.'

'So tomorrow is VE Day. I heard a news flash at 8.30 and went out to see whether anyone else had heard it. A youngster across the street shouted the news to me, not excited, just glad, and he finished: "I suppose that means we don't go into work tomorrow. That suits me fine."

'There were very few flags out in this street at the time, and I immediately went and put my own up, a Union Jack and a rather old South African flag that I have treasured ever since the coronation of Edward VIII. I don't think that the rest of the street had heard the announcement, so at nine I put the radio on full blast and opened all the windows. Heads came up, spades went down and the whole neighbourhood went indoors. Bedroom windows began to pop open, and within a quarter of an hour some dozen flags had been put out. On the average there is only one flag per house, but a few have two or three.

'I cannot say I am wildly excited, but then one needs company for that and I am alone tonight. I can't even go out and join the neighbours for long, because I am on duty, that is to say, my wife is out part-timing at the telephone exchange, and I am left to deal with the children. Just a pleasant feeling of "Well, that's over. What now?"'

'What a queer and confusing day this has been. First, the expectancy that any time during the day Churchill would be breaking into the radio programmes to announce VE Day. This idea was fostered by most of the papers … and the midday editions said it was all a matter of hours. Nearly everyone thought that Churchill would be speaking at teatime, which would coincide with suppertime in Moscow and lunchtime in America. There were many rumours in the afternoon, and we were all confused and wondering how much holiday we were to take if the announcement of the end was made in the evening, after we had left work … Just before five, I managed, by a stroke of good luck, to get a *Mail*, which had a banner headline saying that the Germans had announced the unconditional surrender of all their armed forces at 2.30 this afternoon. I showed this round the office. We left the office still not knowing whether we had to go in tomorrow or not. There was no excitement in town, life was proceeding more or less normally, and there was a sense of diffidence in the way the flags were appearing. I rode home, confidently expecting to hear on the 6 o'clock news that Churchill would be speaking then or later in the evening, but was perplexed and disappointed to learn only that there was no official statement in London … badly wanted to go to the allotment and do some work, but I felt that anything might happen at any minute, so I kept the radio on until the Forces news at 7 o'clock. Then there was a definite enough announcement that Churchill wouldn't be speaking until tomorrow, so I packed up and went to the allotment, firmly convinced that I should have to go to the office in the morning and that we should start VE Day sometime during the day. The kids have been told that they are to go to school until they are told otherwise.

'Dick Masters was on his patch and said he was disappointed, as he had been expecting the same thing as I had done. We both felt that the whole thing was very confusing and poorly handled, and couldn't see any logical reason for the delay in giving the news. Churchill had said previously that he wouldn't hold up the news for a minute, and yet here were the papers with definite statements that the war in Europe was over—and articles giving the highlights of the war—and no word from him. I know in my own mind the war in Europe *is* over, for all practical purposes, and I find it very confusing and perplexing. The ending has been unlike I had pictured it, and this business only adds to the confusion and mystery, and makes it a proper anti-climax. Just before eight, Bill Higgs came and shouted that there had been a news flash on the radio that tomorrow would be VE Day, and that there was to be two days holiday. Fuller details would be given on the 9 o'clock news. We all packed up in time to get home for this, and learned that the day would be a holiday, as would Wednesday. So we know that much.'[12]

Many people were still unsure whether or not to go to work the following day, as this woman civil servant recorded in her diary that evening: 'In the 9 bulletin it was confirmed that Germany has surrendered and stated that the Prime Minister will make the announcement tomorrow and that tomorrow and Wednesday will be public holidays. This put me in a dilemma as official instructions were that we come in unless the Prime Minister *has made* his announcement. Problem—is an announcement that an announcement will be made the same as an announcement?

'As I couldn't make up my own mind, I cycled over to the other side of the town to consult my friend and colleague, as to *her* interpretation. She was as undecided as I and had just been trying to phone another colleague but said the call box was out of order. She suggested that as I had my cycle I should go and ask another colleague—a staff Branch HCO—who might have official information and who lives in yet another part of the town (my friend had her address). This I did, but found her as worried as we were. She had also been trying to phone other senior members of the staff but without success—and other people had been asking her. She made another attempt while I was there—but after sitting with the telephone receiver to her ear for about 20 minutes, without even getting a response from the exchange—gave it up as hopeless. Probably the exchange was inundated with inquiries, and that was why my other friend could not get through from the call box.

'We all decided that our best way was to stick to official instructions and go up to office as usual unless we got definite official counter-instruction. It all seems an unnecessary muddle.'[13]

Gunner Ralph Walton of 4th Surrey Regiment, Royal Artillery, summed up the general disenchantment in a dispirited letter to his fiancée: 'You ask me how I celebrated this, the day we'd been waiting for for nearly six years? Well, darling, I don't think there was a more miserable crowd than the troops in a certain transit camp last Monday when it was announced that VE day would be next day. We had all just returned from leave and there wasn't a drop of alcohol in the camp not even the chance of a cup of tea as the NAAFI queue was nearly a mile long and three deep when I returned from the camp cinema. So I just lay on my bed and went into solitary communion. What was I thinking? Well naturally, sweetheart, my whole thoughts were of you and what you would be doing at this time. I don't think I have ever been so near to tears as I was then and the church very nearly got a convert as I was in a highly introspective mood searching for someone or something to receive my thanks for ending such a lot of horror and torture which the world has endured these last few years. But then I asked myself, who really deserves these thanks? After giving myself a slight pat on the back—you don't mind that small show of ego, do you—I congratulated all the democratic (supposedly) peoples of the world, and mainly the British, who saw this thing through from start to finish.' [14]

There were, though, those who were keenly aware that history was being made. Verily Anderson, the wife of a Ministry of Information official, heard the announcement while sitting at home in St John's Wood with her small daughter: 'Marian, I said, you must remember this all your life. It's history … Come on now we'll hang out flags. I ran with Marian up the drive to hang them on the trees by the road. Now she understood. "The war's over and it's my birthday," she told any passing pedestrians. But nobody seemed quite sure the war *was* really over, except Marian and myself.'[15]

In Nella Last's household history took second place to frustration. 'Steve pooh-poohed the idea that VE Day would come tonight,' she wrote. 'I said, "It *might* have been announced in a programme"—and I put the wireless on at five minutes to nine o'clock. We agreed that, if Stuart Hibberd said, "The King will speak in approximately one minute's time", we *would* have missed an announce-ment—and smiled at each other when it proceeded normally. Then, when he said so unemotionally that tomorrow was to be the VE Day, and that Churchill was to speak at 3 o'clock, we just *gazed* at each other, and Steve said, "*What* a flop! What a *flop!*" We could none of us believe our hearing. It was as if a body of psychologists had been consulted and been told, "Now sort out the events and announcements for us. We want to tell them, of course, but with no dramatic announcement, no build-up. We want to let them know the European War is over, but not to emphasize it. You now, it's only the first half: we *must* keep that in people's minds, not let them maffick and forget what's ahead." We felt no pulse quicken, *no* sense of thankfulness or uplift, of any kind. Personally, I've felt more thrilled on many occasions by news on the air. At intervals, Steve chanted, "But what a flop" as if fresh angles had struck him. I'd heard people say, "I'll kneel down and pray if it's in the streets when I hear it", "I know I'll cry my eyes out", "I'll rush for that bottle I've kept—open it and get tight for the first time in my life", and so on. I rose placidly and put on the kettle and went through to prepare the salad. I looked on my shelf and said, "Well, dash it, *we must celebrate somehow*—I'll open this tin of pears," and I did.'[16]

In London the crowds that had been hanging around all day began to disperse around six o'clock when it was generally thought that there would be no further news that evening. But two hours later, after confirmation that VE Day would be the following day, people began flocking back into the West End looking to celebrate.

The lady secretary of the Hungerford Club, which provided shelter for the homeless in the Charing Cross area, was amazed by the scenes: 'From the windows of my flat just behind St Martin-in-the-Fields, there came a surge of sound, as of a great crowd of people singing and cheering, and the steady shuffling of hundreds of feet ... I rushed down to Trafalgar Square, with my torch. There, an astonishing sight was vaguely visible in the darkness. The whole square was filled with people. One could just see groups of men and women, their arms linked together, whirling round and round. Others leapt about on their own in their irrepressible relief and joy ... An enormous tide, or river, of humanity filled the square in ever-increasing numbers, as others heard the news and flocked in from neighbouring streets. The great lions, occasionally visible in the flare of a torch, seemed the right background to the spontaneous expression of relief of those thousands who, for so long, had endured the shattering sorrows of war, the darkness and gloom contrasting with the light and joy in the hearts of the people.'[17]

Fleet Street reporters were present in strength, of course, mingling with the crowds, and the *Daily Mirror's* man filed a particularly exuberant, on-the-spot report from Piccadilly Circus:

'This is IT—and we are all going nuts! There are thousands of us in Piccadilly Circus. The police say more than 10,000—and that's a conservative estimate.

'We are dancing the Conga and the jig and "Knees Up Mother Brown", and we are singing and whistling and blowing paper trumpets.

'The idea is to make a noise. We are. Even above the roar of the motors of low-flying bombers "shooting up" the city.

'We are dancing around Eros in the black-out, but there is a glow from a bonfire up Shaftesbury Avenue and a newsreel cinema has lit its canopy lights for the first time in getting on for six years.

'A huge V sign glares down over Leicester Square. And gangs of girls and soldiers are waving rattles and shouting and climbing lamp-posts and swarming

over cars that have become bogged down in this struggling, swirling mass of celebrating Londoners.

'We have been waiting from two o'clock to celebrate. We went home at six
when it seemed that the news of VE Day would never come, but we are back
now.

'And on a glorious night we are making the most of it. A paper-hatted throng
is trying to pull me out of this telephone box now. I hold the door tight, but
the din from Piccadilly Circus is drowning my voice.

'It is past midnight. We are still singing. A group of men liberated from German
prison camps are yelling "Roll Out the Barrel". "We sang it when we went to
France in 1939 and we sang it as we tried to get out in 1940," they told me. "Now
we sing it for victory."

'Amid terrific cheers a New Zealand sailor climbed on the bonnet of a bus and
from there to the roof. He stood there swaying above the crowds as the American
army swarmed up after him, but the police fought through the crowd and pulled
them down.

'Traffic tried to push through the crowds, got lost to sight and came out with
civilians, soldiers, airmen and sailors—and their girls—clinging to the running
boards …

'There is a brass band here now. They are banging out all the songs that saw this
war through—and they are even trying, amid the mocking cheers of the crowd,
the song that did not see Germany to victory—"Deutschland Awake" … '[18]

Dame Beryl Grey, then a leading ballerina at Sadlers Wells, went to work as
usual that night: 'We were in the middle of a London Season at the New Theatre
and had been rehearsing, as we always did, from ten o'clock that morning. I am
afraid that dancers become so totally absorbed in their rehearsals and concerned
for the impending performance that everything else comes second to the dance.
Obviously there was enormous relief that the hoped-for end of the war had
finally been announced, but the programme went on that night as usual. It was
Swan Lake Act Two, Festin de L'Arraigne and Comus. I think I was only in *Swan
Lake* that evening and afterwards I went straight home to Islington, to my mother
and father. I seem to remember going straight to bed, not feeling at all well.'

The ATS girl who had confessed in her diary that she was feeling 'fluttery
inside' finished her entry for that day with an account of a trip into the West
End: 'In Piccadilly Circus the crowds are fairly dense, and also down Coventry
Street. We exclaim at a neon sign in Leicester Square and at the lighted revolv-
ing dome of the Coliseum—sights forgotten in these six years. The crowds are
hilarious in Trafalgar Square. Students march by in bands. The chimes of Big
Ben come through loudspeakers, and the 9 p.m. news, but no one listens. Down
Whitehall—and more marching students. ATS duty personnel wistfully watching the merrymakers from a War Office building. A little quiet area around
the Cenotaph. Then Westminster—and the face of Big Ben lit up—another

forgotten sight! Rosy floodlights are being tested on a Government building, but a policeman tells us that the Houses of Parliament floodlights are not going up till tomorrow night. Some of us want to go into Westminster Abbey for a few minutes' prayer, but it is closed. So into a YMCA for a lemonade, all we can get to toast Victory!

'Outside, London is really getting into the victory mood, without waiting for Mr Churchill. The Embankment is quiet, but Trafalgar Square is gayer than ever, dancing and singing, the "Marseillaise" and "Knees Up Mother Brown". The Palais Glide in the Haymarket and little bonfires on the pavements, fed by newspapers. Then Piccadilly Circus again. It is dark now, no street lights and few lighted windows. But it is one mass of yelling, laughing, singing, shrieking people; a small sports car is trying to wriggle through, and its folded roof is in shreds. A brilliantly lit bus is bogged down beside Eros, with people swarming all over it, inside and out. A man has climbed a lamp standard and is beating his hands against the unlit lamp. Most of the men are in uniform—all services and nationalities. The Canadians are noisy, the sailors are merry, the airmen are drunk (or pretend to be), and the Americans have a girl apiece.' [19]

In the suburbs it was somewhat quieter, to judge by this dour report: 'We arrived at my friend's house to find his mother busy arranging about hanging out a string of flags. The man opposite was fixing a crown of lights to his front window.

'Outside the entrance to our flats, a "knees-up" was in progress. A lot of shouting, but not much hilarity. I walked by with the dog, since I couldn't get in, and returned when they had dispersed.

'Found my sister in. She had been to the pub—the first time in years. The fellow upstairs had come to ask her to have a drink and to his amazement she had accepted. She was now with the girl from upstairs.

'I felt browned off. Then Bill came down. He said I looked unhappy. I didn't feel particularly joyful—I could see nothing to jubilate [sic] about. Bill had been over at the Rose and Crown. He said it was flat there too. He said folk were frightened of losing their jobs and didn't feel secure. At this particular time many folk felt that under our present system, having a job and having a war go together.

'May, Bill's wife, went up to bed, but Bill remained. Jess, May's sister, came down. She and I went up to the balcony above to see the bonfires and fireworks. I said it was the sort of incident that Noel Coward will some day perpetuate. She said that she couldn't feel happy since she had had no letter from her husband in the Navy for three weeks.' [20]

Away from London, few of Britain's major cities reported mass celebrations on the same scale, although the *Glasgow Herald* noted a noisy midnight welcome for VE Day: 'Hundreds of ships, war ships, merchant ships, tugs, steamers, motorboats and anyone possessing a horn, hooter or an old ARP rattle opened up in the Firth of Clyde to create the most tremendous victory din likely to be heard in any part of the country. For miles around and far inland the noise was heard and people on the coast, excited by the din ... suddenly defied the coast blackout ban and allowed their lights to blaze out into the streets.'[21]

In Cornwall the writer Mary Wesley's small boy forebore to celebrate: 'I had walked down through the woods to the cliff and the sea with my little boy of three. We were coming up again, nearly there, nearly back at the house, when someone, I forget who, shouted down to me that it was over, the war had stopped. They'd heard it on the radio, it was definite.

'I burst into tears. I said to my child, "The war is over, darling, it's over at last." He stamped his foot and shouted, "I won't have it, I want my war" and he, too, wept. I should explain that I had had to take him to London to see a specialist at Great Ormond Street Hospital during the height of the doodlebug bombs and he simply *loved* them, had never seen anything so thrilling in his life.'

In Somerset, hostel worker Muriel Green was taking part in a pre-arranged cricket match, Ladies *v.* Gentlemen. 'The wireless had been put on out of doors and was going through the match. When Big Ben chimed at 9 p.m. everyone stopped playing and waited in tense silence for the news. A general cheer went up when Tuesday was announced a holiday. After the headlines and beginning of the news, the game went on. It was drawn at 19 runs either side, the men having been handicapped into playing left-handed and bowling underarm.

'We had a snack and went in, to dancing to records. There was more than the usual crowd there and lots of people were the worse for drink already. About 11.15 p.m. an American sailor who was being entertained by some of the Irish girls forced his way up to the platform where the mike was. He, as well as the girls, was obviously the worse for drink. He said he would do an impersonation of Bing Crosby (rousing cheers) and sang "Irish Lullaby" and "Lula-lula". The girls who were sitting beneath the stage asked him to sing "If You Ever Go to Ireland", which he then followed up with another Irish song at their request. The last was unknown to the English people present, who were by this time not so enthusiastic in their applause. In the corner where we were sitting [people] were saying "The Irish haven't won the bloody war" and "It's time we had an English song". A drunk boy beside us said "What English song can we sing?" and E [Muriel's best friend] said, "There'll Always Be an England." In the next interlude the drunken boy led off in this song and in no time everyone in the room was singing it. The social director who was putting on the records on the stage then saw the way clear to get the mike away from the Yank and suggested that we should sing "Land of Hope and Glory", which we did. Then another man (also drunk) clambered up on to the stage and said we mustn't forget the jolly old Eighth Army and started the crowd singing another modern soldier song, "Lily of the Island". This led to another after which the social director gave out appropriate words for the occasion and told of arrangements for the following day. She said she would now put on the last dance as we had two late nights in front of us. I didn't think many of the crowd felt like going to bed.'[22]

Across the Channel in Paris, there were similar scenes to those in London, even though official confirmation of VE Day was not announced there until 10.30 p.m. 'Paris was Bedlam,' the *New York Herald Tribune* correspondent reported. 'Hundreds of thousands of Parisians jammed the streets, pistols were fired into the air from moving cars, planes overhead dropped multi-coloured flares and fireworks boomed in all directions.'

Janet Flanner was in the Allied Servicemen's Club at the Grand Hotel when the news broke: 'An orchestra leader whose men had just finished playing and singing "And the tears flowed like wine" suddenly shouted to the dancers that the war was over, that tomorrow was V Day in Europe. A wild groan of joy went up from the men in uniform. They then began capering extravagantly, their girls in their arms, to the tune of "Hallelujah". Afterwards, tumbling out into the boulevards they started spreading the news to all Joes [GIs] and to anyone French who would listen.'[23]

In Brussels, Captain Ian Carmichael was enjoying the fruits of victory — two days' unexpected leave: 'We hadn't had a day off for months and were incredibly tired and so it was with some relief, and even incredulity, that on Monday my pal John Moore and I were told we had earned a rest and should take a staff car and go to Brussels. The biggest initial thrill was to be able to put on clean service dress once again. I left my battledress almost literally standing up in the corner of my tent.

'On our arrival in Brussels we checked into a hotel on the Boulevard Adolphe Max and went up to our room. It was an extraordinary moment—the first comfortable room in a smart hotel that we had experienced for what seemed like eons. We both stood for a moment in silence. For starters we decided to soak for about an hour in a hot bath.

'In the early evening, refreshed and ready for the fray, we went out on the town. Two days previously we had witnessed and shared the elation of a small town in Holland with its street parties and orange lanterns; now we were in a big capital city with the lights of shops windows, neons, floodlit squares and even fireworks being sent heavenwards off the top of trams. The streets were packed. Everybody loved everybody and rockets and thunderflashes were being ignited on every street corner.

'After visits to innumerable bars, we wandered into Maxim's to watch the cabaret. There we joined the company of two half-cut but friendly GIs with their ATS escorts and after several bottles of champagne we emerged an hour or so later feeling in pretty much the same condition ourselves. Nevertheless, no time for bed yet, we decided to sample a few more cafés, in one of which we got tangled up with two young Belgian married couples who shared a flat and insisted that we went back to it for further celebratory glasses. Somewhere about 1 a.m., unable to keep up with John's fluent French, I finally passed out on the sofa.'[24]

In Naples, Cicely Courtneidge, darling of the musical-comedy stage, was entertaining the troops at an ENSA concert at the San Carlos theatre: 'I was singing "Home is Where Your Heart Is" when the news of the victory reached the theatre. A British soldier got hold of a huge Union Jack from somewhere and rushed up over the orchestra and on to the stage and hung it round me. I went on singing, and soon it seemed the whole of Naples was singing that song, with tears streaming down many a cheek, including mine.'[25]

Betty Donaldson, a widow at the age of 21, was on a boat travelling back to India to be with her parents after her husband, an army officer, had been killed in action in Holland. 'I had never taken much notice of the war, other than that it was a dreadful thing. I had no idea that when I left England to go back to India that the war was almost over.

'This was a Dutch boat, the *Teborsch*, and the Dutch had a custom that all widows had pride of place in society for the first year of widowhood. Consequently, at dinner I always sat on the Captain's right-hand side. I was treated with particular deference and kindness because my husband had been killed in Holland, and it was a Dutch crew. The officers and crew were wonderful; none of them had seen their families for the full six years of the war.

'One night at dinner the Captain rose from the table resplendent in his tropical uniform, and said he had an announcement to make. Slowly, in his clear English, he said "We have been informed that hostilities in Europe have ended." He paused and then he continued, "We shall now be able to see our families." He could say no more and his white handkerchief came out.

'I looked around the dining saloon and several hulking sunburnt and manly officers had tears coursing down their cheeks. The Captain, knowing how I would feel, just turned to me and said, "I'm sorry, my dear." I had to leave my seat as their joy and my sorrow were too great, and leaning over the rails under the gaze of the moon, my own tears dropped into the sea. Peace in Europe held no allure for me, the way I was feeling.'

Pilot Officer Anthony Wedgwood Benn was enjoying a brief spell of leave with two friends in Palestine when he heard, from an unlikely source, news of the victory. He described the events in a letter to his parents: 'We hired a rowing boat and rowed out into the Sea of Galilee, trying to pick out Capernaum on the side of the lake further up. Coming in, we entered a little Arab restaurant for refreshment and as we walked towards the place, a Jew hurried up with a smile and said, "The war is finished!"

'We didn't know whether to believe it or not so we smiled back. It seemed to be confirmed by a special edition of the paper. So we solemnly celebrated with an orange squash and ice cream each—hardly believing it could be true, hardly thinking of it, it seemed so remote. Returning later to Shaar Hagolan, via another settlement, we found them preparing for a festival to celebrate peace.

'It was nearly ten o'clock and we understood that the King was to speak, so we asked to listen to a wireless. As you know, he didn't, but in consequence we missed the gathering on the lawn when the leader of the settlement gave an address of welcome in Hebrew to "the three English officers". Think of the wonderful opportunity for replying with a speech—what we missed! I was disappointed.

'Outside on the grass an effigy of the swastika was burned and the settlement crowded into the eating hall, where a little wine and lots of biscuits and nuts were laid along tables. I asked for an orange squash and was given one, however one old boy emptied half a cupful of wine into it, and I drank it up—it was practically communion wine—rather an appropriate beverage to celebrate peace.

'Then the national dances began—German, Czechs, Poles, Turks, Yugoslavs, all did their national dances. Then there was a pause and an announcement in Hebrew. Everyone looked at us and it was explained that the RAF officers would do an English national dance. Hurriedly deciding to do the boomps-a-daisy, two of us took the floor—it was an instantaneous success and everybody joined in.' [26]

Back in London, Elizabeth Layton, Churchill's secretary, was on late duty at 10 Downing Street: 'There was an atmosphere of great excitement in the office; we knew that the unconditional surrender terms had been signed. The war in Europe was not yet officially over, but everyone seemed to know that it would be by tomorrow, and as I walked round St James Park during the dinner hour there was a good deal of shouting, cheering and singing going on. Crowds were gathering, wearing silly paper hats and blowing whistles and waving flags—throwing confetti, playing banjos and mouth organs, banging cymbals, whirling crackly things round and round—anything to make one feel joyous and carefree. Later that night, when I went into the study for dictation, Mr Churchill looked up and said, "Hello, Miss Layton ... well, the war's over, you've played your part." As the evening progressed, a terrific thunderstorm broke—flashes, bangs and crashes. Once or twice he looked up and said, with a twinkle, "Was that an explosion?" or "Might as well have another war." It was 3.45 before he went to bed and 4.30 by the time I had finished off the typing.' [27]

Tuesday 8 May Morning

Victory, At Last

'It had dawned a perfect summer day. No cloud had touched the blue sky. No breeze stirred the peaceful warm sunshine. The few churches left undamaged in Eastbourne chimed the joyous message that peace in Europe had come. Fighting in Europe had ceased. Germany in defeat had surrendered to the victorious Allies. For the second time in my life, now aged 50, there had been proclaimed a national holiday to celebrate an Allied victory over Germany.'

No one described preparations for VE Day in more colourful detail than Wynne Lewis, a former teacher from Eastbourne who had spent the war delivering homely little lectures to the troops to counter defeatist attitudes.

'I had dressed carefully in my nicest clothes, none needing mending except my one and only pair of corsets, dating back to 1939, which had steadily torn its silk covering into shreds. Silk stockings and silk underwear had all been new; the last remaining silk garments of pre-war quality that I had carefully kept unworn, reluctant they should become worn out, the last reminders of days when life in Britain had been pleasant, happy, abundant and of good quality and when new garments had been within reach of every average purse.

'Five shillings and elevenpence I had paid for that pair of sheer silk stockings in Harrods in 1939, in the days when the "wicked" Tories governed Britain. Thirty shillings for the set of silk underwear in Harvey Nicholls in 1938. The fine grey flannel suit lined with pure silk grey crêpe-de-chine they had tailored for me in 1938 for nine guineas; completing the order within two weeks.

'That summer day of Victory celebration in May 1945, the suit looked as good as new. The fine, smooth flannel had been a joy to touch; the sheer silk lining an even greater delight, for such materials had long since completely disappeared from British shops, obtainable perhaps by black market methods at exorbitant prices, but not over any counter in a normal way.

'Britain after nearly six years of war, had been reduced to harsh utility textiles, mixtures of glass and grass and heaven knows what! Wiry utility silks and satins had shone like bright enamels and guaranteed us just the same amount of warmth.

'A pair of pre-war perforated, hand-made summer shoes of black box calf as soft and as flexible as a pair of kid gloves I had bought in Harvey Nicholls in 1939 for forty-five shillings. They had looked an elegant pair of aristocrats beside the shoddy, useless, shapeless utility shoes that had cost me forty-nine shillings and sixpence, plus seven precious coupons, out of an allowance of thirty-two to clothe me for six months.

'A grey chiffon blouse, made for me in 1938 to match the grey flannel suit at a dress-maker's cost of five shillings had totalled altogether with two yards of material at six shillings and elevenpence a yard, a sum slightly under eighteen shillings.

'A luxurious pair of long suede gloves, fastening at the wrist with large grey pearls I had preserved from 1939, when they had cost eighteen shillings and sixpence. A black calf handbag filled and lined in black moiré silk had cost only fifty shillings. The grey felt hat I had bought for two guineas.

'So dressed in my last remaining outfit of best quality clothes, costing altogether less than £20 before the war but valued at that time of Victory Day in Europe at least a £100: each garment a reminder of the world renowned high standard and famous hallmark stamp of British quality and workmanship that we had fought to keep the right to produce in our pleasant island home, I went down into the drive of the block of flats at Downscourt, Meads, thence out into the sunlit, merry village street ending at the foot of Beachy Head, to see how Meads village had started to celebrate VE Day, feeling that for once I was well clothed in fresh garments on which I not been forced to spend precious hours in mending, darning, patching and turning as had had to be done to almost every garment I had possessed, every time I attempted to dress myself.

'Clean and bright and happy the pleasant village street looked. Flags had been draped from every window and flown at every garden mast. Our Union Jack and all the flags of our Allies. Lines of gay bunting had been stretched across the village street. Not a breeze stirred them. Drenched in sunshine their brilliance had competed with the gay flower beds and the bright window boxes making the clean village street, nestling at the foot of green-turfed, white-faced ancient Beachy Head, look happy and proud, dressed to celebrate in the midst of her bomb shattered dwellings that had long since been tidily cleared of rubble and gently left to a profusion of wild flowers, that had endeavoured to soften the stark ruins with dainty blooms.

'Shopkeepers and residents, all dressed in their best, exchanged happy smiles, soldiers and sailors gathered at the porch of the "local" sang "Roll Out the Barrel" as they waited for it to open. Children in fancy dress had formed impromptu processions and had come dancing along the centre of the road singing and laughing as they passed. Young girls, arm in arm, had come swinging behind in a wide curve, all dressed in their best, all rosetted, all tied up in streamers of red, white and blue. The sunshine had been filled with laughter, song, music and dancing.

'Instead of a time and labour saving lunch direct from stove or fridge to kitchen table, we had on that great day of peace in Europe, laid an elaborate luncheon table in the dining-room. Best lace table mats brought out from precious reserves of fast disappearing linen, utterly irreplaceable; handsome silver and cutlery unwrapped from parcelled canteens hidden in cupboards; normal possessions that had become of fantastic value in their scarcity. Beautiful china and glass that we had been afraid to use because England had ceased to make such things and had instead been filled with ugly white mugs and utility cups and saucers all monotonously white and thick.

'One precious bottle of sherry we had kept for the occasion. It had with due ceremony been opened. Friends and neighbours had come to share the toast to our gallant country and our brave Allies. We had filled the sunny drawing room with massed sprays of white lilac and handsome purple iris, demure blue forget-me-not, gorgeous pink tulips and a bowl of white lillies-of-the-valley, cool and pure amongt the green leaves, their fragrance mingling with Chanel perfume, each of us had received from Brussels, gifts from our jubilant soldiers who had liberated that joyous city. From the large, wide open windows of the flat we had draped our enormous Union Jack and the equally large Stars and Stripes, side by side.

'We ate in our pre-war grandeur of table appointments the meagre rations of a tuppeny slice of corned beef; a salad made from an eighteen pence lettuce; a quarter pound of tomatoes sold at the controlled price of 1s 4d a lb but so scarce that they were only sold in 4oz allocations to each customer, a bunch of radishes at ninepence, half a cucumber at three shillings and sixpence and a bottle of utility mayonnaise, made from an ingredient we did not question too closely.

'Rhubarb bought at eightpence a pound we had stewed and made really sweet that day by rashly dipping deeper into our month's ration of two pounds of sugar. Custard we made from dried egg powder, part of Lease-Lend arrangements with the USA. We had ceased to question after our first suspicions of that gaudy yellow mixture, guaranteed pure "yolks", whether they had been pure yolks of snakes' eggs or of the Dodo. Hungry Britons were glad by 1945 not to look gift horses too closely in the mouth …

'I had been sitting on a sofa turning a pre-war grey felt hat inside out to make it do another summer, when I jumped to the terrific, actual realization that it definitely was VICTORY DAY IN EUROPE.

'That day of glorious peace for which we had worked ceaselessly for nearly six years; that tremendous victory that we had struggled and staggered towards through heart-breaking setbacks; that rapturous day of brilliant sunshine and peaceful blue sky towards which we had groped through six years of terrifying black-out! That great day had come at last!'[1]

Naina Cox was aged 17 and a half and was a part-time Red Cross nurse: 'Portsmouth, where I lived, had borne its share of everything—severe bombing, daylight raids, V1 and V2 rockets included.

'We awoke to the official announcement "This is VE Day" about eight o'clock in the morning. We didn't know what to do. Should we do anything? Should we do everything?

'Mother said to go to work as usual. Father had already gone to work in the dockyard knowing that he would pick up the very latest news. I walked to my office job in a dry cleaners about 8.40 a.m. There wasn't the usual bustle of people about, just several women standing at their garden gates, not really caring if they went to work or not.

'The Manageress was waiting for me when I arrived. She exclaimed, "Oh, I'm glad you've come. Now you can take over everything. I'm off to the Guildhall Square, there is sure to be some sort of celebrating going on there." And with that she rode off on her rickety old bike.

'I was lost for words and furious, having been told a few days previously that I was not experienced enough to take charge of anything. I pulled myself together, tidied the office, tried to get on with unfinished book-keeping, but nothing seemed to add up, so went to look out of the shop window. Nobody came into the shop. To me all the passers-by were completely wrapped up in themselves, at a complete loss, too frightened to exclaim anything in case it was not true.

'No more blackout restrictions someone said, rationing will get worse as we have to feed Europe now. I tried to work out that one. When customers did come in to pay bills they told me that only about half the shops were open that day, causing more confusion.

'Perhaps by mid-day other parts of Britain may have been shouting, singing, dancing or trying to get drunk, but not here. Generally, it is forgotten that in Hampshire we had a far higher quota of lost men. Hundreds went down on warships, hundreds were killed or still prisoners-of-war in the Far East, never a word about them. Is it any wonder the women in our High Street were not laughing?'

Like so many war widows, Pat Hazlehurst had mixed feelings on VE Day. She had married her husband, Jack, in 1939 on his first leave from France. He was 30 years old, a company sergeant major in the North Staffs Regiment, when he was killed in 1944. Pat, then 29, was working in the Army Pay and Record Office in Shrewsbury.

'Jack was a regular soldier when I met him. My father had been a regular soldier, so I was used to the army background and army thinking was: you marry a soldier and you go where fortune takes you. Jack was in France and was wounded in 1940 and I really thought, without giving it any logical thought, that he'd done his share. But he came home, recovered, went back to France and was killed.

'I think my greatest rage was—and I still think this—the starry-eyed people who thought that by laying down our arms and being meekly co-operative with the whole world, that that would stop the war. I thought then, and I think now, had we been prepared to defend ourselves in 1938, when Chamberlain waved his bit of paper …

'The war was over for me, really, with Jack's death. I was in this accountant's office, and on VE Day I had to take some work into the boss, who was a darling man and he said to me "This is a sad day for you, Pat" and I said "Yes sir, but nobody, nobody, can alter what has happened to me, but whilst people are rejoicing on VE Day, they must remember those men who are fighting in the Far East." That was my main thought, that really we ought to be girding up our loins and doing more in the Far East than flag-waving here.

'There was no reason for me to rejoice, first my husband was dead and second because the war in the Far East was still going on. Men were still at risk of being killed, like my husband was killed.

'I was tied to the office all day and then I went home and put my head under a pillow. There was nothing for me to celebrate. I mean, I was glad for the folks who were coming back home, of course. I didn't feel particularly sad that day, because the sadness never leaves you. You learn to live with it, you cannot live at the same pitch of misery.

'I was one of those women who was fortunate enough to have met someone who had everything I wanted in a man—a good brain, a wonderful sense of humour. There is always the sadness, but always the deep, deep gratitude that I had him, even though it was for such a short time.'

A disaffected teenager living in Kenton, Middlesex wrote in his diary: 'I woke up at about 8.30 a.m., after a fearful night, with probably the noisiest thunderstorm for years. I got out of bed feeling worse than when I'd got in.

'The atmosphere in the house was peculiar to say the least. My father had already gone to work—but only for an hour, apparently—and my stepmother was up, having seen my father off and agreeing after the shopping to go and meet him … My sister was also up, to my surprise, and her main theme was the attraction of two days' holiday away from school. She was already dressed and on the verge of dashing off, so coming down amidst the rush, I sat in the armchair in my pajamas and dressing gown, reading about the capitulation in the *Dailey Telegraph* [sic] listening to the wireless and consuming tea and toast.

'Later. I played some of my jazz records, but tiring of them, I turned the wireless on again, dressed myself up in my riding breeches and had a shave. I felt distinctly ill and restless. I wanted to lie down, but I thought I ought to be doing something, so I entered up my diary. Eventually my father returned from his shop, with the amusing remark that he'd sold one tin of boot polish! We all laughed, for by now, for some mysterious reason, the family were all re-assembled in the dining room again. My father had brought home a fair-sized flag for my sister, and there ensued a lively discussion whether or not it ought to be hung outside the house, because there was a picture of ex-King Edward VIII in its centre. I was horrified at the thought of a flag outside the premises, and I expressed my opinion force-ably [sic] saying that it was a form of reaction, my sister piped up that people want some form of pleasure, and this was the time for celebration. My father felt that we could not hang a flag of an ex-King out of the window, in the circumstances he suggested cutting all the little flags out of the main one, and hanging them outside, which my sister did finally. I shook my head sadly.'[2]

Frederick George Cockman, aged 43, was the manager of a small insurance office and a special constable: 'On May 8, I shut the office in Peterborough and gave the typist the day off. I wanted to get back to my wife and family in Bedford and drove back home in the office car on what little petrol I had. What struck me was the uncanny silence. I had not expected to see much traffic as motorists were allowed only two and a half gallons of petrol per month (pro-vided you could convince the authorities that you were engaged on work of national importance).

'It looked so odd. Everywhere was terribly quiet, there were no aircraft, noth-ing. What was more strange was the absence of pedestrians in the towns and villages. On reaching home, I discovered the reason. Everyone was indoors preparing for the celebration teas which were held everywhere.

'Children were in school, not to learn, but to help with decorations while housewives were busy turning out their precious stores of things they had put by—dried fruit, dried egg, flour, butter, real eggs, nuts and all the other ingredi-ents of homemade cakes. The men were out searching for tables and chairs.

'My wife was also making cakes, for this great big tea party that we had in Balmoral Avenue, where we lived. We men set up the tables, putting them end to end along the road. The ladies brought out their table cloths and cakes. This experience really broke down British reserve. I spoke to people in the road I had never spoken to before. In my road people were never more than formally polite, but that day all reserve was broken down and there was an upsurge of warm friendship which was perfectly genuine.

'As I wasn't a soldier, I felt it wasn't really my place to talk about the war on that day. Plenty of people had done more than I had. I hadn't been called up partly because of my age and partly because I was, through the government's war risks insurance scheme, doing work of national importance.

'I don't look upon myself as a very brave man, I was glad not to be in the war but on the other hand, I did whatever I could to keep things going at home.'

Twenty-one-year-old Edna Seymour remembers VE Day in Hayes, Middlesex, rather better than most: 'I was working in the Air Ministry during the war, which being a reserved occupation, prevented me from joining the WRENs. My fiancé, Paddy, was an able seaman serving on the battle cruiser, HMS *Renown*, and had been away for about 16 months. He came home suddenly in the first week in May and we obtained a special licence to get married on Tuesday May 8th. Of course, we had no idea it would be VE Day.

'It was a tremendous rush, making all the preparations. Neighbours helped with supplies and coupons. I went round to the local baker and begged him to make us a wedding cake, but he said he couldn't do it. He hadn't made a wedding cake since the beginning of the war because he couldn't get any dried fruit. Then I found out that Paddy's ship had called in at South Africa on the way home and for some reason he'd bought a lot of dried fruit. I rushed it round to the baker and he made us a lovely two-tier wedding cake. As it was the first he'd done since the start of the war, he took enormous care with it.

'I wore a navy blue suit which I had bought specially for 18 coupons and a pair of new shoes which I had kept for getting married in. Unfortunately we don't have many photographs because it was very hard to get film those days. I asked the local newspaper if they would send a photographer round, but of course he was out covering the celebrations. After the wedding someone dragged a piano outside and we all danced in the street. We had a wonderful day.'

Edith Pargeter, also known as the thriller writer Ellis Peters, has similarly fond memories: 'I was then a Petty Officer Wren in the Signals Office of C-in-C Western Approaches, Liverpool, and in the Birthday Honours of 1944 someone had recommended me for a BEM. Recipients were expected to apply to attend on any one of the future dates fixed for presentation of medals, and because of work pressure I delayed applying rather a long time and finally applied for 8 May 1945.

'I travelled down to London with a Wren friend who was one of my two guests!—my brother came down to join us next morning—and we two spent the night in Wrens' quarters in town. And that evening the announcement came out of the blue that the morrow was to be, officially, the close of the European war. We were a little afraid that in the general celebrations the presentation might be cancelled, but no, it went ahead as planned.

'So at ten o'clock on VE Day I was in Buckingham Palace, second in line after one Wren officer, receiving my BEM from King George VI, whom I hugely admired for his enormous moral courage. Afterwards my brother had to catch a train back to Shropshire. My friend and I spent the rest of the day rushing about London, dancing in the streets and embracing anything in a uniform. I am never likely to forget any detail of that day.'

Ipswich postwoman Rose Bell, aged 19, had delivered many a telegram bringing bad news. On 8 May it was different: 'I consider VE Day one of my most enjoyable days I ever spent at work. Volunteers had been asked for to deliver telegrams, but the only telegrams being taken were from ex-PoWs who had been released. Some of the homes I visited were not even sure their loved ones were still alive, so it was wonderful news I was bringing them.'

A 34-year-old woman teacher from Thornaby-on-Tees noted in her diary: 'Very quiet and ordinary early. The buses are running. Many men go to work, having been told to work until Mr Churchill declares the European war ended.

Rag and bone man comes round as usual, and the butcher's boy brings meat. I go out to buy bread and see other people doing likewise. Decoration of streets is proceeding at a leisurely rate, and street discussions are taking place about having teas. Eg, "I can bring the sugar", "We've got a lovely victory cake, all red, white and blue decorations". Some groups of mostly older women are very thoughtful. "It isn't as if the war was really over, when there's Japan." "I'm only doing it for the kids." Most people are using their Coronation decorations—the little streets have done the best, some even painting lamp-posts, steps or window sills, but most of the larger houses are sporting a flag of some sort. Young girls are wearing hair bands of red, white and blue, and older people have rosettes. Many people have gone to great trouble to give enjoyment to their children—red, white and blue dresses (I see three beautifully made from bunting, the children being sisters), decorated tricycles, toy motor cars. Most dogs have bows and horses are gay too.

'I walk towards the aerodrome. A group of RAF officers are having drinks outside the open window of a pub opposite the drome. They secure a cart and horse. A woman brings bunting and they drape the cart and the horse. They wear bowler or top hats and one has a Brittania helmet. One has a trumpet and the other a mouth organ. They mount the cart and one gets astride the horse. Singing and playing they set off into town. Someone says, "They only returned from Germany last week".' [3]

The opera singer, Constance Shacklock, was at home in her studio in Kensington on the morning VE Day: 'I can remember hearing the church bells ring. It was so wonderful you felt you wanted to go out in the street and dance. One could hardly take it in, believe it was true. It was as big a shock as when they announced the war.

'I was very committed to doing concerts, keeping up the artistic side of life. During war years I was member of CEMA, the Council for the Encouragement of Musical Arts. I sang in factories and hospitals and for the troops. It was quite an experience, I would say the best experience a young singer could have because if you could sing under those conditions you could sing under any conditions.

'One always got a warm reception from the troops, yes, but the factories, no. Having to sing for the night shift at half past two in the morning was my idea of purgatory. They had to give me black coffee to keep me awake. One felt they really didn't want us at that time in the morning. The hospitals were also trying experiences: one saw terrible sights one will never forget.

'One occasion I remember with great joy. I was singing somewhere in the south of England to one of the camps and as I had finished my second song the door opened at the back and three young boys came in on crutches. Afterwards I went and had a chat with them and one of them said, "Will you pinch me Miss Shacklock?" and I said why. He said, "Well at 9 o'clock this morning we were fighting on the Normandy beaches and we were wounded and here we are back in England at a concert. Is it true?"

'I was the first British singer to go into Germany after the war to sing in a Wagner season at the Opera House in East Berlin. I remember I stayed at the Adlon Hotel. It was a moonlight night and as I looked out of my window there was the bunker where the whole crowd had committed suicide. I must admit it was quite a frightening experience.

'VE Day I just sat back quietly and thanked God it was all over. It had been like a nightmare; one had seen so many of one's friends go to the war. I had been in London throughout the war. Some of the experiences one had had been quite terrifying, but one took them in one's stride. War was like a horrible dream. Afterwards you wondered, did it really happen?'

Muriel Green, shop assistant in a Somerset hostel for war workers, observed:

'The weather was unsettled and showery when we came over to breakfast at 9.30 a.m. There was a large crowd in between 9–10 a.m. and they were queueing for boiled eggs to be cooked. Breakfast is usually staggered from 5.45–10 a.m., there was a rush later when everyone was not at work. After breakfast we sat in the foyer talking and looking at the closed shop with delight. There was a sharp shower before the most glorious sunny day, as though the heavens were weeping for the dead before rejoicing. Two elderly women were saying, 'It was just like this on the last Armistice Day." At 11 the staff had coffee, biscuits and cigarettes given them in place of the usual tea. After this, J [sister], E [best friend] and I decided to cycle into the town to see the decorations as the sun had come out by then. The town is decorated well considering the five years of shortages of flags, bunting, etc. The streets were very narrow so that the pendants across the street could easily be put up. Most of the shops which were closed had red, white and blue window dressings with a number of photographs of Churchill, Stalin, Roosevelt and the King and Queen. There was a lot of people walking the streets. We decided to take ourselves to the best hotel in town and have a drink. We had a glass of good old sherry which made us feel just too jolly. The hotel bar was crowded but we managed to get served with difficulty. We drank to "Peace in the future".' [4]

A coal miner, injured in an accident in the pit four months earlier, describes his morning in a Welsh village: 'Our street is a cul-de-sac, 16 houses. Streamers of material, dyed red, white and blue, was being placed across the street. The lady opposite us had been busy, she had a red flag in centre. I had drawn the hammer and sickle for her and she had done a good job. Prices for streamers were outrageous. The women said they were not paying it, so had bought dyes. We had an old red curtain, and the wife made it into a flag, the "People's Flag" she calls it. An old broom handle, and we hung it from the upstairs window. We were watching flags going up, down the street. Two Russian flags and one streamer with large flags of all nations (against Jerry).

'The Pit was off and I spoke to others out for a stroll. One had a son, a prisoner of war, had heard nothing of him for two months and was rather anxious. Another man had heard that those of us on compensation would not receive the £1 a day men at the pit were receiving for the two days off, so what are we going to do about it?

1 Soviet soldiers hoist the Red Flag over the Reichstag, 30 April 1945

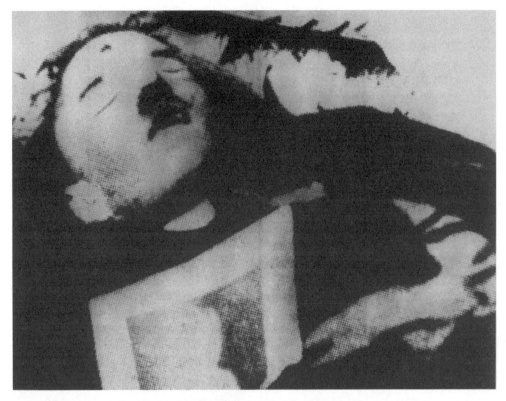

2 A picture purportedly of Hitler's corpse shortly after he shot himself

3 US and Russian troops link up at the River Elbe, 27 April 1945

4 General Dwight D. Eisenhower and a party of high-ranking officers, including General Omar Bradley and Lieutenant-General George Patton, witness the evidence of Nazi cruelty to prisoners at Ohrdurf concentration camp, Germany, April 1945

5 British Honey tanks patrol the streets of Hamburg, while unarmed German troops look on, awaiting the official surrender, 4 May 1945

6 Delegates from the German armed forces visit Field Marshal Montgomery's 21st Army Group Headquarters: General Admiral von Friedeburg, Commander in Chief German Navy; General Kinzel; Rear Admiral Wagner; Colonel Pollek and Major Freidel

7 Field Marshal Montgomery reads the surrender terms to General Admiral von Friedburg and Rear Admiral Wagner

8 At Rheims on 8 May, General Dwight D. Eisenhower makes his victory speech in front of the newsreel cameras, with Sir Arthur Tedder, Deputy Supreme Commander

9 Eisenhower holds the pens in the form of a Victory 'V', with which the Germans signed the unconditional surrender at Rheims. At left is General Walter Bedell Smith, Chief of Staff; on the right Sir Arthur Tedder

10 The *Daily Mail* announcement on 8 May 1945

11 A crowd of twenty thousand people cheer the Royal Family, who appeared on the balcony eleven minutes after the Prime Minister made his official announcement of Germany's unconditional surrender

12 The Royal Family with Winston Churchill acknowledging the huge crowd outside Buckingham Palace

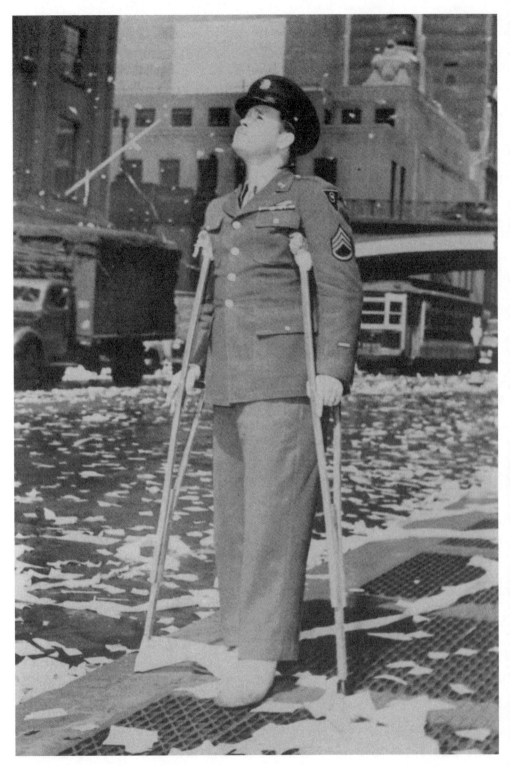

13 A wounded American serviceman watches ticker tape rain down in New York on 7 May 1945, as the people of the city celebrate following the Associated Press report that Germany had surrendered unconditionally

14 Servicemen and civilians celebrating in Manchester

15 A Parisian crowd celebrates VE Day at the Place de l'Opera

16 St Paul's Cathedral, floodlit during the victory celebrations in London

17 Alan Ritchie's sketch of the evening of 8 May in Hemslo, north-west Germany. Young Nazi activists continued on the offensive after the official surrender

18 The author (front, third from right) at a street party, demonstrating an original version of the victory salute

19 Winifred Watson and her husband outside St Andrew's Church, Greenwich on Saturday 5 May 1945. They didn't realize at the time that the day was also special for another reason

20 Private John Frost, who was in the 11th Armoured Division in north-west Germany

21 David Langdon's cartoon catches the VE Day mood

Opposite above: 22 *Evening News* vans waiting to deliver newspapers on 8 May

Opposite below: 23 Local women dancing for joy in Charlton-on-Medlock, Lancashire

Left: 24 A car-load of merrymakers throws caution the wind

Below: 25 The happy and not-so-happy

I said if so, then all of us on Comp had better all get together, crutches and sticks, and have a procession next Friday with a black banner chalked on it "The Forgotten Army". Boy oh boy, I said, what propaganda. Personally, I think we will get it, but if we don't, well "Sufficient unto the day".

'By now, others were passing and glancing down the street, saying it was the best. One said "Look at this street, it's bloody red." Lads were coming through from the distant wood, carrying branches of trees, for bonfires. Ninety per cent of people wore rosettes of red, white and blue. I went for a short walk. I should say 60 per cent of Union Jacks were upside down. Many women were very dressed up. Paper Xmas trimmings were being used. They were preparing a V-sign over the picture house. I bought 20 Gold Flake, 2s 4d, at a shop, remarkable perhaps only because that was ALL I spent during the day.

'The weather had been sunny, it was now getting dull. Anxiety for the streamers and flags was expressed. Everyone wore a cheerful expression; 'twas a day off from the pit anyhow. Everyone I spoke to intimated that our relief could hardly be equal to those in the rocket and V-bomb areas. Those people with relations in France were over-flowing with gratitude and those without were not backward in expressing their approval of the end of the war.

'Arrived home about 12.30 p.m. Rain was evident now. Another two ladies were collaborating about a streamer. One had materials and a dye and the other had dyes. Later on, a knock at the door and "Would Mr J please cut out in paper a pattern of hammer and sickle?" I obliged and waited for news.'[5]

John Forrest was an 18-year-old recruit at 63rd Training Regiment, Royal Armoured Corps, based at Barnard Castle. He was out on exercise completely oblivious to the fact that the war was drawing to an end in Europe: 'VE Day came as a complete surprise to us, we were so involved in our training. I remember it very well. We were out training with our tanks on a combined five-day exercise with the poor old infantry and a message came over the wireless in the tank that all training had to cease and we had to report back to the camp, which we did. We formed up on the parade square and the commanding officer got up on the saluting base and shouted out that he had some very good news, that the war in Europe had ended.

'There was not a movement in the ranks, probably because the sergeant major was going round saying "Stand still!" I can always remember, to be honest, feeling a little bit disappointed that I was not going to be involved. Quite a few people felt like that. We were only 18, hadn't seen war, didn't know what it was like. Everyone got onto 15 cwt trucks and we were all taken into Bishop Auckland to celebrate. I didn't drink in those days, but we had a jolly good time. The Geordies are a very, very friendly lot and a lot of us, including myself, were taken into their houses to celebrate.'

A Leicester office worker wrote in her diary: 'Tuesday 9.0 a.m. Housewives hurrying off to do their shopping while the shops were open. Some grumbled that the arrangements for getting in food, the length of time shops were to be open etc, were confused and inadequate.

'10.0 a.m. People still putting out flags and decorations. Children in the street with paper hats on, but most of them playing in the normal way while others just stood about. Groups of neighbours gathered and dispersed again. Some people were "dressed up", others were in working clothes. People keep coming out of their houses into their gardens or the street, and then going back again. There is no dancing, music, games or animation of any kind.

'I feel that I should like to celebrate in some way but don't quite know what to do. Although it is a joyous occasion that the war with Germany has ended and a halt has been called to that slaughter, one feels that today does not really mark the first day of peace as we knew it before the war. Japan is still fighting, most of the wartime restrictions are still imposed on us, we are short of many essentials and have so few luxuries. One feels the battle is but half won. There yet remains the peace settlement, "Post-War Reconstruction" of all kinds, future organization for peace, radical domestic and international political adjustment and so on. These problems, as they are now being approached, give some cause for apprehension. All this tends to make the present victory only victory with a small "v".'[6]

A local council worker, Haverfordwest, Pembrokeshire noted in her diary: 'Like most of the people, I spent the day quietly. In the morning, having visited two friends from the office to discuss the news, I walked round this small town to see what was going on. The thing that struck me most were the flags. Large flags, small flags, bunting, flags carefully stored since the Coronation, all served to turn the grey stone buildings of the town into a rainbow-like world. The three commercial streets had a really tremendous display, while one of the poorer residential streets had a turn-out almost as good. The Union Jack and the Welsh Dragon flew side-by-side on the public buildings and the castle and in the streets were Russian, British, American, Dominion and other Allied flags. There were also a large number of Scottish standards, though nobody seemed to be able to explain why this should be in such a remote corner of Wales. Red ensigns fluttering from many houses gave proof of the number of past and present Merchant Navy men in the district, while many paid tribute to a great ally by flying the Chinese flag. The tricolour was also much in evidence: 'The streets were crowded with people, who, having finished their own decorating, were strolling around to see what others had accomplished. Most of them wore red, white and blue favours, while dogs, with and without their owners, sported the national colours on their collars. Many people were hanging out of their windows to fix coloured lights and I was really surprised to see how many people had gone to their place of employment for the purpose of doing a little decoration. The showmen at the fair, adding even more flags and lights to their already heavily burdened booths, were evidently hoping for a record attendance. This fair is the annual May Fair, being held for the first time since the outbreak of war and by a coincidence, its opening day turned out to be VE Day.

'As I passed on my way, a police car, decorated with coloured ribbons and presenting an appearance of a limousine at a wedding, drove slowly round, its loudspeaker blaring the arrangements for services and functions.'[7]

An office worker from North London recalled the weather: 'Precisely at midnight last night a violent thunderstorm broke—it seems as if the clerk of the weather had better and more striking ideas of marking Victory than our human authorities. It was a marvellous storm and I enjoyed it. The lightning was intense and almost continuous and there were torrents of rain. And it lasted at least till 3.30 (I went to sleep more soundly then, and didn't wake till 6, so don't know how much longer it went on).

'My first thought when the storm broke was how lucky for me that it didn't come two hours earlier (for it broke very suddenly) while I was chasing round the town on my cycle. The next—what a shame that the heavy rain came just after the decorations had all been put up and it would spoil them all. Then, more seriously, I felt how fitting it was and how it seemed to have an almost biblical significance—a kind of symbol of the clash and breaking of spiritual forces. In so many of the Old Testament stories great historical events have been accompanied by violent storms, and it seemed that this was following suit.

'This morning I felt still more that the storm had been symbolic for it has cleared off all the heaviness and mustiness. It is a perfectly glorious morning—clear and fresh and invigorating—even at Holloway.

'It was announced on the wireless again this morning that today is to be a public holiday, but I thought I had better stick to my plan of going up to the office to see what arrangements have been made.

'I started out therefore as usual. It was all very quiet—few people about—only about a dozen on the station—and heaps of room in a train that is usually packed. It felt like going out early on Sunday morning.

'As I had really expected, the office was open only for special duties—but am glad I went to make sure. Met several colleagues who had also come up, according to official instructions. One agreed with me that the wireless announcement had made a muddle of it—another blamed the office for their instructions.

'I should have had to wait an hour for a train back so came home by trolley bus—incidentally this gave me a view of what was going on. There were long queues at all the bakers' shops—smaller ones at all provisions dealers and greengrocers. Decorations were up, or being put up everywhere. But it was all quiet. People were going about their business calmly and silently as usual. I did a little shopping myself on the way—buns, sausages and a lettuce—at shops where there was no queue; it was later then, presumably the queues had been served. There seemed plenty of everything for everybody except for greens, which were almost unobtainable. We had intended getting a dinner from the British Restaurant, but our New Barnet one is closed for both days.

'I spent most of the morning and afternoon taking down blackout. It was a bigger job than I expected as curtains and strips of paper round the edges of windows had all been fastened carefully with tacks and drawing pins—dozens of them—which had all rusted in. It looks so much lighter and more cheerful in the house now.'[8]

Phyllis Horton, aged 26, was a junior sister on an orthopaedic ward at Hammersmith Hospital: 'Well, VE Day was a public holiday, but for nurses it was literally an ordinary working day, no off duty. I worked from 7.30 in the morning until 8.0 p.m. that night.

'There was a great atmosphere of frivolity in the hospital, lots and lots of talking and also, next door to the hospital, was Wormwood Scrubs. We had our nurses' home there and some of the windows looked across to the cells in the Scrubs and we had to have blackouts, of course, and we were told particularly to keep the blackouts drawn because all the prisoners wanted to see the nurses getting undressed. On VE Day, they were all terribly, terribly lively and then they all disappeared, they were transferred somewhere else in the night. We took the blackout curtains down on VE Day but we didn't have any other curtains.

'Otherwise, we nurses didn't celebrate at all. Some of the nurses lived out, but most lived in and we did absolutely nothing.'

Dr Christopher Starey, 26-year-old junior doctor in the same hospital: 'A sense of anticipation was building up that the war was coming to an end and we were all pretty fed up with the rationing. We discussed it very little indeed, if you are living in the hospital mess and having your meals in the hospital, you tended to talk nothing but medicine. It was only the very big headlines, such as the sinking of a battleship or a new landing somewhere, would perk people up a bit. But medicine did seem to take precedence over everything else.

'I hung a flag out on VE Day. There were three or four of us who got together and decided we must put something up somewhere. We decided to hang a flag on the front of the hospital, on the large gable. Unfortunately, we did it without any authority and got into a bit of trouble afterwards. Once we had got it up there, I think we climbed up through the attics and never actually got up on the roof, I happened to look down and there was the Medical Superintendant, a chap called Sir Thomas Carey Evans—he had married Lloyd George's daughter, and she was a frequent visitor to the hospital—and they were down there with the Matron and quite a few others watching us. We didn't actually see them until we had done it, so when we came down we were promptly called to order—not very seriously.

'We were very relieved when it was over, of course, but having lived with it for six years, it took quite a little time to sink in. It made not a scrap of difference to the way we were living, rationing went on for some years after the war. But there was the lifting of the stress, the bombing stopped and you could get around more easily.

'I think, if anything, one worried rather more about the war in the Far East, particularly towards the end. One had expected the war with Germany to end but one was somewhat anxious about how long it might go on in the Far East. Pearl Harbour was an awful shock and the Japanese seemed to get the upper hand very quickly. They were all over the place. On the one hand, it was an awfully long way away but on the other hand, we seemed to get a lot of bad news about what was happening to the armed forces. There was an awful lot of news and talk about the concentration camps, the Japanese torture.'

Sir Henry 'Chips' Channon lunched, as usual, at the Ritz: 'Before lunch I walked through the Ritz, which was beflagged and decorated: everyone kissed me, Mrs Keppel, the Duchess of Rutland and Violet Trefusis all seized me alternately ... The streets were almost empty, as there is a bus strike, and taxis refused to go out—there were a few singing people, that's all.' [9]

The Prime Minister lunched at Buckingham Palace with the King, who noted in his diary: 'We congratulated each other on the end of the European War. The day we have been longing for has arrived at last & we can look back with thankfulness to God that our tribulation is over. No more fear of being bombed at home & no more living, in air-raid shelters. But there is still Japan to be defeated & the restoration of our country to be dealt with, which will give us many headaches & hard work in the coming years.' [10]

Tuesday 8 May Afternoon

Good Old Winnie!

Harold Nicolson lunched early at the Beefsteak Club, near Leicester Square, and left in what he thought was plenty of time to walk to Parliament to hear the Prime Minister's victory speech, due to be broadcast to the country and the Empire at three o'clock. 'When I had finished my luncheon I found the whole of Trafalgar Square and Whitehall was packed with people. Somebody had made a corner in rosettes, flags, streamers, paper whisks and above all, paper caps of the comic variety. I observed three Guardsmen in full uniform wearing such hats. Through this cheerful, but not exuberant, crowd I pushed my way to the House of Commons. The last few yards were very difficult, as the crowd was packed against the railings. I tore my trousers in trying to squeeze past a stranded car. But at length the police saw me and backed a horse into the crowd, making a gap through which, amid cheers, I was squirted into Palace Yard. Seeing that it was approaching the hour of 3 p.m. I decided to remain there and hear Winston's broadcast, which was to be relayed through loudspeakers.' [1]

A social worker from West London with the same objective was encountering similar difficulties: 'After we have cleared away a cold lunch, we all set off for Whitehall in a party—nine of us altogether, two men and seven women and girls! We board an 88 bus, almost empty at this end, though it quickly fills up as we approach the West End. Everybody on the bus seems in high spirits, exclaiming at the decorations, etc. As we approach Piccadilly Circus, the streets become very congested, and in the Circus itself the traffic is held up for some time. We watch the crowds surrounding Eros and climbing to the top. We see several sailors and girls sliding down the boarded up part of the statue and also several Yanks perched on top of lamp-posts, etc. The bus proceeds slowly along Whitehall and we get off near the Cenotaph, where large crowds are already lining the street. It is about 2 p.m. and we join the crowd assembling between the white lines in the middle of the road.

'Nobody seems to know if or when Churchill is coming past, but we stand near where we can see some amplifiers, so that we shall at least be able to hear his speech broadcast. In the meantime, we watch the crowds, etc. Occasional little processions of students, or service men and women, march down the street, cheering, etc. There are arguments about which side of the street Churchill will come, and everybody keeps a sharp look-out, especially when the traffic is stopped. A car does come down the road and a feeble cheer begins, but it does not appear to be him. At last three o'clock approaches, and there is still no sign of him, so we settle down to hear the speech broadcast. Everybody quietens down ... '[2]

In Downing Street, Elizabeth Layton, Churchill's secretary, could barely contain her excitement. She had attended a thanksgiving service at St Paul's Cathedral that morning and put her heart into 'Praise my soul, the King of Heaven'. By three o'clock she was waiting anxiously for her boss to make his historic broadcast. 'The entire staff turned up at Number 10 from the Annexe for the occasion, and we all stood outside the Cabinet Room door. Just before 3 we heard a great trumpeting sound over the loudspeaker as he blew his nose, then some remarks—"Pull down that blind," "What are you doing with that? No, leave it there," "Move a little further away please," etc. But of course, this was only coming out to us, he was not yet on the general air.'[3]

As Big Ben struck three, the familiar voice began:'Yesterday at 2.41 a.m. at General Eisenhower's headquarters, General Jodl, representative of the German High Command and Admiral Doenitz, designated head of the German state, signed the act of unconditional surrender of all German land, sea and air forces, in Europe, to the Allied Expeditionary Force and simultaneously to the Soviet High Command.

'Today, this agreement will be ratified and confirmed at Berlin ... Hostilities will end officially at one minute after midnight tonight, Tuesday, 8 May, but in the interests of saving lives, the "Cease Fire" began yesterday to be sounded all along the fronts.

'I should not forget to mention that our dear Channel Islands, the only part of His Majesty's Dominions that has been in the hands of the German foe, are also to be freed today.

'The Germans are still in places resisting the Russians troops, but, should they continue to do so after midnight, they will, of course, deprive themselves of the protection of the laws of war, and will be attacked from all quarters by the Allied troops. It is not surprising that on such long fronts and in the existing disorder of the enemy, the commands of the German High Command should not, in every case, be obeyed immediately.

'This does not, in our opinion, with the best military advice at our disposal, constitute any reason for withholding from the nation the facts communicated to us by General Eisenhower of the unconditional surrender already signed at Rheims, nor should it prevent us from celebrating today and tomorrow, Wednesday, as Victory in Europe days.

'Today perhaps we shall think mostly of ourselves. Tomorrow we shall pay a particular tribute to our Russian comrades, whose prowess in the field has been one of the grand contributions to the general victory.

'The German war is therefore at an end.

'After years of intense preparation, Germany hurled herself on Poland at the beginning of September, 1939, and, in pursuance of our guarantee to Poland and in agreement with the French Republic, Great Britain, the British Empire and Commonwealth of Nations declared war upon this foul aggression. After gallant France had been struck down we from this island and from our United Empire maintained the struggle single-handedly for a whole year until we were joined by the military might of the Soviet Union and later by the overwhelming power and resources of the United States of America.

'Finally, almost the whole world was combined against the evil doers who are now prostrate before us. Our gratitude to all our splendid Allies goes forth from all our hearts in this island and throughout the British Empire.

'We may allow ourselves a brief period of rejoicing, but let us not forget for a moment the toils and efforts that lie ahead. Japan, with all her treachery and greed, remains unsubdued. The injustice she has inflicted upon Great Britain and the United States, and other countries, and her detestable cruelties call for justice and retribution. We must now devote all our strength and resources to the completion of our task both at home and abroad.

'Advance Britannia!

'Long live the cause of freedom!

'God Save the King!'

Vere Hodgson, a social worker in West London, listened to the speech relayed on loudspeakers to the crowds in Whitehall: 'People hung on to every word he said. When he told them that as from midnight hostilities would cease, there were loud cheers and a waving of hats and flags; and then a louder cheer when he said: "The German war is therefore at an end." People began to cry and laugh and cheer at the same time. He ended his speech with "Advance Britannia", and the buglers of the Scots Guards sounded the ceremonial cease fire. Then the band struck up the National Anthem and looking round I saw everyone, young and old, civilians and soldiers, singing with such reverence that the anthem sounded like a sacred hymn.'[4]

Jane Gordon, a VAD nurse in a London children's hospital had decided to listen to the speech in one of the wards with the children: 'As soon as I had put on my cap and apron I went straight up to the ward, where I found Matron and the sisters, as well as the out-patient and in-patient nurses. Outside on the green a brass band was playing rather lugubriously to a fairly large crowd. As the hands of the ward clock neared the hour, the nursing staff automatically moved apart. For once the ward was silent—the children stopped chattering and not one of them was crying. When the Prime Minister's voice came on the air I glanced at the women in uniform. Each one stood quietly and you could tell by their eyes that their thoughts were far away from the hospital. Even the youngest nurses looked strangely subdued. The ward staff nurse came from Guernsey and her family had lived there throughout the German occupation. When Mr Churchill referred to "our dear Channel Islands" her mouth quivered for a moment and her eyes were full of tears.

'So it was ended. Germany had officially surrendered and the announcement finished. I felt a tug at my hand, which was being held by a small girl in the cot I was standing by.

'"What does it mean?" she asked anxiously.

'"The war has ended," I tried to reassure her with a smile.

'"What does that mean?"

'"Well it means," I hesitated for a moment, searching for some thing she would understand. "It means you will see lights at night in the streets and windows lit up." She looked dazed and I stumbled on: "It means you will never hear a siren again."

'"Never hear a siren again?" she repeated in a voice of utter astonishment. "Never again?"' [5]

Elizabeth Layton remembered: 'After his statement, we all rushed downstairs and out into the garden to line the path to the garden door, and when he came out to go to the House to give his statement again we clapped and clapped, and I think there were tears in his eyes as he beamed and said, "Thank you all, thank you very much."

'Outside, through the Horse Guards Parade, along Birdcage Walk and Great George Street, through Parliament Square, the whole place was cram-jammed with people waiting to welcome him. They cheered and shouted "Good old Winnie", and some pressed forward to pat the car and jump onto the running-board, so that it was almost impossible for it to move and it took quite thirty minutes to drive the quarter of a mile.' [6]

Churchill's bodyguard, former Detective Inspector W.H. Thompson, recalled VE Day as one his toughest jobs ever: 'The crowds knew that the Prime Minister was to visit the Commons and they waited in their tens of thousands to see him. No engine power was necessary. The car was literally forced along by the crowd. Everyone seemed determined to shake his hand.

'In Parliament Square the cheering thousands closed right in. Mr Churchill came forward to stand on the front seat of the open car with me while mounted police cleared a way. Eventually we reached the House after a terrible struggle which Mr Churchill, looking very happy, thoroughly enjoyed.' [7]

Somewhere in the crowds jamming Whitehall as the Prime Minister left Downing Street was Geoffrey Howe, an 18-year-old officer cadet, who, as a Member of Parliament and government minister would later become very familiar with the area. Howe and his friend John Lowry had come up to London for

the day from Exeter, where they were both on a university short course as poten-
tial officers, prior to joining their regiments.

Lord Howe:'I can remember an extraordinary sense of bewildered exhilaration.
London was pretty much *terra incognita* to us in those days, we had never roamed
at large there, and so the whole thing was a tremendous miscellany of experiences
and adventures. One thing that sticks in my mind is that when we were trying to
get down into the underground through these enormous crowds, Jack suddenly
passed out. I managed to bundle him into a train and when he recovered he saw
these lights flashing in front of his eyes and said "Are we in heaven?"

'When we got back to Exeter our group whitewashed the statue of General
Sir Thomas Redvers Buller on the main road above the station and left him with
a jerry on his head. Neither Jack nor I were involved, but when our group was
identified as culprits we had to pay a collective fine to Exeter City fire brigade to
get the statue cleaned.'

Shortly afterwards, John Lowry wrote a detailed letter to his parents describing
their day:' ... Yes, I went up to London for VE Day! Geoff Howe and myself
caught the 1.20 a.m. train from Exeter on Monday night. It was packed like a tin
of sardines. We travelled up with a gang of Norwegian airmen, some of whom we
already knew.

'We arrived in London at 5.30 a.m. on Tuesday morning. From Paddington
we caught a tube to Piccadilly. The streets at that hour were deserted. We walked
up East and called in at a Milk Bar for a glass of milk on the way. A policeman
directed us to a public lav where we got a wash and brush up. Then we came
back West to the Waterloo Bridge and watched all the ships and barges with their
bunting and flags. Everything that had a hooter was blowing it. From Wat. Bridge
we went up the Strand and got breakfast in a restaurant. After breakf. we went up
to Hyde Park Corner where we had arranged to meet John Cox, but he didn't
turn up.

'Then we went down to the Palace where a crowd was beginning to form.
By 12 noon there were thousands of people present. We got lunch free (we were
in uniform) at a Lyons Corner House just off Piccadilly Circus. From there we
walked, or rather pushed our way down to Parliament Square. By this time there
must have been hundreds of thousands of people blocking all roads and squares.
Flags were flying everywhere, thousands of them. We waited beside the House of
Commons from 2.30 p.m. and then the P Min. made his speech from the Public
Health Buildings just opp. Immediately after his speech everyone went raving
mad. Thousands of people cheered and shouted, threw things in the air, climbed
up lamp-posts and railings, clambered onto cars, buses and lorries; there was
absolute chaos.

'By some stroke of good fortune, Geoff and I happened to be standing near by
the gate through which the PM was to pass to go into the H of Parl. Suddenly
across the Square the cheering got even greater, hats went up into the air, rattles

screeched, trumpets blew and out of the din and roar emerged Winny in an open car. The Police on horseback cleared a path through the crowd and left us right in the very front. He passed within 10 yds of us. A camera man was taking pictures of it and I believe we might come out on the film. If you see the newsreel watch for the time when PM entered the H of C and look out for us on the right at the gate as he went in.

'You might also see us rushing around in a body in Westminster, Piccad. and Leicester Square with a crowd of other Yanks and British soldiers and Norwegian airmen.

'After the PM had gone into Parl. we pushed ourselves back through the multitude to Piccadilly Circus. Here it was almost impossible to move. Bands were playing and we danced arm in arm with Officers (majors and captains all included), men and girls round and round the Eros monument. Soldiers were up on top of it blowing trumpets and waving flags with Policemen vainly trying to persuade them to come down. From the roofs of all the shops and offices ticker-tape, bunting, flags and streamers AND bundles and bundles of LAV PAPER (!) cascaded down. We got free meals and lemonade at a canteen, had rosettes and coloured paper pinned all over us, and the terrific din continued all the while.

'It was then after 4 p.m. and after another rush around the city on top of a double-decker bus we landed up in Leicester Square. Things were now getting out of control. Thunder flashes, blanks and rockets were being let off, people were climbing up the sides of the offices and the crowd got even more hilarious. We attempted to get down to the Underground but found this impossible. A Policeman directed us up a side street where we eventually reached an accessible tube. Down underground it was still the same. People were singing and shouting, yelling and screaming and making the most infernal row.'[8]

The writer Vera Brittain was also there, in Whitehall, that afternoon: 'On the afternoon of VE Day, I went to Whitehall alone. I had promised, after hearing the announcement, to go to my mother for tea … No doubt, through friends in the Government, I could have watched the crowds from the comfort of a ministerial window, but I preferred to join them on the pavement … In spite of the flags, bells and streamers, the now harmless bombers circling Westminster Abbey, and the sense of danger departed which London at the close of the First War hardly knew, the waiting multitudes never surged into that outburst of relief known to history as Armistice Day.

'When Winston Churchill, complete with bowler hat and cigar, left Downing Street for the House of Commons, they surrounded his car and cheered him with an enthusiasm which convinced him that he was destined to remain their Prime Minister in the years immediately ahead. But they listened to his voice announcing the end of the war in a silence which, for a long moment, remained unbroken.

'It is only civilians far from the line who burst into noisy rejoicing. The people of London had seen their fellow-citizens killed and their homes destroyed; they had known danger, terror, apprehension and relief. Because of these things, their attitude to war's end resembled the attitude of soldiers at the front.' [9]

The press of the milling crowds in Whitehall delayed Churchill's arrival at the House to such an extent that there was a danger of the sitting being adjourned before he could get there. Eileen Harris, the Reuters reporter in the Press gallery, explained: 'The business of the week had finished, which automatically meant that the Speaker calls for the rising of the House. "Those in favour?" "Aye." Then everyone's off. So, somebody had to keep it going. One member after another talked and talked, and then somebody would butt in and say a little bit, and they kept this going, more or less a lot of nonsense, just to keep the House sitting.

'In the meantime, word had arrived that Churchill was trying to get through from Number Ten, but he couldn't get through the crowds. It took him, well, I don't know how long, even at walking pace he couldn't get through. The House was packed, as you can imagine, not a space anywhere. All got their question papers and parliamentary papers. As Churchill walked in, a great cheer went up all the way round the House and then there was silence as he reached his place. Then he rose to say how happy he was to bring the news that the war in Europe was now at an end.

'To my dying day, I shall never forget it. I couldn't have moved, couldn't have done anything, whatever had happened. Although we had known this great day was coming, the House itself just went into one great roar of cheers, papers went up in the air and they kept up the roaring and cheering for some time. I just sat there and the tears were rolling down. There was nothing I could do about it. It was the relief, you see, after all this long time.' [10]

Harold Nicolson: 'I enter the House. The place is packed and I sit on the step below the cross bench. I see a stir at the door and Winston comes in—a little shy—a little flushed—but smiling boyishly. The House jumps to its feet, and there is one long roar of applause. He bows and smiles in acknowledgement. I glance up at the Gallery where Clemmy (Churchill) should be. There is Mrs Neville Chamberlain there instead. And thereupon Winston begins. He repeats the short statement he had just made on the wireless ending up with "Advance Britannia" and then he lays his manuscript aside and with more gesture and emphasis than is customary to him, he thanks the House for its support throughout these years. He then proposes that we adjourn to the Church of St Margaret's, Westminster. The Speaker then leaves his seat and the mace is fetched before him. He is in Court Robes with gold facings to his gown and his Chaplain and the Sergeant-at-Arms are also in full dress.

'We file out by St Stephen's entrance and the police have kept a lane through the crowd. The crowd are friendly, recognising some of the members. I was with Nancy Astor, who is, I feel, a trifle hurt that she does not get more cheering. We then have a service and very memorable it is. The supreme moment is when the

Chaplain reads out the names of those Members who have lost their lives. It is a sad thing to hear. My eyes fill with tears. I hope that Nancy does not notice. "Men are so emotional," she says.

'We all go to the smoking-room, Winston comes with us. Passing through Central Hall, he is given an ovation by the crowd. A tiny little boy, greatly daring, dashes up to him and asks for an autograph. Winston solemnly takes out his glasses and signs. He then pats the delighted little boy on the head and grins his grin.' [11]

James Lansdale Hodson, the war correspondent, was back in London in time to join the celebrations: 'This afternoon I went into London to walk through Whitehall, Trafalgar Square and Piccadilly. The sun came out, and London was gay, gay and densely thronged but, in a sense, comparatively quiet. I saw only half a dozen people tipsy, and these hung from second-storey windows in Piccadilly Circus, one woman beating time and wearing a large imitation policeman's helmet. American soldiers were throwing oddments down from the windows of their club in Piccadilly; suddenly a great streamer of paper came down, and for a moment we wondered how this had been contrived; then we saw it was a roll of toilet paper, and everybody laughed. Streets were crowded, and looked, from a short distance off, impassable. But in the main one could move about. It was a crowd light-hearted, wearing its red, white and blue rosettes as on a Cup Final Day, and wearing, too, a host of comic little hats, silver cones, tricoloured cones, and in one instance, small royal crowns. Some hats had "Welcome Home" written on them. Two soldiers sported a badge "Pity the poor unemployed". There was little singing or jigging about, but I heard "Marching Through Georgia" in Whitehall, and the Volga Boatmen's song in the Haymarket ... In the heavens a number of Flying Fortresses were moving on, pleasure bent. From Trafalgar Square five or six in formation seemed to be flying up Northumberland Avenue. Over the Admiralty one dropped two cerise flares and later I saw a Lancaster let fall a Verey light over St James's Park. Girls had climbed on to various clumps of stone and turned themselves into living statues; the lions' heads in Trafalgar Square were being sat upon, and in Whitehall a girl had clambered onto a stone ledge twenty-five feet above the street. In Piccadilly we skipped into a News theatre and here heard the only bitter complaint, from a woman taking our tickets, who said: "All celebrating like fools and the war not over yet." Maybe she had a husband or a lover in Burma ... ' [12]

The writer John Lehmann had slightly less evocative memoriese: 'My chief recollection of VE Day is of queueing for a bus to Paddington that never came, and finally having to walk right across Hyde Park with a heavy suitcase in one hand and a briefcase in the other, pouring with sweat. The crowds were more dazed than excited, and they seemed to gather and move in a slow groundswell, no wild battery of waves, good-tempered, a little bewildered and awkward about celebrating, like cripples taking their first steps after a miracle healing, not fully grasping yet the implication of the new life ahead of them.' [13]

Decidedly not celebrating was the Methodist minister and veteran orator at Speakers' Corner, the Reverend Donald Soper, now Lord Soper. 'I was by that time a convinced pacifist and a socialist, and for me, the outbreak of the Second World War was the vindication of the fears I had, and the beliefs I had, that unless we eradicated war, it would contribute to our own eradication. It was an experience which was deepened with the catastrophes at the beginning of the Second World War. Over and over again, I had the unhappy but complete conviction that the Second World War was an inevitable consequence of the behaviour patterns of those who might have learned the lessons of the First World War.

'No, we did not mark the peace with any celebration. You see, in one sense, we were extremely fortunate. I hadn't brothers who died on battlefields, we had then two girl children and we were able to send them to the Methodist School in Harpenden and I hadn't to make great sacrifices and therefore I didn't feel entitled to throw my hat in the air and say "How marvellous it all is!" I felt that the war, at its lowest level, was an impermissable waste of time, that it prevented the fulfillment of so many things that belonged to the nature of the Christian evangel and that now we had to get down to missionary work.

'VE Day for me was the re-establishment of the compact that I had made, however irreverently and however badly; I had a mission to try to fulfil and I had a course to take and VE Day opened the door or opened the gate to that continuation of the journey which had been made impossible by six years of war.'

Charles Kohler, a 34-year-old Quaker and conscientious objector, suffered similar reservations. He was working as an accountant, a 'reserved profession' and need not have enlisted, but chose to go through the rigours of a tribunal for exemption from the military, in order to make his objections known: 'At about half-past four on the afternoon of VE Day I had finished my auditing work at the Piccadilly Hotel, packed my briefcase and left through the big swing doors. At once, I caught the mood of elation, church bells clanging, cars tooting, shops blazing. The newspaper hoardings read "Victory in Europe", "Unconditional surrender".

'The pavements were crowded with troops, ordinary soldiers, ATS girls, WRENs, WRAC, some Poles and a few Free French, all linking arms, singing. One man waved a child's Union Jack. This was a spontaneous outburst by those men and women who had fought and bought victory. It was their day. Joy filled me: peace, relief, no more rockets, no more fire-watching on the roofs of my London office, no more mass bombardments, no more slaughter.

'And yet, I stood outside the communal rejoicing. I could not link arms with comrades-in-arms; I had taken no active part in the fight for victory. I had refused military service and registered as a conscientious objector, a CO. Why? Although I was half German, my deepest loyalties, like those of my mother and older brother were fervently English. I was no fanatic or extremist. I was willing to do relief work, fire service, ambulance, farming.

'The tribunal dealt with me lightly, probably because they knew I was a Quaker. I was given conditional exemption, conditional on either continuing in my own work as an accountant or doing work on the land or in the Friends' Ambulance or other relief work. But I need not join the Home Guard or the non-combatant branch of the Army. I was free very much to lead my own life.

'Why did I refuse to fight? There are many threads. I come from a divided, broken family—father German, mother English, my parents separated. My brother Wolfgang, born 1913, spent all his life in Germany. At the outbreak of war, he was working as a journalist and joined the Luftwaffe on sorties as an observer.. He was an idealist and I remember his telling me that he believed Hitler had in mind a united Europe with a kind of "pax Germanica" in which there would be full employment and peace.

'At that stage he knew nothing of the Nazis' deeper objects, he knew nothing of the killing of Jews, he knew nothing of the persecution of minorities. Soon after joining the Luftwaffe, he was wounded but when he recovered, he rejoined his unit and was shot down in Kent at the Battle of Britain. He then became a prisoner of war in Canada for the duration.

'My brother Hermann, born 1909, spent most of his life in England, although foolishly, he never applied for naturalization. He was fervently British and when there was an opportunity, for those who wished, to join the Pioneer Corps, he was among the first volunteers. He quickly stood out in the Pioneers and was placed in the RASC, then he got a commission and served with distinction in France and Norway.

'That leaves me, Charlie, the middle one. Nearly all my life I have spent in England. I am a Quaker by convincement and probably that is why I registered as a CO. What were my motives, underlying promptings? They lie too deep for coherent expression, but include my Quaker faith. I am a pacifist by nature, a reconciler, a conciliator.

'The historic peace testimony of Quakers appealed strongly to me, but I did not want to stand aside from danger. I was very ready to do fire watching or any relief work that came my way. What other motives? I think, although it may not be very logical, my mixed parentage—the thought of fighting actively against my father and brother in Germany and my other German relations somehow seemed to me to be wrong. Naïve, perhaps, but that is how I saw it at the time.

'But it was not an easy choice. I felt the majority of all those I knew in the office and in life, were making great sacrifices for their ideals and to lean on my Quaker faith and not register as a CO was a temptation, because I didn't need to tell my boss or clients or colleagues, none of whom were happy with my position. I could have kept mum, taken the easy path, but I felt that was wrong, if I was standing for peace, however naïve, then I must pay the price and suffer in a different way like others did, I couldn't escape suffering.

'I felt great guilt, I think I generally kept mum about it although it leaked out. Part of me, like my brother Hermann, was fervently English and all the ideals of the war appealed to me and somehow, if I went into pubs or those I was fire watching with, were all the time talking about victory, I felt I wasn't really wholly integrated, I wasn't really with them. Part of me was standing aside from the war—and that gave me a great feeling of guilt. There were two or three times, I remember, when I passed an RAF recruiting office and felt a great urge to go inside and volunteer as a rear gunner, but I resisted this temptation and remained true to my Quaker faith.

'I did not parade the fact that I was a CO and to that extent, I was cowardly. On the few occasions I did, I met with great antagonism. A neighbour was talking about what he would do to any German who landed in this country by parachute. He said he would knife him and tear him to pieces, wouldn't you? I said, "No, I wouldn't. I'd better be honest with you, I am a conscientious objector." And he raised his umbrella and said, "I am going to kill you." I knew that he was a gentle man, older than I was and that he wouldn't. So I stood absolutely still with my arms down and his anger abated. "I'm never going to talk or walk with you again," he said, and walked away.

'There were those who said cruel things, and being a softie, having a gentle kind of nature and wanting to be loved, I found it difficult.

'Throughout the war, I felt the isolation of being a CO. I felt I was not really accepted in the community. So, VE Day, I felt I had no right to link hands with comrades-in-arms. I rejoiced in the peace, the end of the war, but I was not among those had risked their life for victory.'

In fashionable Kensington there was little public rejoicing to be observed, as Cecil Beaton, at home in Pelham Place, noted in his diary: 'It is as quiet as a Sunday. Flags are hanging from the balconies of the houses opposite. Some young people have gone to the West End to let off steam, but there is no general feeling of rejoicing. Victory does not bring with it a sense of triumph—rather a dull numbness of relief that the blood-letting is over. Hitler's reign of terror has left behind it a ruined and exhausted Europe, and throughout the world a desperate uncertainty about the future.'[14]

By five o'clock in the afternoon a crowd of more than 20,000 people were gathered outside Buckingham Palace chanting 'We want the King! We want the King!' At 5.25, to wild cheers, the King, Queen and the two princesses stepped out onto the red and gold draped balcony. A few minutes later they were joined by Churchill, bareheaded in the late afternoon sunshine. 'The people went frantic, delirious with joy,' the *News Chronicle* reported. 'Their cheers, their laughter, their whistling and shouting marked the consummation of victory … This was the proudest, happiest moment in the lives of all who waited. And this, surely, was the greatest, proudest, most unforgettable of all the mighty moments in the life of Winston Churchill.'

It was a rather unforgettable moment, too, for a small boy in the diligent care of his nanny in the crowd outside the palace railings. Winston Churchill, the Conservative MP, was born in 1940 a few months after his grandfather became Prime Minister. 'I was literally brought up in a bomb shelter in London.

My father, Randolph, was in the army and my mother and I had no real home. But I do remember being taken by my nanny, Mrs Martin, to Buckingham Palace in the afternoon, clutching a tiny Union Jack.

'A large crowd can easily seem intimidating to a child, but the British on VE Day afternoon were simply happy and excited and glad to be alive. At about 5.30 there was a momentary hush as the French windows were opened and my grandfather stepped onto the balcony with the royal family. The King was bareheaded and in uniform, the Queen and Princess Margaret were in blue and Princess Elizabeth was in ATS uniform.

'I don't remember being in the least surprised to see my grandfather in such company. Every small boy believes his grandfather to be the most important person in the world.'[15]

Meanwhile, another crowd was impatiently waiting outside the Ministry of Health building in Whitehall, where it was reported that the Prime Minister would be speaking at five. A Mass Observation observer recorded a detailed account of the atmosphere:

'Time passes. Sporadic bursts of shouting from crowd. "We want Winnie! We want Winnie!" There are occasional shouts of "Here he comes!" but the balcony is still empty. Now and then people look up enviously to those sitting at windows opposite or sitting down on the roofs above. A few people pipe up weakly "He's a jolly good fellow" and there are more shouts of "We want Winnie!" The minutes seem to pass very slowly in the intense heat. More people keep feeling ill, and the crowd makes way for them, sympathetically. A stout man collapses and is helped out. Shouts of "Hurry up, Winnie, old man!"

'The crowd gets restive. Voice from the back: "Why don''e come out?" Another voice, ironically, "He's 'aving a drink, dear."

'People fan themselves with newspapers and handkerchiefs. "Be nice if it starts pouring." "Be cool, anyway." There is discontent about. Seven or eight voices start singing, softly, clearly, and with some hostility, "This is a lovely way to spend an evening." They start up several times, but it is not taken up by the crowd. By and by some male voices start shouting "One, two, three, four. What the hell are we waiting for?" Then there are wild bursts of applause, cheering and clapping, and the crowd falls silent again.

'A paper plane, very well made, sails out over the crowd from an upper window, and heads turn to watch its flight and hands stretch out to seize it. Somewhere in the crowd a woman says, "I've never seen one better made. Leonardo must be about somewhere." There's another burst of cheering and clapping, and then the chorus starts up again: "One, two, three, four. What the hell are we waiting for?" Somebody else adds on "Five, six, seven eight. Mr Churchill's always late."

'Rattles sound occasionally. Another paper plane sails down. The time is now 5.40. People faint or file out pretty constantly, as the heat is really appalling, though there is a light breeze. Someone says bitterly, "Perhaps it was six o'clock, not five." More clapping and shouting. A sudden burst of Yoo hoo! Yoo hoo! An old cracked, but very resolute, voice shouts "Come on Winnie. We shan't want you for long!" In the restless state of the crowd, this sounds like a *double entendre*.

'Man at the side of the balcony suddenly puts up two fingers in the V-sign and instantly there is a terrific burst of cheering: people wave handkerchiefs, fags, fans, hats, umbrellas, gloves, anything. Churchill appears, wearing a hat. Gives the V-sign. Crowd roars itself hoarse. Waves white handkerchief. Crowd roars again.'[16]

It was nearly six o'clock before Churchill made his appearance in Whitehall but it was, it seems, a *tour de force. The Times* claimed it was 'one of the most moving and remarkable scenes' of the day: 'Mr Churchill spoke from a balcony in Whitehall to a great crowd, whose self-disciplined orderliness and gaiety were so typical of the proud, unconquerable spirit of London through the dark and perilous days now left behind. This was London's own joyous meeting with the nation's war leader and with other Ministers who have worked at his side through five exacting years. Mr Churchill spoke to this assembled multitude of citizens only a few sentences, but they were deeply expressive. "This," he said to them, "is your victory."

'The vast crowd filled the whole of the wide roadway and the pavements from the end of Downing Street to Parliament Square. Above the balcony hung prominently the flags of the allies. Mr Churchill appeared on the central balcony accompanied by a group of Cabinet colleagues. Mr Churchill's appearance was greeted with a loud and sustained cheer and this was renewed when the crowd heard his voice—carried resonantly by the loudspeakers—saying "God bless you all." After further cheering, waving and singing by the crowd, Mr Churchill said: "This is your victory. It is the victory of the cause of freedom in every land. In all our long history we have never seen a greater day than this. Everyone, man or woman, has done their best. Everyone has tried. Neither the long years, nor the dangers, nor the fierce attacks of the enemy, have in any way weakened the independent resolve of the British nation. God bless you all." The Prime Minister's words were heard distinctly throughout Whitehall, and when he had done there was another great outburst of cheering. With Mr Bevin beating time, the crowd sang "For he's a jolly good fellow" and Mr Churchill repeatedly waved his acknowledgements.'

Twenty-four-year-old Private Peter Ustinov of the Royal Army Ordnance Corps had had every intention of joining the crowds in the West End but was beaten back by their numbers: 'I had a sleeping out pass and lived near Knightsbridge. That afternoon I made my way slowly to Trafalgar Square to watch what was going on, but found it rather too oppressive because it was so crowded. In the end I walked back to Knightsbridge and solemnly opened a bottle of champagne which I had bought in North Africa for just this occasion. It was a herald of post-war conditions because I opened it with great solemnity and there was only the slightest puff as the cork came out. It was as flat as a pancake. Perhaps it was a herald to post-war conditions.'

Tuesday 8 May Evening

Bonfire Night

At precisely nine o'clock in the evening of VE Day a hush fell across Britain and much of the Empire as the uncertain voice of King George VI crackled from what was then universally known as the wireless: 'Today we give thanks to Almighty God for a great deliverance.

'Speaking from our Empire's oldest capital city, war-battered but never for one moment daunted or dismayed, speaking from London, I ask you to join with me in that act of thanksgiving.

'Germany, the enemy who drove all Europe into war, has been finally over-come. In the Far East we have yet to deal with the Japanese, a determined and cruel foe. To this we shall turn with the utmost resolve and with all our resources. But at this hour, when the dreadful shadow of war has passed from our hearts and homes in these islands, we may at last make one pause for thanksgiving …

'Let us think what it was that has upheld us through nearly six years of suf-fering and peril. The knowledge that everything was at stake: our freedom, our independence, our very existence as a people; but the knowledge also that in defending ourselves we were defending the liberties of the whole world; that our cause was the cause not of this nation only, not of this Empire and Commonwealth only, but of every land where freedom is cherished and law and liberty go hand in hand.

'In the darkest hours we knew that the enslaved and isolated peoples of Europe looked to us; their hopes were our hopes; their confidence confirmed our faith. We knew that, if we failed, the last remaining barrier against a world-wide tyranny would have fallen into ruins. But we did not fail. We kept our faith with ourselves and with one another; we kept faith with our great allies. That faith and unity have carried us through to victory …

'There is great comfort in the thought that the years of darkness and danger in which the children of our country have grown up are over and, please God, for ever. We shall have failed, and the blood of our dearest will have flowed in vain, if the victory which they died to win does not lead to a lasting peace, founded on justice and established in good will. To this, then, let us turn our thoughts on this day of just triumph and proud sorrow … '[1]

The King's broadcast interrupted countless street parties, almost all of which were due to end with a bonfire. Effigies of Hitler replaced the traditional Guy Fawkes and homemade fireworks fizzled and banged in the night. Children raced hither and thither, their parents danced around the flames, potatoes were cooked in the ashes, couples embraced at the edge of the flickering light and some young women lost their virginity in the heady abandon of victory.

A young firewoman called Eunice perhaps wisely withheld her last name when she made her contribution to a local history group in Portsmouth: 'I lost my chastity on VE Day: victory over Eunice! In the field at the back was a big bonfire. They'd been making it for ages. Rumour had it that the war was about to end, and it was all building up. What we felt when we realised the war was coming to an end was relief. Everybody went mad. We all made cups of tea and sang songs and all sorts of things, and it ended up with this particular firewoman's pants on top of the hose drying tower! It was a 40-foot tower.'[2]

Similar, although slightly less saucy, stories were told about parties and bonfires in every town, village and community.

This was the bonfire party on a bombed site in Hannover Road, Willesden: 'The young people gave the affair due publicity. They made their own posters and affixed one either end of Hanover Road and pinned handbills in adjoining roads. The children were instructed to bring as many friends as they could, while the older boys made their own fireworks, flares, etc. Everybody participated in the making of Hitler. One lady gave the jacket, another the trousers, and so on until Hitler's rig was assured. A dressmaker living on the road gave the dressing up the professional touch. Hitler's clothes fitted to perfection. The chief fire-watcher in the road made the face, and the boys fitted up the gallows, but one of the men erected it for them.

'When the gallows were erected and Hitler's body strung up, the foundations of the bonfire were laid. One of the men suggested they burn Goering too, and he volunteered to make him. Goering, complete with medals and two Iron Crosses, was seated on a chair at the foot of Hitler. Lying nearby was a battered doll, face and body daubed with red paint, as a reminder of the misery Hitler and Goering had brought to humanity.

'Two Union Jacks and bunting was hung from wooden posts in front of the bombed site. From about seven o'clock onwards children collected round watching the proceedings, and making sure they weren't going to miss anything, despite the fact that the proceedings were billed to start at 9.30 p.m. Two planks supported by bricks were intended as "Reserved" seats. At 9.15 p.m. a gramophone and records, light music, was obtained. By this time there must have been about

50 children and 20 adults, standing about in the road watching the goings-on, the adults encouraging the young people and giving them every assistance.

'The chief fire-watcher was invited to light the bonfire at 9.30 p.m. One of the boys handed him a long pole at the end of which was a rag soaked in paraffin. Immediately the bonfire was lit a cheer went up. Hitler started to burn too quickly and there were cries of "Don't let him end up so soon, let him linger" and the boys promptly doused him with a hose in order to prolong the burning. Soon Goering's chair collapsed and a cheer went up.

'The children danced round the bonfire yelling at the top of their voices. Flares were let off and with each bang the crowd caught fright. At 9.40 p.m. a piano was carried into the roadway and a lady sat down and played popular songs—"Roll Out the Barrel", "Tipperary", "Daisy-Daisy", "The Lambeth Walk", "Knees Up Mother Brown", etc—and things did really liven up. At first people were rather shy and sang very quietly, but they soon plucked up courage and within a short time their voices were ringing out and could be heard a good distance away.

'Grown-ups and the young people joined hands and danced and sang and altogether there must have been about 150 people. Neighbours were standing outside their front gates in small groups and they too joined in the singing. At about 11 p.m., the smaller children left, but the older boys were very unwilling to go, despite repeated calls of "Come on, you've got to go to bed."'³

'What a day!' a young Cardiff mother wrote in her diary. 'We gathered together on our bombed site and planned the finest party the children ever remembered. Neighbours pooled their sweet rations, and collected money, a few shilling from each family … and our grocer gave his entire stock of sweets, fruit, jellies, etc. All the men in the neighbourhood spent the day clearing the site. The church lent the tables, the milkman lent a cart for a platform, and we lent our radiogram and records for the music. We all took our garden chairs for the elderly to sit on. Someone collected all our spare jam jars. Blackout curtains came down to make fancy dresses for the children. Everyone rummaged in ragbags and offered bits to anyone who wanted them. That evening, ninety-four children paraded round the streets, carrying lighted candles in jam jars, wearing all manner of weird and fancy dress, singing lustily, "*We'll Be Coming Round the Mountain When We Come*", and led by my small son wearing white cricket flannels, a scarlet cummerbund and a Scout's hat, beating a drum. In the dusk, it was a brave sight never to be forgotten.

'Later we wandered into the city centre. Outside the City Hall, thousands and thousands of people gathered, completely covering the gardens and lawns. A choir sat on a stone parapet and began to sing what seemed to be a prepared programme, but the people, led by a policeman, outsang them with the old Welsh favourites, "Gwlad", "Aberystwyth", etc. To be there was to know real Welsh fervour and is another never-to-be-forgotten experience. Back in the suburbs, fires were lit in the streets, fed from the rubble of the bombed houses and aided by a door from the air-raid shelter that came too late.'⁴

In the Coventry suburb of Radford, as in many other places, local people had been making preparations for days: 'During the rumour days previous to VE Day, money had been collected all along the street, also offers of all kinds of food. Quantities, large and small, of fat, sugar, etc. was turned into cakes by some residents so that on the great day itself, although this food had been collected "for the children", there was enough to spare for everyone living in the road.

'It was a lovely day, no rain threatening and warm enough to stand about till far into the night. Tables and urns, borrowed probably from some church hall, were set up on the brow of the hill on the pavement. All the children were given more than they could eat, including jellies (goodness knows where from!) trifles and such like. Food was also taken to invalids and the old, and anybody who didn't come out and join in the throng …

'"Musical arms" for children, boys, girls, ladies, gents, over 50s, over 70s, mixed etc, took place in succession to the music of a piano which had been hauled onto the pavement, the winners in each case getting an egg.

'This took a long time. It was followed by dancing till dusk looked like approaching.

'Two days previously, a life-sized image of Hitler, stuffed with straw had been suspended by the neck in the middle of the street from bedroom window across to bedroom window.

'As dusk came near, a self-appointed "mayor and wife" both men, conducted the effigy's funeral. A builder, the fattest man in the street and the jolliest, was the "mayoress", dressed in a very tight dress with white frillies showing and with a wig made from pulled out rope. Some "bearers" brought some planks, the effigy was let down solemnly and placed on them and the whole procession headed by the "mayor and mayoress" and forming a long crocodile of all the residents and anybody else who liked, marched singing to the common at the bottom of the road.

'Here there had been built a huge bonfire, with all sorts of things which any other time wouldn't have been burnt. The image was put on the bonfire ready for lighting.

'As dusk was not till 10.30, a programme of sports was arranged. Races for all ages were arranged, the three winners in each getting respectively three eggs, two eggs and one egg. Goodness knows where all the eggs came from! The two ladies who won the over-50 race for ladies were the thinnest and fattest in the street and they ended up with the thin one submerged by the fat one to the amusement of all.

'By this time it was dark enough to light the fire, which the "mayor and mayoress" proceeded to do, the "mayoress" catching her "lovely blonde wig" alight.

'An hour later about, the procession returned to the street and the piano, every window illuminated. Ordinary light was enough to do this, after memories of the blackout and the care needed by fuel shortage—still needed of course, but waived on this occasion.

'From then until midnight dancing, orderly and happy, filled the time. There was one window, kept open, from which drinks were served, mainly soft, also soup, free. At 12.15 all joined in singing "God Save the King" and brought to a close a day which will never be forgotten by any who were there.'[5]

The broadcaster Ralph Wightman, reporting for the BBC, waxed positively lyrical when he described the sleepy scene in his own village, Piddletrenthide in Dorset: 'On Victory Night outside this village inn in Dorset, through the open window, you can hear men in the village relaxing after six years of toil. I can see the bar through a thick haze of smoke … The room looks very much as it does on a normal Saturday night when the week's work is over. Charles Battick is here—he's thatched most of the cottages in the village. His father was a thatcher before him and there are sons to follow him, though one has been missing since Arnhem. Trooper Clark is here—he is on sick leave from Germany. His father is the village haulage contractor. Then there are Tom Woodsford, a roadman, Charlie Briggs, a tractor driver, Jack Groves, a shepherd, and old Herb Clark, a professional rabbit catcher who may have done a bit of poaching before now.

'Just opposite the inn a byroad climbs diagonally up the hillside until it reaches a little plateau on a cliff above the road and stream and valley. It is quiet up here. This is one of the places which come into my mind whenever I hear the name England … From here you can see or hear or smell all the things which in their season are given to decorate our homes. Hedges of whitethorn, banks of primroses, sunshine through young leaves, bluebell woods, violets, primroses, honeycups, anenomes, apple-blossom, woodsmoke in the evening, hoar frost on grass, the scent of hay, the dawn chorus of birds in the spring. Up in the valley you can see the church tower set against the woods of Morning Well. Below is the manor house, glimpsed through its horse chestnuts and elms and copper beech …

'A few lights are lit in the cobb-walled thatch-roofed cottages. These were the lights I missed. It was a hellish thing to have blackness over them all as if death has passed over. Of course death did pass over us. One bomb destroyed the butcher's shop, a shower of incendiaries fell at White Packington, a stick of HEs crashed across the meadows behind South House, and a landmine on Bellamy's farm shook the whole village. We had one German plane down in the Battle of Britain, but we'd no history to compare with Kent or Sussex … We are a completely ordinary village.

'Here by the stream you get an impression of things going onward forever the same. It is a very ordinary stream. It has seen every man in the village disguised in the uniform of the Home Guard or ARP or the NFS, which is like every other stream in every other village. This is the England for which a handful of us have worked in a way we never believed it was possible to work. This is the England we saw for the first time with open eyes in 1940. This is the England for which the most worthy of our handful have died.'[6]

'Went to Divisions,' Leading Wren June Last wrote in her diary on 8 May. 'Had to work hard until half-past five. Had supper, then went to the Palais, had gin and lime. Went out of there, went along the Prom, had fun and games round bonfire.'

June worked in the billeting office at the Patrol Service Central Depot in Lowestoft, which co-ordinated small boats guarding the coastline, and was not pleased to have to work on the day everyone else was having a holiday: 'On VE Day we had to go to Divisions, as they called it, a parade, and had a speech from the Commodore and we thought, "Oh well, at least we won't have to go to work any more today" but we did have to, and were quite surprised and what's more we had to work until half-past five.

'Then, when we'd finished, I had to go to a rehearsal for a concert party we were putting on at the depot; I was a dancing girl. After that we heard there was going to be a dance in town. One of the good things about being in the Wrens was that you didn't have to wear uniform unless you were on duty, so we could go out wearing our own clothes. I went along to the dance with some girl friends and there were masses of people there, nearly all Naval people. The dancing itself was quite calm but when we walked back along the front, some of the sailors who had been billeted in the Royal Hotel, which was right on the front, were getting furniture out and burning it on the beach in a bonfire and they were all dancing around it and singing, all round this bonfire.

'We thought, well the war IS over, but we've still got to live here, and there they were, bringing all the furniture out of the hotel where they were staying and burning it.'

Twenty-four-year old John Henry Scoby, a sapper in the Royal Engineers, had been wounded in Italy in 1944 and was waiting for an operation in the North Riding Infirmary, Middlesborough: 'I had permission to go to other wards to shave patients too ill to shave themselves and on the morning of VE Day, having done this job, I was walking back to my own ward when I was greeted by three off-duty telephone girls who invited me out for a VE Day celebration drink at a pub across the road. I had no cap, but knew if I went back to the ward I would not get out again, so took a chance, as it was only about 100 yds away.

'We crossed the road and had just got to the pub door when two redcaps stopped me and asked for my name, rank and number. I gave them the details and they then asked for my leave pass. I had to admit I didn't have one, but I explained I was just going out for a quick drink and then returning to the hospital.

'They would not listen or understand how important it was to me to share a drink on VE Day with friends. The girls pleaded for me to be allowed to go back to the hospital, but they were adamant I had to be taken in a jeep to their HQ near the Town Hall. There I was grilled and locked up in a cell until the facts were verified. I grumbled a lot and said it was one of my first outings since coming home from Italy and it had been spoilt by their actions on such an important day.

'At 6 p.m., they unlocked the cell door and put me in a jeep and took me back to hospital, telling Sister that I would face a charge of being out without a pass and being improperly dressed. So I got a good telling off and was told I was grounded and confined to the ward.

'As the ward filled with visitors, some came to chat to me and I explained what had happened and how I was not going to get a drink on VE Day. Some of them invited me to join them if I could get out and I decided to ask the night nurse to cover for me when she came on duty at 8 p.m. As soon as she arrived and the hand-over had been completed, I approached her about going out and promised to be back before the Night Sister's visit at about 12 p.m. She agreed.

'Dashing off to my new-found friends' house just a short distance away, I arrived just as they were going out and we all set off on a tour of Middlesborough pubs. Beer was in very short supply and you were lucky to get one drink in each pub. I don't know how far we walked but we ended up about 11 o'clock in the house of an Army sergeant on leave from Italy, where snacks and drinks were laid on and they were dancing to records in the street.

'I was enjoying this when I suddenly passed out; I don't know if it was my war disability, or not being used to the drink, but anyhow, I ended up in the sergeant's daughter's bed.

'They woke me at 5 a.m. to get the workman's bus into town and back to the hospital. The night nurse greeted me with great joy. She had managed to cover my absence, but was on the verge of having to report a missing patient. I said how sorry I was to upset her and thanked her for allowing me out and everything was OK, no harm done.

'I was operated on the next day and so it was about ten days before the major came to the hospital to try my case for going out without a pass and being improperly dressed. The trial took place in the ward kitchen, with me being marched in and the charge read out. When I explained what had happened the major just smiled and said "Case dismissed!" A month later, I was discharged from the army with a 100 per cent war disability pension but I had to stay in the hospital for two more years. Of course, I was not allowed out, so I never saw my friends with whom I spent that brief period. Thanks to them, I have happy memories of VE Day and night.'

'Did you have any excitement on 'V' Day?' Mrs Rose Martin from Rochdale wrote to her sister in Buckinghamshire. 'I suppose it would be rather quiet at Bledlow Ridge. We ourselves did nothing very exciting, but Rochdale was decked in style. The Church at the top of the hill was floodlit in red and blue and really looked like a picture of fairyland. There were peacocks and butterflies illuminating the gardens beneath the church; the Town Hall was floodlit; there was a bandstand right in the centre of the Town Hall Square all lit up and the roundabout in the middle of the town was bedecked with fairy lights and looked like a maypole. The whole effect for the town centre was grand. I believe it was one of the best 'V' night displays in the whole of Lancashire.

'We went down town at night to see the lights go on at 11 p.m. and there were crowds and crowds of people; the whole Town Hall Square was absolutely packed. The band was playing in the middle and people were dancing all around. It was a scene I would not have missed for anything. It was the same on the next three nights, but on Saturday night—well—Rochdale must have been saving fireworks for the last ten years for this time. I never saw such a scene! There were fireworks all over the show. Some were like miniature flying bombs. They skimmed the heads of all the people, swooping and rising and then suddenly landed on somebody with a terrific bang. There were screams and laughs and dashing about, mainly lads and girls about 18 to 25. They were having the time of their lives.

'Our friends from Bury came over for tea so we took them down town and they thought it was grand. Bury has been in mourning all the week. The Town Council in Bury say it is not a time for rejoicing and too many people have been killed but they seem to forget that Peace means there will be no more killing and millions will be saved. Even Heywood did better than Bury and that wasn't much. Daddy went to Heywood and thought it was exciting there but if he had seen Rochdale, well, he would have been flabbergasted.'

Irene Rees, aged 20, turned down as medically unfit for the forces, was working 12-hour shifts in a munitions factory in Cardiff: 'I was very aware of what was going on with the war, though of course we only had the radio and newspapers then. There was a period in the war, when everything was black and I was convinced we were going to lose at one stage and that we were going to be occupied by the Germans.

'I lived in Cardiff, which was bombed, and we slept in air-raid shelters. You weren't living properly, you were working, you feared for your lives all the time. You wondered every day, am I going to be alive next week? Quite a few friends used to say "I wonder will this war ever end, will we ever see normal life again?"

'I realized the war was coming to an end when we started to get better news, when the raids actually stopped and we were able to go to our beds at night.

'That day (VE Day), I didn't really feel the war was over. I was still working the long shift in the munitions factory which was not particularly pleasant. That was the rule at that time: once you reached the age of seventeen and a half you had to do work of "national importance", unless you had young children or were disabled.

'For somebody young, it was quite demoralizing. You couldn't do anything— you were either at work or were in the shelter. You couldn't go anywhere. The relaxation side of life wasn't there, you were afraid to go into town, you were discouraged from gathering in large crowds and most young people of 19 or 20 want to be with their peers. You were full of life, yet you were trapped.

'At the end of the shift, I was aware from the radio that things were well for us in Europe. We all prayed for peace and the return of our loved ones from far distant places. But bed was inviting, so I retired as soon as possible. A short time later, my mother came into the room and told me to look out into the street. It was dark, but people were thronging in the street, kissing and hugging and dancing. It was a happy sight. I joined them and with the rest of the family, joined the festivities. We could hardly believe it after so long.

'There were many tears also, many would never return. People's lives had been affected in so many ways. There was the boy on crutches, who had lost a leg and was at home in blue, convalescing with his family. There was a young woman, whose husband had been drowned at sea and her parents and baby had died when a land mine fell on the street while she was at work. Many neighbours had lost their homes on that night, some their lives. We could not forget those tragedies.

'Some of us had friends or close relatives still fighting in the Far East. That war was still in progress. My boy friend was still in the Far East with the Navy and we didn't know what he was doing. I had a brother who was a paratrooper and two cousins—one who never returned—away in distant places, so for many people, anxiety still remained. To me, the war wasn't over.'

Kathleen Barnett was living at home, in Moor Common, Buckinghamshire, looking after her sick mother and was exempted from war work, but spent a lot of time doing voluntary work for the WI and the Red Cross: 'I got involved with the war effort because I felt I ought to be doing something. I was motivated by patriotism, I suppose, the sense of excitement of doing something different. In fact, they weren't exciting times, they were fearful times, we could hear the bombing of London from out here. On the night they bombed the docks, you could see the searchlights over London.

'By the time the war was coming to a close, the people round here were absolutely fed up with it, they were longing for it to finish, but we were determined to win, our whole idea was to win. The village worked together extremely well during the war, everybody forgot their differences working for a common cause. I don't think we have ever got back to that again.

'When the war ended, it was a complete surprise to me. We knew when the invasion started and everybody got their hopes up then and we thought, well, it won't be long now. Of course, in fact it did go on for almost another year. It seemed never-ending and although we were taking places all over the world, when it did end, it hadn't finished in the Far East.

'When we heard about the death of Hitler, we just cheered, we were so glad to get rid of the blooming man. I suppose then I began to think it must end because he was, after all, the leader and all the others seemed to be running away. He was the one who kept it all together.

'I remember the Prime Minister's speech and the King's speech on VE Day. I remember putting on all the lights in the house—you couldn't put enough lights on, everyone did.

'In the evening, I went out celebrating with Morris (her boyfriend, later husband, whom her parents had forbidden her to meet because he wasn't "suitable", but whom she continued to meet secretly) to Northend, a nearby village. We spent the evening up there and had a whale of a time in one of the little pubs, drinking anything we could get. It was packed out that night. People were singing, and having a tremendous time, they were all so relieved it was over.

'I was able to drive up there. I was lucky because I had a permit to drive because of delivering wool to the women who were knitting for the war effort and it just so happened that I had a knitter up there in Northend, so it was even the right route. And of course, we had a wonderful policeman in those days, who used to shut his eyes everytime he saw ABL 155 (my car) coming up the road. He used to say to me, "I saw ABL 155 parked so-and-so." You couldn't get away from PC Harris in those days.

'That was the fun of the thing. We actually had a lot of fun out of the war, you could always see the funny side of things, you had to.

'When the war ended, the future held very little for me. I knew what my life was going to be—just as it had been before the war, looking after my mother. Morris was the only love of my life and I would have gone on waiting for him, until the end of time.

'Living in a small village, the end of the war made little difference, not like those people living in towns. We had extra food, we could scrounge around for food to eke out the rations, we had our own eggs, we were never short of milk, things like that. The towns suffered much more.'

Elizabeth Denham, a 19-year-old trainee nurse was on night duty at the Royal Devon and Exeter hospital: 'When we reported for duty that evening, at 8.30 p.m., the night sister said she would allow the whole staff out in bits—the more senior ones went out together, but the junior ones she felt she had to look after, so she sent us out in groups with a young house surgeon, or with the porter to see the VE Day celebrations.

'I went in a group with the senior porter. The hospital was very near the centre of the city, near the cathedral. We went down the streets and I remember seeing dancing in the cathedral close, lots of people about and lights everywhere. We were out there for just over half-an-hour, enough to get a taste of what was going on, to have something to remember.

'The night went on quite quietly until the early hours, about 3 a.m, I had to go to casualty because there had been an accident and they were expecting a good many casualties. A Jeep, carrying too many American soldiers and girls had collided with an army lorry. Each of the Americans, except the driver, had had a girl on his lap. We had four girls admitted, one of whom was dead—she'd been in front and gone through the windscreen. Three of the soldiers were dead. It was such a dreadful thing to happen on a day of celebration. They obviously had been celebrating a bit too generously.

'It was my first encounter with anything quite so horrible. I'd entered nursing too late to experience war wounded, but I thought this was particularly horrid because of the day. The irony was very great.'

A 23-year-old ATS clerk from Norfolk stationed in London described VE Day in her diary: 'We all went home for VE Day. All through the East End the battered little streets are gay with bunting—recent V2 damage, barely tidied up, borders the bravest shows of all. My home town looks bright in the sunlight, the shabby paint-work masked by flags. Housewives are getting their rations in for the holiday, and in one queue I hear a woman say, "Wouldn't I like a lorryload of Jerry prisoners to go by now." Again, the gloating note is so unfamiliar that I have to record it, and it was the last of its kind I have heard throughout the celebrations.

'VE Day was very quiet at home. My father came home from Liverpool, and we stayed in listening to the radio, and had a family party at teatime. In the centre of the table was a dish of canned pineapple which Mother had saved through all the long years for this day. We went to the village church for a short service; it was full, and everyone sang "Onward Christian Soldiers" with might and main. Back home to hear the King's speech and the news. The children have built a bonfire, and, unable to wait for darkness, have a lovely blaze at dusk, under the watchful eye of an NFS man. At intervals during the day, the ships and tugs in the river set up a lively chorus on their hooters and sirens — the traditional "Cock-a doodle-oo" and the "Victory-V". This usually signifies a BLA leave ship coming alongside.

'Feeling rather flat, I was ready for bed by midnight; none of my friends is left locally, and others live too far away. I watched the signs of other festivities from an upper window; at midnight, when the Cease Fire came officially into force, searchlights went mad all over the sky, rockets and flares went up, the ships started off again, and a group of youngsters danced and sang in the road. Feeling rather out of it all, and wishing I were in London, I went to bed.'[7]

Hostel worker Muriel Green from Somerset wrote in her diary: ' ... After dinner Jenny [sister] and K [her boy friend] went for a walk to the favourite country inn two miles away. E [Muriel's best friend] and I arranged to follow them. We talked about the future most of the way there. We found Jenny and K already drinking. We each had a pommia, a refined bottled cider and the strongest drink I know. After one we were giggling and after two we had made ourselves weak, partly I suppose we imagined we were tight but we didn't have to imagine very hard. E never stopped talking and each time I spoke I thought what a silly thing to have said as I found myself speaking without thinking! We were sitting in the sun in the back garden on a long grassy bank and when E said she wanted to hear the King's speech I came down the bank on all fours. We stood in the bar to hear it and afterwards I couldn't have told anyone a word he said, as I felt in too much of a dream. The inn was crowded but shortly after 9 p.m. when we left there appeared to be no one drunk. We walked home by way of the woods, still very talkative but quite sober by the time we got back to the hostel for snacks and to see the bonfire lit at 10 p.m.

'It was a roaring blaze and seemed to have a significance in saying "Goodbye" to many wartime restrictions. Dozens of village children appeared on the scene with fireworks and crackers (squibs). We stood watching it for a long time and about quarter to 11 went into the dance hall. Here I have never seen such signs of unrestricted merry-making. People who in the usual way never unbend were simply romping like healthy children in circles, with joined hands. They were all young people with a larger proportion of women than men and they were simply letting themselves go in a way most joyful and unselfconscious to behold. Some had the necessary amount of alcohol to make them like this but most of them were drunk with the spirit of victory. Everyone in the room, which was packed, had a smile on their face. The romping continued till the end of the radio music and with exhaustion the circles were broken up. Dance records were put on and dancing began but "Jitterbugging" and "Conga" type of dancing was the rage, most of the crowd being at a pitch too high to concentrate on serious ballroom dancing. This went on until 12 o'clock when the ballroom was cleared. The next move was out to the bonfire. Until 3 a.m. dancing round in a circle of joined hands, one of the crowd, went on tirelessly. I went to bed after looking for a while at the others. I was very tired and had no male escort in the fun. All manner of songs were being sung, the old ones being popular.

'Years of monotonous clocking-in to war factories had brought this feeling of supreme elation to the young workers, many of whom have turned yellow with their work. They have given vent to their suppressed feelings tonight as never before. They would not go to bed while the last ounce of energy could be summoned to carry on. The night nurse told me afterwards that at four she crossed the site in her duties and there were about ten couples round the dying embers of the fire.

'Several people today have said that as they had relations in the Far East they could not celebrate properly. That has been in everyone's heart that more fighting, more dying and more atrocities are still to come. Also that all the flag waving and dancing will not bring alive the dead to their homes. Men that have lost their sight and limbs cannot be the same. Life will always be sadder for those of us who think. If we knew this had been a war to end war we would feel jubilant but when it may happen again without extreme care, it makes life seem a dilemma ... '[8]

Joan Kendrey, a 21-year-old WAAF meteorological assistant at Bomber Command, Rufforth, near York, gave little away in her diary: 'Morning with Nina [another WAAF] 0800 to 1500. Five course lunch. Terrific rain. Duty NCO but locked the picket post because of party in No 3 hangar. Met Officer and his wife were there. Bonfire, followed by a party in Flying Control. Squadron Leader went and the Group Captain till 4 a.m. No sleep at all, but on duty next morning at 0800.

'My main memory from this party in No 3 Hangar was that they had hung up on a flagpole some WAAF "twilights". It was a great standing joke with the men, they always referred to our knickers as "blackouts". They weren't black, they were air force blue rayon directoire knickers. But the "twilights" were for winter, interlock drawers in a very pale grey and always referred to as "twilights". Anyway, they had these strung up on a flagpole. It was a wonderful party, lots of alcohol, not that I am a drinker, but it says next day in my diary "All flying scrubbed." I should have thought nobody could have found their way to the planes, never mind fly one.'

Diary of a young woman civil servant from New Barnet: 'I went to church in the evening—at that time (8 p.m.) there was quite a crowd (for New Barnet) collecting in the centre of the town, where a number of men wearing coloured paper caps were dancing in a ring. I heard they were going to have a bonfire later. The Salvation Army marching through with band playing looked rather out of place.

'In the next road to ours, the boys had collected all sorts of junk ready for a bonfire and were busy making a guy. Later in the evening, when we were going to bed, there were dozens of bonfires going—red glows in a circle all around— sometimes one flaring up, sometimes another. Also what pleased me still more —there were bright lights all over the place from uncurtained windows. Lots of people about in the streets and the noise of singing, "music", shouting and dancing from various directions. To the south there was a steady whitish glow, I thought it was some special bonfire though it seemed a strange colour for one. For a long time I did not realize that this was the "lights of London" visible again after all these years. I suppose it was partly from the floodlighting.

'A little street (almost a slum) which runs end-wise on to the end of our garden was beautifully decorated (as it is for every public event) with streamers and flags across the street. And they evidently had a street party all night. (I am finishing these notes in the morning.) The party was still going strong when I went to sleep long after 12. There was a piano being played in the street—joined later by other instruments—communal singing, shouting and laughing. Occasionally a short speech, apparently, followed by further singing and cheers.

'Fireworks were going off all over the place (I don't know where the people got them from) and there were many loud "bangs" which sounded to me too loud for ordinary fireworks. It made me wish I were up and out among the crowd—but Mother and Father would certainly have objected very strongly to any suggestion of going.'9

Mary Grice, a 16-year-old Oxford schoolgirl: 'We got the day off school because it was, of course, a national holiday. It was in many ways a traumatic time as my grandmother was dying of cancer and I was studying for the equivalent of O levels, so my recollection of what happened during the day is a bit blurred but that night time and the lights, that was memorable.

'My parents took my sister and I into the town that night. There was a huge bonfire in St Giles by the Martyr's Memorial and we joined in the dancing round it. Then we went on to a large bonfire in the High, between Queen's and University (colleges) and they were bringing furniture out of the university to burn. Goodness knows what they burnt, in hindsight I'm thinking about antiques, I think they even brought out a piano. The streets were totally blocked, we walked down into the town and progressed from one bonfire to the other.

'It was an extremely good-natured crowd, people were hugging each other and dancing with each other and the police were not trying to intervene at all. They floodlit Magdalen Tower, it was simply fantastic. After six years of blackout, the only lights one had seen at night were the stars. You can't imagine what the lights were like. I mean the mere fact that you could show lights at all was miraculous. I remember you even had to put out your garden bonfire before it got dark.

'Wartime had really taken over the whole of our lives. To start with, we had to cart our gas masks around with us all the time, but I don't think we were particularly frightened. There were all these drills. We had to go out into the playground where they had built these brick shelters with a concrete roof. Inside there was a bench along each wall and one in the middle and we had all sorts of drills to go and sit in these beastly things. There used to be a joke about all the things that were said "behind the air-raid shelter". Priscilla Tolkien, who was Tolkien's daughter, was not allowed to go to biology classes so we used to get her behind the air-raid shelter and tell her what had gone on in biology classes. The Tolkiens were very staunch Catholics and didn't think she should know the facts of life.

'We took the war very seriously, even as young children. The whole of one's life revolved around it. The blackout was terrible, you couldn't even have a crack in the curtain. My father was an air raid warden, so he was partly responsible for going round making sure nobody had a crack in the curtain. It was absolutely dreadful, you cannot imagine.

'We had maps (of Europe) on the walls at home, marked with little flags which progressed back and forth. My father was an Oxford don and I went on to graduate from Oxford, so there was a great deal of discussion about the war in the family. We listened to all the news bulletins and went to the cinema at least once a week to see the newsreel and we had newspapers every day. We were very much concerned with it.

'We felt we had to join in the war effort in some way, absolutely. They used to bring the head injuries hospital to St Hugh's College in Oxford, to the most prominent brain surgeon, and that was just round the corner, so on a Sunday night we would go and do the washing up there. That was absolutely horrific, for a teenager, to hear men screaming. It was dreadful.'

Betty Hockey ran a concert party of 16 amateur artists who performed for the troops in the Bournemouth area five nights a week: 'When peace was declared, we were under canvas at Arne, near Wareham, playing to a small army unit. During VE Day itself, we spent the day on our boat, a thirty-foot motor launch. Near the camp was a place called Redcliff Farm, and there was a cutting that Billy Cotton had had made to keep his boat, *Wakey-Wakey*.

'When Billy went out on his boat we used to go in there and moor up. We were actually in there, moored up, nearly all day relaxing before the show. I remember that because my daughter, who was only about six, fell overboard into the mud.

'That night, I think everybody went almost mad. We did the show, our Number One show, in which the first half was just one artist after the other and the second half was in revue form, which consisted of a French bar scene.

'I was the naughty one doing the can-can, which was the most popular with the lads. Then I did the Seven Veils and the veils were thrown out to the lads and I didn't get them back. Being on clothing coupons, I had to wait until granny opened up her attic before I was able to do that dance again.

'Then I did the feather dance until I lost all the feathers and you couldn't replace those. It was a wildly appreciative audience.

'After the show, I think all the boys congregated with us at Redcliff Farm, where the farmer had opened up his barn, quickly got a band and put it in there and we had music and beer and what not. Everybody went completely crazy. There must have been two to three hundred people there altogether.

'Hard to describe a thing like that, but perhaps what I felt most was the great sense of relief that things were now finishing at last. I thought I would probably have to stop doing the concert party, but then I thought, why should we? The boys are still there and they still want us.'

A WAAF sergeant from Swinderby, in Lincolnshire, left a nostalgic account of a VE night party on an RAF station: 'We promised to help collect wood for a bonfire in the afternoon, but it suddenly clouded over and rained, so we decided to rest ready for the Big Dance at night. We all got in dressing-gowns and cold creamed our faces and curled our hair or pressed our uniforms. In our hut, Gwen wrote a description of everything to her sailor-husband, Audrey and I top and tailed it in my bed and went to sleep and Wendy and Edna turned the radio on and listened to the accounts of the crowds in London, Edinburgh etc, and Churchill's speech.

'I felt a bit sentimental and put out James's photograph (her brother-in-law, who was killed at Gibraltar) and thought of his poor mother and hoped she wasn't feeling too awful and I also thought of Toby and Paul, my two friends overseas and wondered what they felt like. We got up at teatime and had baths. I got in a temper because I had lent the others my iron and pressed Audrey's shirt for her and when I wanted a bath, the water was cold, Edna having had the last hot one. However, after frightening them very much by being fierce, which I seldom am, I got over it and we went to the Mess and bought each other four whiskies in rapid succession.

'I don't know whether it was the emotional upset, but I seemed to become very cheerful very rapidly and was in the mood to kiss everyone and sing loudly. We went to the dance for a while, which was held in No 1 hangar, all decorated with flags and bunting. The effect of the whisky wore off rather quickly and a suggestion was made that we go over to the Mess for further supplies, so we all crowded into the Flying Control car and drove over. Unfortunately two Squadron Commanders leapt on the running board and one of them insisted on taking the wheel leaning in through the window. He drove us madly all over the grass hockey pitch in front of the Mess and presently the Group Captain was to be seen emerging with a stern air. We tried to flee but too late. However, he was not very cross and only said that the car must be immobilized. So we had to walk back.

'We then went over to see the bonfire which was roaring sky high—it was a lovely, starry night and the sparks flew up into the sky—red and green rockets went off, and we could see the flicker of ack-ack guns going off all round the horizon, firing Victory salvos. We all danced round and sang "Auld Lang Syne" and things. A large party were singing "The Red Flag" and an airman had a red flag on a stick with which he led a procession. The Sgts Mess also had a large notice with "Joe for King" written on it.

'After the bonfire, we went to the Dance and danced until we were tired out. About 1 o'clock about 14 of us came back to the Ops room and made tea. I washed up madly and poured out wildly as more and more people drifted in and out. Also, I regret to say, I kissed a lot of people in a vague sort of way but only in public! We cycled up to the Waafery about 3.30. It was still a lovely night and a nightingale was singing in the May trees in Waafery Lane. We tumbled into bed, tired absolutely out.'[10]

Sir Henry Tizard, president of Magdalen College, Oxford, and former scientific adviser to the Ministry of Aircraft Production, wrote in his diary: 'Shops and factories were closed, and the streets filled with cheerful crowds. Plenty of flags, and bell-ringing. Little disorder, no "mafficking". We had a special dinner in Hall on 8th—free port for all, but no speeches. Afterwards we had a bonfire in the Meadows. Well, it certainly is a great day: a great historic day. It is hard to realize now, but we shall know better later on. I feel rather like a patient coming round after a severe but successful operation. Deep down there is a feeling that all is well, and that a great oppression has been lifted, but other feelings are not so pleasant, and the nurse who pats one on the arms and shouts that all is over is excessively exasperating. All is not over by any means. There is a secondary and still serious operation to follow, after which will come a long period of convalescence and slow recovery for the nations of the world and everyone knows how fretful patients are in convalescence. We shall want all our stock of courage, forbearance, and hope for many years. Memories crowd in on me; memories of acute anxieties and tragedies—memories too of absent friends—and of the dismal prophecies of utter destruction of the cities of England which proved in the event so greatly exaggerated. I wonder if the part that scientists have played will ever be faithfully and fairly recorded. Probably not.'[11]

A social worker from Chiswick recorded in her diary: 'In arriving home [from a visit to take part in the celebrations in the West End] we have tea in Mrs H's garden, and then have a wash and change and go to the Thanksgiving Service in the local church, which is not so well attended as I expected. The church service is normally very "high", but there is little of that sort of thing tonight. The vicar, who was leader of the local fire guard, shakes hands with us all as we came out, and seems pleased to see us all, though we are not regular church-goers. We then go home and listen to the King's broadcast. Some of the others criticize me for knitting whilst this is going on, and also for not standing up when "God Save the King" is played, but I do not take much notice of them.

'Shortly after this is finished, we go out again in search of a drink, but again there is nothing to be had but beer and ginger wine, so I decide to have a shandy. We then wander round, looking at the local bonfires, fireworks, etc. A few small groups are dancing in the streets, doing "Knees Up Mother Brown", etc, and one or two seems to have found enough drink to be slightly "merry". In Ravenscourt Park there is a band playing, and organized dancing, but not very many are taking part in it. Amongst those who are dancing we notice some of the nurses from Queen Charlotte's Hospital, in uniform. There are bonfires being lit in many of the streets, including one in the main road not very far from here. It is lit just near a tree and does not look very safe: After the others have gone to bed, I sit up for some time in my own room, listening to the dance music on the wireless.'[12]

LAC Brian Poole wrote to his penfriend in Miami from Rivenhall in Essex:

'Dear Trudie,

'It's all over now and we are so back to normal. I sometimes forget that the war with Germany has come to an end. I'm a little on tenterhooks, too, because if I am to go to South East Asia Command I'd sooner go now instead of beating around here. Now the future doesn't seem so terrifying we can see a way, a clear way to complete victory.

'I know you will tell me how VE Day was celebrated in Miami. So I'll tell you what I did. I had made up my mind to go to church previously but had decided to celebrate with a certain amount of restraint as the war wasn't really over. I did the first, being thankful for the preservation of my life so far. But as I went out with the boys, the drink began to flow in what could be called a torrent. You couldn't help but notice that all the cares of nearly six years of war, the fear of imminent death, were all being cast aside and a new spirit was in the air. By the time that we were all very merry we ran into some friends. A woman whom we met in a canteen that we frequent and her husband invited us to their home. Then the party grew hot and furious, we drank, danced and sang and drank still more and then lit a big bonfire in the street, danced round it until we were dizzy. After they took us to some of their friends where the same process continued. When you realize, Trudie, that I don't drink a lot and I never touch spirits, but I had beer, whisky, gin, sherry, cocktails and champagne that night so by midnight, I was well under the "weather". By 1.30 a.m. I went out flat on my face, consequently causing them to put me to bed. The next I knew was being awakened at 9.0 a.m. by Mrs Loveday with tea and many aspirins. I couldn't face breakfast though my head was like lead. Later I was informed that I had been making violent love to one of the chap's wives (a woman aged 34 with two children). I had to blush and everyone else laughed their heads off. I am not ashamed of all the drink I had because it was a special occasion, wasn't it, Trudie. Say yes, please!'[13]

Elspeth March, the actress recalled: 'I was in a play called *Duet for Two Hands*. Mary Mills wrote it and John Mills and I and Mary Morrison and Edward Brook-Jones were the stars of it. We had quite a long tour and my recollection is that on VE Day, we were in Blackpool.

'Anthony Pelissier, Fay Compton's son, who was the director, threw his hat into the sea as a gesture of triumph when we were all walking along the beach, but I don't really remember huge celebrations going on.

'I never really felt frightened in the war. There was such wonderful camaraderie; our daily was bombed out three times and she'd still turn up and say "That old bugger Hitler has done it again!" I remember towards the end, I heard one of these doodle bugs cutting out and my then husband threw me down on the pavement in Chelsea and lay on top of me and I was furious because he spoilt my one and only pair of nylons, which were like gold dust.'

LAC Frank Last, aged 24, an airframe mechanic posted to Stornaway remembered: 'How most of us summed up Stornaway at that time was "the three Ks"—kippers, chaos and queues, because you always had to queue for your meals in the main mess.

'We always kept tabs on what was going on with the war. There was the local cinema, where they put on newsreels, and every billet had its radio. We sensed that the Allies were gaining ground all the time and that some sort of result couldn't be far away. But when you are young, you've got other things to do, you've got the whole island to explore, on a bicycle, you've got girl-friends to meet and take out and I had a wedding coming up. Every letter matters and that is what you looked forward to, first of all, not when the war was going to end.

'But I thought it was going to happen, and I suppose, in a way, maybe I was a little saddened by it. Because it was a jolly good job I had. Here you were, travelling around, albeit in the British Isles, meeting lots and lots of people from different callings. Life would be very different once the war ended, though at the same time, there was something to look forward to, because June and I were going to get married.

'We heard that the war in Europe was over on the tannoy, the public address system. We were in our billet, a Nissen hut—you'd hear a sheep or a bullock rub up against them in the night—when we were told that the Germans had surrendered, up near Kiel, the Lüneburger Heide, that seemed to stick. They said, more or less, the war with Germany was at an end and that tomorrow and the next day, the CO had given permission for a 48 hour stand-down, only essential personnel to remain … blah, blah, blah … and wrap things up. So you knew then that there wasn't going to be any more war flying, the kites weren't going to have to go off.

'We thought about the war going on with the Japanese and we knew that until that ended service life would go on. The end of the war in Europe, however, to me personally, meant relief, I suppose, because one did worry for one's parents. My parents still lived in Essex and so did June's and all the time there was the risk of anybody coming over and bombing, Heinkel, Dornier or whatever. Till that threat had been eliminated and the threat of the Vs, the reprisal weapons, had been removed, you couldn't help worry.

'In the billet itself, it was great. There was swearing and shouting and whatever and the cooks, they did us proud. The air force thinks a great deal about its food, its stomach, and the cooks on this place could work wonders! They could bring in the bacon and the where with-all to cook it. There were stoves in the billet and if your bed was near them you were warm as toast, if it wasn't, you froze.

'On that day, they did us a slap-up meal, we had a good old fry up, and then we thought, what do we do tonight? We'll go into Stornaway, a little gaggle of us. It was cycling distance away, so we went down there. The main place to go to for a meal in Stornaway was known as Kipper Annie's because she sold kippers. You could have kippers and kippers, or kippers, kippers and kippers!

'So, we went down to Kipper Annie's and there, where it had previously been very dull, you couldn't have lights on as lighting was restricted, we saw that the lights were on and they formed a "V", which was great, and the locals had brought out their bagpipes. You didn't get much of this usually, they were very stolid citizens there, but they were really in a party mood. They were so relieved, I suppose, because they had had us lot on their island and they couldn't get on with their sheep rearing and their turf digging, not easily, anyway.

'Well, anyway, we went down there. I went down with my "oppo". There was dancing in the street, literally everybody was out. The air force had its caps off and tucked into their belts. You weren't allowed to wear civilian clothes off duty, as it was still war time. I couldn't do these eightsome reels but it just didn't matter after you had a beer or two. At that time I was practically teetotal, in fact I still am, so this made me feel a bit heady. Dammit, I thought, this is the end of the war, let's cut loose.

'Now these girls, three of whom I'd seen before, they said, well, you come and join us. A wonderful evening, all round. Then, early hours of the morning, time to go home, we went to their place, which was a pub and it was closed up. "She's locked us out!" So, what to do? They didn't know. Can't you climb in? No, no, no. So we went to a bus shelter and stayed there until the early hours, which was damp and cold and all the euphoria drained away. My oppo had gone somewhere else. I am sure there were five girls, well, you had a snog. What else was there to do? The poor girls had to keep warm! And that lasted out until the early hours when back we went to camp.

'A couple of days later I got selected to play football in the Victory Europe Cup and that meant us going to the mainland as they couldn't come and play on our grotty pitch on Stornaway. On the way to Thornaby-on-Tees in a Warwick I saw half-a-dozen U-boats coming up the west side of Scotland, going to Northern Ireland to surrender, and we flew over the top. The crew said they'd go low-level so we could see them and that's what they did. It really impressed me, this sight.'

Norris McWhirter and his identical twin, Ross, were both sub-lieutenants in the RNVR — their naval paths crossed only once in the war when Norris's ship collided with Ross's in the harbour at Valetta, Malta. Norris described VE night in Liverpool:

'At 0001 hours, on 9 May I was standing alone by the binnacle of the nearly deserted frigate HMS *Labuan* in Gladstone Dock, Liverpool. The captain, Lt Cdr Vivien Bidwell DSC RNR had given early shore leave to two watches and two parts of a watch thus leaving only a skeleton care and maintenance crew aboard under a single Officer. Being at 19 both the most junior and a virtual teetotaller, his choice easily fell upon me.

'From the bridge I watched a blizzard of rockets, coloured star shells and Verey Lights loosed off amid a cacophony of hooters, sirens and whistles. After an hour or so the first libertymen began to wend their way back to their bunks and hammocks along the dockside towards the gang plank. Some lurched to within inches of the vertical granite dockside walls and near certain death if they had toppled on to the oil-saturated catamarans 20 feet below.

'In a curiously reflective way I felt, in the absence of my twin Ross on the other side of the country with a minesweeping flotilla in Harwich, that I was quite detached from the revelry because I had no one there with whom to savour the moment.'

A young mother from Slough wrote in her diary at midnight: 'Exhausted now, but wish very much I were in London at one of the Victory night dances with some of my friends, but there has been no time to make any arrangements … When the baby had been put to bed we decided we would go forth on our bicycles and see the local sights. Meg said she felt exceedingly flat and not at all as though it were VE Day. She had made a pennant for the car in which they pro-pose to visit her parents tomorrow and a rosette for herself out of odd pieces of red, white and blue material. She had been to Slough in the morning—the food shops were open—and she said that everyone seemed to be wearing something. The town was crowded and women were loading themselves with provisions as though stocking up for a week at least.

'It was a lovely evening. There had been one or two showers during the day and I had brought my mackintosh but I did not need it. I had without thought for patriotic colour schemes put on a bright royal blue jumper with grey slacks and a short white jacket. A scrap of Meg's red felt made into a bow and pinned to the lapel of the jacket provided the finishing touch and we sallied forth.

'People were strolling in the streets in their best clothes and red, white and blue emblems, rather as though it were a Sunday. All sorts of different red, white and blue touches—rosettes, bows—flowers in the hair—flags and bunting on many houses (not all). We went to a nearby village green where an enormous pile was ready for lighting at dusk. People were gathering on the green—a party of RAFs and WAAFs got together in a circle on the grass and began singing, drawing the crowd around them. Sunset was unusually lovely, filling the sky with a storm sweep of lemon and orange, with little grey fluffy clouds streaking across it. We had a drink—it was early and people were standing about outside the pub chatting happily and quietly, although we had passed other pubs where singing had already begun.

'As it grew darker the lights came on—fairy lights that one hadn't seen for years decorating private doorways, arranged in V formations at windows surrounded by bunting. In the High Street some buildings with all their pre-war lights glowing, some shop windows lit and the Town Hall greatly beflagged, floodlit in a deep red rose with the clock tower at the top in lime green—it was like a stage set and very effective. Bonfires were flickering now, here, there, everywhere in waste spaces and allotments. We had seen one or two effigies of Hitler awaiting destruction (will this day become another Guy Fawkes day?) The singing in the pubs had increased. It was like a dream out of the dead past. Lights again. Something one had forgotten for a little while but now back, were familiar and would soon be accepted as they were of old.'[14]

John Dossett-Davies, aged 22, an aircraft inspector at De Havillands in Oxford wrote: 'My mother and I had hung the flags out from our bedroom windows and the town was made gay by coloured bunting, streamers and even towels of the right colour. There were happy crowds in the warm sunshine and a great feeling of relief, especially after hearing Churchill's broadcast at 3 p.m., although my friends and I felt a shiver of anticipation when we heard him say "We may allow ourselves a brief period of rejoicing, but let us not forget for a moment the toil and efforts that lie ahead, Japan with all her treachery and greed, remains unsubdued ... "

'There had been a torchlight procession from Wood Green, a bonfire on the Leys at which the crowd joined hands and danced around and long-hoarded fireworks let off. Some people wore paper hats and a few dogs wore a coloured ribbon. There were rosettes and streamers all saved up. The finale on that warm spring evening was a grand open air dance in the Market Square to a services dance orchestra. Even before this started there were impromptu dances to a man playing an accordion and people kissed each other quite freely.

'My friends and I had fortified ourselves by some illicit drinking of cider and port in our homes and later in the Royal Oak, where the obliging landlady had accommodated us.

'The dance had been going some time when we arrived. There were Land Army girls dancing with Land Army girls, servicemen in black and maroon berets, Poles and free French, airmen, sailors, a plethora of Americans dancing with everyone in skirts—a Gordon Highlander was lucky to escape! There were girls in trousers and girls in thin light summer dresses, some wore flowers in their hair or had red, white and blue ribbons in it or round their waists. The dancing was lively, the veleta, waltzes, the palais glide, boomps-a daisy and jitterbugging by the Americans and from time to time a very long conga wound its way round the square.

'This was the milling scene my friends and I surveyed, which we looked down upon from the canteen windows of the Corn Exchange. Two searchlights were in the Square to give unaccustomed and somehow improper floodlighting, and lights for the first time in six years were put on in some of the buildings around the Square to the terror and wonder of two small girls. There was no organization and it was a spontaneous finale. The King's speech relayed to the crowd at 9 p.m. was the only formal moment and once he'd finished the dancing resumed on through the warm night.

'It was from the canteen window that I first saw the girl in the white silk dress. It was the dress that first caught my eye—it was full length and shimmered and flowed like water in the unaccustomed lighting. It had bands of sequins at the waist, hem and wrists. I don't think I had seen a girl dancing in a long dress before—certainly not under lights in the open air. I was enthralled and knew this was a memory I'd always recall however long or short I lived.

'For me she epitomized the future: peacetime, adult life, goodies in store. A plenitude of love and sex—just around the corner. Eventually, boldly, my reticence and shyness driven back or certainly held at bay by the romantic nature of the occasion (or the effect of the port and cider) I found myself dancing with her. She guided me round the square. She had a particular sinuous way of dancing, and had long golden hair worn turned under in a roll at the ends—a wartime fashion. She was an American nurse from a nearby Air Force base, her name was Linda and she came from St Louis. We had two dances and a brief snatched conversation and I got a smile and a wink later in the evening and that was all.'[15]

Rabbi Lionel Blue was evacuated during the war, but by the time of VE Day he was back in London, aged 14: 'I burst into tears on VE Day. It was the end of childhood. It hadn't been a bad war for a child, so long as you never looked further ahead than half a day. Every morning we came out of a communal shelter in the East End and returned to our house on Windward Street to see if it was still standing.

'One morning in 1941 it wasn't, so we moved in with relatives and I was evacuated yet again. As an evacuee I spent nearly every afternoon in the cinema, staying there from 2 p.m. till the National Anthem at the end of the last house. I saw *One Night in Rio* with Don Ameche and Carmen Miranda 20 times.

'But with VE Day the bottom dropped out of my world. I had to plan and think about the future. All this hit me at our street party in Jubilee Street E1. The talk was of Belsen and Auschwitz, which had just been liberated.

'We'd all brought out the best we had in the larder. I was asked to sing a song. All I could think of was an awful temperance song taught to me by some teetotal Rechabites I'd stayed with as an evacuee.

'My grandfather was raising a large glass of whisky to his lips, given him by an American serviceman, when I sang the chorus of the song in my piping treble "My drink is water, bright from the crystal stream". He cuffed me soundly for that.'[16]

Pat Howard, a young switchboard operator at ARP headquarters in Ealing wrote: 'I was just 17 when the war ended. I had a very strict father who wouldn't let me go into the armed forces so I was terribly envious of all those people who were a little bit older than I was, who managed to get into really doing something. The political implications of the war and the war itself went over my head a bit and I am ashamed to say that what I was interested in, was the glamour.

'I was intensely patriotic and wanted to help, but I was just that much too young. My enthusiasm was rather greater than my usefulness at that point and so that is why my father sort of compromised. He was a dentist but he was also an ARP warden and he heard that there was a switchboard job at the ARP headquarters in the Uxbridge Road and that was the nearest I got to helping the war effort.

'I was rather sheltered, my father wouldn't let me go out with boys, but I met a chap in the air-raid shelters that were deep under Walpole Park, very deep, row upon row of bunks. I realize now that the young man was probably a homosexual, but my father didn't have any qualms about my going out with him.

'On VE night, I remember going out with him to the gates of Walpole Park and there were a lot of folk dancing round fires, big bonfires that had been built and there were people from every walk of life, every kind of person. It was evening and we were dancing round and round.

'It was a wonderful crowd, there were armed forces there, every one you could think of, children. Good natured? Good Lord, yes! Everyone was tipsy on nothing, exhilarated.

'I have no doubt we had a drop of cider and things and what happened to me, was, well I think I was caught up with the excitement. Not drunk exactly, but caught up, as one would be at 17. There was this Polish officer and we linked hands and everyone danced round the fire.

'I remember him pulling me and saying "Come on! Let's run!" At 17, I suppose, with all the excitement, it was fun just to run and we ran through Walpole Park and it was there that I very nearly got raped by this Polish officer. I expect that he was caught up with it as well. He was very dashing and I thought he was wonderful until he lay on top of me and I got a bit scared.

'If it hadn't been for my lovely homosexual friend calling through the park, "Where are you, Pat? Your Daddy will be so cross!" I don't know what would have happened. Luckily he did deter the Polish soldier and got me back safely. The Polish soldier was being pretty forceful, but he didn't get my knickers off!

'I sobered up a bit after that, not that I was truly drunk, but the atmosphere was intoxicating.'

Central London was, of course, the focus of the nation's celebrations that evening and no one was making his way there with more expectation of adventure than 15-year-old Derek Lambert and a group of his chums from public school in Surrey.

'We went to the West End for VE-Day with victory one pound notes in our wallets, a grim determination to celebrate and no thought of thanksgiving. We hugged ourselves with anticipation as the train trundled through the Claphams and Balhams of London; past boarded windows, clawed roofs, severed spires, playgrounds of rubble, walls still clinging with stairs and chimney flues, craters filled with water, propped up bridges, empty charred houses.

'The sandbagged West End was already throwing off its inhibitions. Cars backfired with hoarded petrol, beer frothed and slopped in victory toasts, soldiers tore off their ties and flung high their caps while the MPs looked the other way. Gaggles of girls, arms linked, sang "Roll Out the Barrel" and "We're going to get lit up when the lights go on in London".

'We went to a restaurant off Tottenham Court Road where Peter's father dined. We ate Wiener Schnitzel, drank champagne which we pretended to enjoy, and stood on a table singing our school song, feeling solemn.

'"Let's get some women, man," said one of us and out we went into the dusk. The crowds were thickening, dancing, singing, swearing. Girls kissed soldiers and sailors and GIs. One kiss between a girl with a blonde streak bleached in her hair and a hatless GI lasted eight minutes (we counted) before they surfaced, breathless and carmine-chinned, and wandered thoughtfully up a side street. In the pubs girls jived and plump women did the knees-up showing long drawers from which we averted our eyes. Youths struggled up lamp-posts and split their trousers sliding down, trumpets blew, rattles rattled, tempers flared, heads broke, blood flowed, women cried, bottles smashed, fireworks exploded.

'In Trafalgar Square some girls grabbed us to dance the hokey-cokey; sheepishly we put our left legs in and our left legs out, we did the hokey-cokey and we turned all about. The girls were plump and flushed, liquid stockings streaked with spilt beer, hair escaping from cardboard sailors' caps. "You put your whole self in, your whole self out …" We laughed inanely, banged rumps, winked hugely.

'Into the crowd fell a thunderflash hissing fire. The girls screamed and threw themselves into male arms. I found myself with an armful of wriggling flesh, freckled and squealing. She smelled of strawberries and beer as she put her face up to be kissed. The firework exploded, there was a wetness and a banging of teeth and the kiss was over.

'"You're a one you are," she said.

'"You're not so bad yourself," I said.

'"I bet you're one for the girls," she said.

'"What about a drink?" I said.

'"Whoopee," she said.

'We led the girls across the square, lost them near the fountains and swaggered into a pub. Inside a soldier thumped out the songs of war on a cigarette-burned piano. We swayed and sang and waved our half-pint pots at the port and lemons. "There were rats, rats ... " and "There'll always be an England ... "

'Relief and pride and patriotism swelled inside the blue-hazed saloon. We stood to attention, overcome with emotion and alcohol.

'Arms slipped round acquiescent waists, tears slipped into gin and gin turned into tears. A wounded soldier in Reckitt's blue wandered in and was given three pints of beer and two whiskies. He drank slowly and thoughtfully.

'"Watcher, mate, where d'yer cop yours?" shouted a soldier.

'The man in blue shook his head. "I forget," he said, and left.

'We followed him into the chiming night and moved with the crowd to Piccadilly. In a pavement arena two men fought, growling obscenities. Blood oozed from one's nose; their collars were torn and their jackets dusty.

'"You filthy bloody Irishman," said one. "To think I fought for the likes of you."

'"You pacifist bastard. You never fought for no one."

'Fists flayed and missed. A policeman proceeded along the pavement and they thankfully parted.

'Up the Haymarket we went, past war films and war plays. I remember a small lost girl, unaware of war or victory, sitting on the kerb, squeezing an orange and repeating with gathering anguish, "I want my mum." If she ever remembers VE night, there will be no recollection of festivity or inanity or glory, just a needle of pain recording first awareness of insecurity.

'There was no escape now: we moved with the throng and stumbled at our peril. We were propelled to Rainbow Corner, London haunt of the GI on furlough, near the Windmill Theatre which never closed or clothed. A band played and rival choruses bellowed their own songs.

'"There'll be blue birds over the white cliffs of Dover ... When the lights are on again all over the world ... Kiss me goodnight sergeant-major, tuck me in my little wooden bed ... Silver wings in the moonlight ... Roll out the barrel ... Why do you whisper green grass ... Now the first is number one and the fun has just begun ... "

'The songs merged into lachrymose, belly-laughing babble. Beer-tuned sailors sang the Navy-bluest of songs and a cluster of ATS and WAAFS replied with tender love lyrics.

'From windows and rooftops fell newspapers and apple cores and pages of telephone directories. Chains of conga dancers side-kicked their way down the road, squeezing each other and tickling. We tried to sing another chorus of our school song, "*Deo non fortuna* ... " but our voices broke with wind and adolescence and joined the twittering of the starlings above.

'Rockets festooned the sky with plumes of fading stars; green, red and silver, the spangles melted and vanished in skies that had recently erupted with gun-fire. Crackers exploded at our feet with the gunpowder smells of war and many winced before laughing.

'The crowd, welded into festive togetherness, heaved and ejected us into a side street. Couples clung to each other in doorways swearing lifelong devotion that would last at least tonight and drunks spied the rockets through beer bottle telescopes. Men argued the next war, women emerged from retirement to solicit, clubs beckoned, spivs sold black market nylons hidden between newspapers.

'With sly grins and self-conscious swaggers we tried to get ourselves solicited.

'"Go on, man, you first."

'"No, you—you're the oldest."

'"Oh, all right. But you've got to try as well."

'The woman had dark hair, grey near the roots. Lipstick doubled the width of her mouth and powder levelled her craters. She wore ankle straps and a fox fur and radiated desiccated sex, cupidity and Evening in Paris. Effervescing with beer and victory, I approached her.

'"Excuse me … "

'"Bugger off," she said without removing the cigarette from her mouth. "Bugger off or I'll tan your backside for you."

'The others were full of admiration. "What did she say? Did she say you could?"

'"We discussed terms," I said, "but I told her it was too much."

'"How much did she want?"

'"Twenty pounds," I said.

'"Gosh, man," they said.

'We stopped at a stall and drank sugarless tea before returning to Victoria. In Piccadilly they were still jiving and kissing and singing and drinking. We skirted the jubilation and walked through silent streets trying to resurrect our failing zest with jokes. But the spectre of tomorrow's unrehearsed Latin and calculus walked with us … '[17]

Mass Observation's incomparable reporters were, of course, out on the streets in the force that night, watching, listening and taking extraordinarily detailed notes. This was just one vignette recorded in Trafalgar Square: 'A very pretty girl about eighteen dressed in a red frock with white polka dots, a blue neck square, and shoeless and stockingless, stands on the edge of the fountain. She's been fooling around with three pompous-looking officers of the Norfolk Regiment. Lifting up her skirts she paddles into the water. Two of the officers roll up their trousers and follow suit. They climb to the very top of the fountain, carrying the girl. When they reach the top they get a cheer from the crowd, and the pretty girl kisses them. British movietone cameramen take photographs. After a while, they paddle back. Lifting up her skirts she calls: "Oh my, I've never shown so much leg in my life." Male cries of "Don't mind us." The captain (one who remained behind) lifts her shoulder high. She puts her arms around his neck and the crowd sing "For she's a jolly good fellow". And so perched on the captain's shoulder, the party leave. A middle-aged woman says: "I bet she'll catch it when her mother sees it in all the pictures."

'Fireworks are being released among the crowd. They go off with a bang and screams from the crowd. Lines of girls and Servicemen arm in arm fill the width of the roadway singing "Oh, you beautiful doll" and many other songs. A Jeep passes, direction of Haymarket. It's filled with girls and American soldiers. A girl is sitting on the bonnet waving a Union Jack and the Stars and Stripes. Two Yanks pass. The face of one is smothered with lipstick markings. As he passes an attractive girl he calls "Won't you join my collection" and pushes his face forward … '[18]

The lure of the West End was an extraordinarily powerful one. Margaret Goult, aged 22, had spent the final years of the war in an ATS searchlight regiment, the only one operated by women: 'On VE Day, we were in Hammersmith on a Victory Parade and as we got near to Hammersmith underground station, I can hear myself now saying to my friend Grace, "Have you got any money in your pocket?" and she said, "Yes" and I said "Well, what about hopping it?" We just about-turned smartly, walked off and got on the underground and went up to London.

'We just wanted to be where the action was. We knew that things would be happening in London we wanted to see and sure enough, they were. It was chaotic, I can still feel the atmosphere to this day. It was mind boggling, I don't think anybody who was there would ever forget that feeling, all those millions of people, milling about in the streets, cheering and shouting, climbing up lamp-posts.

'We were there all night. There was nowhere to sleep, all the undergrounds stopped because they couldn't cope with the sheer volume of people, so there was no way of getting back. I can't remember exactly where we slept, I think it was in an air-raid shelter. There really wasn't much to eat as everything was closed down.

'Next morning we had to go back and face the music. The sergeant said she was going to put us on a charge for being AWOL. She said she was going to report me to the officers and this that and the other, but discipline was breaking down at that time. We all knew it was over. We didn't get put on a charge, but I had to do a lot of extra duty on that damn searchlight, I can tell you. But it was worth it to have been out with crowds on VE night in London.'

Captain Michael Denison of the Intelligence Corps and his wife Dulcie Gray had taken the trouble to book a table at the Savoy Grill, which was offering a special Victory Dinner of soup, chicken and iced peaches for five shillings and one shilling cover charge. (Meals of more than three courses were still illegal.) 'Every time I was on leave we would go to the Savoy, whether we could afford it or not. In those days it was remarkably cheap, one got out with change from a fiver for two.

'I was stationed at Latimer in Bucks, interrogating German prisoners, who had suddenly become very, very co-operative. Dulcie was then quite a considerable film star—her picture was on all the buses.

'We booked a table at the Savoy as soon as we realised VE Day was imminent. I think we found ourselves at a table with some congenial spirits and had a wonderful night. There was a remarkable bandleader there, an American called Carol Gibbons, who played all through the Blitz and was a lovely man and a great friend.

'Afterwards we wandered up the Mall with the rest of London and cheered the King and Queen outside Buckingham Palace.'

The broadcaster David Jacobs was there, too, along with his friend the actor Jon Pertwee. 'I was actually on embarkation leave as I was due to go to Ceylon in a couple of days, so I was living at home in Streatham. I always remember my mother saying "What have I got to celebrate, you're going off to the other war." But I was as excited about going to Ceylon as I was about VE Day—I had never been out of England before. Jon and I, both in our sailor suits, took a tram up to the West End and just wandered around in the crowds. We saw Churchill but couldn't hear a word he said because of the cheering, then we went to Buckingham Palace and waited for the King and Queen to come out.'

Even Noël Coward strolled along to the Palace after drinks with the company at the Duchess Theatre, where *Blithe Spirit* was playing to packed houses. 'We all had cold food and drinks at Winnie's [Winifred Ashton's house in Covent Garden] … We listened to the King's broadcast, then to Eisenhower, Monty and Alexander. Then I walked down the Mall and stood outside Buckingham Palace, which was floodlit. The crowd was stupendous. The King and Queen came out on the balcony, looking enchanting. We all roared ourselves hoarse. After that I went to Chips Channon's "open house" party, which wasn't up to much. Walked home with Ivor [Novello]. I suppose this is the greatest day in our history.'[19]

The Royal Family made no less than eight balcony appearances during the day. Earlier in the evening, the two princesses, aged 14 and 19, were allowed to slip out, mingle with the crowds and join the fun, escorted by two young Guards officers. 'Poor darlings, they have never had any fun yet,' the King noted in his diary.

Many people milling around outside the Palace that evening recall a trumpet being played with considerably more expertise than the so-called instruments being beaten or blown by the other merry-makers. The trumpeter was a young Grenadier Guards officer by the name of Humphrey Lyttelton.

'When the end of the war with Germany came I was still at Caterham [the Guards' depot] and I travelled up from there to London for the celebrations on VE Day. I had a feeling it would turn out to be an uninhibited sort of occasion, so I took my trumpet with me. I was not mistaken. Having roamed the streets all day with a party of friends, I finally finished up outside Buckingham Palace. All the afternoon the crowds around the Victoria Memorial were packed tight like sardines, all facing the Palace in expectation of the King and Queen's appearance on the balcony. In the evening people wandered off to other parts of the West End and the Palace crowd was able to circulate more freely.

'Inspired by the informality of the occasion—and a picnic champagne supper in the Park—I took the trumpet out and started to play. A crowd gathered round and one or two couples started dancing. Soon other instruments began to materialise. A man appeared out of nowhere with a big drum strapped to his chest, a soldier turned up with a trombone, and then an extraordinary grunting noise heralded the arrival of a sailor carrying what looked like the horn of an enormous old-fashioned gramophone. He puffed away into the small end and produced a convincing, if monotonous, bass note.

'After a while we got the wanderlust and set off in procession round the Memorial, with a huge crowd amassing behind us, to the tune of "High Society". Then someone brought up a handcart and I was lifted bodily on to it, still blowing lustily. There was only room for one on the cart so the rest of the band had to footslog beside it. They pushed me along the Mall, by St James's Street, to Piccadilly Circus, on to Trafalgar Square and back to the Palace.

'On the route I caught sight of the startled faces of several senior Guards Officers, who were clearly uncertain what to make of the sudden appearance of one of their subordinates in full service-dress uniform playing a trumpet on a handcart. I think, if the occasion had been anything other than the end of a six years' war I should have been court-martialled. Back at the Palace there was more dancing and a further appearance of the Royal Family on the balcony. I dimly remember blasting a chorus of "For He's a Jolly Good Fellow" in the direction of His Majesty. After that, with lungs aching and lips red and raw from so much trumpeting, I went to bed.'[20]

At around 10.30 p.m., Churchill, who was clearly having the time of his life, made another appearance on the balcony of the Ministry of Health building in Whitehall and conducted the singing of 'Land of Hope and Glory'. His speech was vintage Churchill.

After referring to the victory celebrations, he boomed, '"We must begin the task of rebuilding our hearths and homes and do our utmost to make this country a land in which all have a chance, and in which all have a duty, and we must turn ourselves to fulfil our duty to our own countrymen, to our gallant allies, the United States, who were so foully and treacherously attacked by Japan. We will go hand in hand with them, and, even if it is a hard struggle, we shall not be the ones who will fail.

'"One deadly foe has been cast on the ground, and awaits our judgement and mercy, but there is another foe who occupies large portions of the British Empire, a foe stained with cruelty and greed—the Japanese." (Loud boos.)

'"We were the first in this ancient land to draw the sword against Germany." (Cheers.) "After a while we were left alone against the most tremendous military power that has been seen. We were all alone for a whole year. There we stood. Did anyone want to give in?" (A great shout of 'No!') "Were we downhearted?" ('NO!')

"The lights went out, and the bombs came down, but every man, woman and child in this country had no thought of quitting the struggle. London could take it. So we came back after long months, back from the jaws of death, out of the mouth of hell, while all the world wondered when shall the reputation and faith of this generation of English men and women fail?

"'I say that in the long years to come not only the people of this island, but from all over the world, wherever the bird of freedom chirps in human hearts, they will look back to what we have done, and they will say, 'Don't despair. Don't yield to violence and tyrany. March straight forward and die, if need be, unconquered.'" (Loud and sustained cheering.)'

Elizabeth Layton squeezed onto an adjoining balcony to watch her boss's performance: 'Flags and bunting had been put up, and floodlights were directed upon the balcony. A crowd which some estimated at 20,000 stood below, the roar of their cheering seemed almost to lift one off one's feet. It was just a sea of faces and waving arms. As Mr Churchill emerged, the noise increased almost to deafening point.

'I shall always remember Mr Churchill as he was at that moment—spick-and-span in a black coat and striped trousers, a flower in his buttonhole, his face smooth and pink, a man medium in height and somewhat round of figure, a man whose character contained all the elements of greatness and whose knowledge of human nature made him understand equally the reactions of his valet and of Heads of other States. That was Mr Chuchill's hour. Whatever was to come, nothing could take it from him. The entire nation came forward to show its gratitude and affection for the man whose courage had been an inspiration in its darkest hours … '[21]

Apart from the sheer size and spirit of the crowds in London, it was the unaccustomed lights—shop and theatre lights, street lights, floodlights—that those who were there most remembered. Tom Driberg spent much of the evening wandering around the West End. 'Of all the buildings floodlit when night fell, I thought the National Gallery—indeed, the whole pillared group about Trafalgar Square—the most majestic.

'Besides the official illuminations, many big cinemas had managed to light up their beflagged façades. A red light in the sky no longer, now, meant incendiary bombs or flares.

'In the orange glow that streamed down from the Tivoli to the pavement of the Strand, a buxom woman in an apron made of Union Jacks and a man of respectable middle-class and middle-aged appearance did an exaggeratedly Latin-American dance while a passing accordion played "South of the Border".

'The trees in Leicester Square were silvery-green in the festive light. The police, civil and military, took their smiling ease (though the Americans' white helmets seemed to have a certain souvenir appeal). There were many drunks, of course; but jolly, not tiresome, drunks. The Yanks, acclimatised to English undemonstrativeness, were stunned into being, for once, the quietest folk around.'[22]

This is how a woman working at the WVS headquarters described the evening in a letter to a friend: 'We all walked to Buckingham Palace. As we got in front of it the flood-lighting flicked on. It was wonderful ... magnificent and inspiring and it seemed we had never seen so beautiful a building. The crowd was everywhere and yet one could walk through it. We edged our way to a good view of the balcony, which was draped with crimson, with a yellow and gold fringe. The crowd was such as I have never seen—I was never so proud of England and our people. It was a crowd of separate individuals. There was never any mass feeling. Everybody spoke quietly or was silent—everybody looked just relieved and glad. We waited. Coloured rockets went up behind us. Then the King and the Queen and the two Princesses came onto the balcony. We yelled and yelled and yelled and waved and cheered. They waved back to us. It was wonderful ... Then we began to walk. We went to a huge bonfire in the Park. People joined hands and were circling round it. We walked by the lake—there were coloured lights in the trees and bushes reflected in the water. We came out of the Park by the Middlesex Guild Hall. It was floodlit in a warm yellowish light and looked medieval with flags from what looked like the battlements. We went to Big Ben. It was floodlit and looked magnificent. I heard myself say, "Dear Big Ben! Dear Big Ben!" The Houses were floodlit from the river and all the lights alight along the Terrace. What moved us all beyond anything else was the great Union Jack on the Lords. It, alone, was floodlit by lights going straight upwards. It was just a great, lovely Union Jack, flying grandly in the sky by itself ... We walked to the middle of Westminster Bridge and stood there. Searchlights were all rotating and making a kaleidoscope pattern all over the sky. County Hall was lit in two colours and their training ships in the river strung with coloured lights ... We walked back to Parliament Square and turned to face Big Ben. It was a few minutes to midnight ... At one minute past, all fighting was to cease. The crowd all faced Big Ben. It was absolutely silent. Big Ben struck. Just before the last stroke it had reached one minute past. A great cry went up and people clapped their hands. Something went off with a bang ... The tugs in the river gave the V sign. It was unforgettable.'[23]

At Broadcasting House, Stuart Hibberd, the duty announcer, admitted to a lump in his throat as he started to read the midnight news: 'As these words are being spoken, the official end of the war in Europe is taking place ... '[24]

XII

Tuesday 8 May

Just Another Day

For most of the British troops still in Germany, VE Day was just another work-ing day; they could only listen wistfully to the BBC's on-the-spot reports of the celebrations taking place at home and, no doubt, curse their bad luck for missing the party.

As Private John Frost with the 11th Armoured Division in Lübeck wrote in a plaintive letter to his mother, being among the victors hardly compared with being in Piccadilly Circus.

'Dear Mum, It's VE Day, fighting has ceased. It finds Stan [his brother] and I safe and well—we have much to be thankful for. Our celebration will come when we walk up the garden path …

'This afternoon we all listened to Churchill broadcast over the radio—it put the official touch to things that it was all over. It's now eight o'clock, at nine we shall be hearing a speech from the King.

'From the radio news we have all learnt of the wild celebrations going on in London and other cities. Wish I could see all the flags flying and hear the bells pealing—the rings sound nice over the wireless.

'This morning on first parade we had three special orders of the day read out to us. They were congratulatory messages from Army commanders on our achieve-ments in Germany. One from Gen Dempsey was addressed to this Div only and he congratulated the 11th Armoured on their recent capture of Luebeck and the advance to the Baltic Sea.

'I am writing to you, Mum, from a village situated in Northern Germany. It is permissible to tell you because all the newspapers have told the news of this Division's capture of Lübeck.

'The weather today has been glorious, I am getting quite tanned—this may be due to the fact that every time I drive my vehicle, I keep the windows open. The crossing of the great River Elbe was by pontoon bridge—it was very bumpy but

I managed to get across safely but I must admit to feeling hot under the collar. I have now driven over 1200 miles from Normandy to Northern Germany.

'The other day I had the pleasure of driving a jeep to Hamburg—people were actually waving to us—we must not reply.

'Along this road today have passed thousands of more German soldiers and airmen. They drive their own vehicles, they look battle-worn and completely tired. They prefer to give themselves up to us than to the Russians.

'Also on the roads making their own way away from the Russians are hundreds of German civilians. Those that have horses and carts have household belongings piled up on the carts, many are walking, women and children too. VE Day is very different in Germany.

'There is not much victory to be seen here in the Army—today we have been holding the usual parades and working as usual. We still carry our loaded rifles everywhere we go—you can't trust every German to surrender quietly.

'This is our third week without bread—it's biscuits and bully beef, not forgetting good old tinned sardines, pilchards and powdered potatoes. There is no beer for the boys—so VE day is just another day out here...

' ... In a few moments, the King will speak—the hut here is crowded. There are several German beds in here for it was formerly a German soldiers' billet. The radio is German too—the reception is excellent. Some of the boys are in bed writing letters, others are sitting up and all ears are open. The Anthem has just played—the Major is present—the speech is over. The King has certainly improved in his manner of speaking. The news is now on—I'm sure you too are listening ... '[1]

BBC correspondent, Edward Ward had been told to cover VE Day from the OKW headquarters in Flensburg. Driving there in a small convoy consisting of a heavy BBC transmitter van with a generator and radio masts on board, a staff car and a jeep, he was surprised to find the town packed with fully armed German troops still giving Nazi salutes to officers and still conducting themselves as if in a well-disciplined garrison.

That evening, after broadcasting his report, the closest he could get to celebrating was watching the fireworks being lit across the border in Denmark.

'It seemed off to be sitting out on Flensburg airfield and listening to what was happening in Piccadilly Circus and outside Buckingham Palace. Over there British people were celebrating in their millions and we were sitting in a little group on a German airfield, surrounded by German planes and transport and with the remnants of a fully armed German army concentrated only a few miles from us ... It was a strange, almost uncanny experience. Nothing had made any sense in Flensburg. It was just the same on the airfield. It was pitch-dark by this time, and as we drove along the perimeter runway German trucks flashed by us with their headlights full on, coming in to join the already vast number of vehicles which had gathered on the airfield. Mysterious red flares shot up from time to time from the centre of the field. Nobody knew what they meant or who was doing it. Nobody seemed to be controlling the German vehicles ... We couldn't make out where the German trucks were coming from. Over the Danish frontier a bare two miles away flares and rockets kept shooting up. The Danes were celebrating VE night in a big way. I wished we could have been over there with them. We'd have known where we stood with them. Here in Germany it was all so strange. Nobody seemed to know what was happening.'[2]

In Kiel, the Sixth Armoured Guards Brigade was ordered to provide a display of 'armoured might'. It was intended to dissuade the German Navy from any thought of rebellion.

'The Coldstream had been chosen for the job and by 12 o'clock on VE Day they were lined up outside the shattered town, preparing to make a triumphal entry. During the previous 24 hours Germans had been press-ganged into cleaning all the tanks for the drive and large gangs of prisoners had been made to fill in bomb craters and clear rubble along the route. The German police had been given instructions for traffic control ...

'At 1.30 the leading vehicles started to enter Kiel. The tanks glistened in the sunshine and the colour fastened to the Commanding Officer's aerial fluttered in the breeze. Slowly and majestically the long column wended its way through the town, the German police saluting as the officers drove by. By 2 o'clock the procession had reached the northern end of town and the expressions on the faces of the German civilians and sailors who were watching left no doubt that it had achieved its object. There would be no trouble in Kiel.'[3]

Perhaps not in Kiel, but elsewhere the so-called 'werewolves'—diehard Nazis who refused to accept the surrender—caused some bother. They received short shrift, as Alan Ritchie, aged 21, a REME engineer with the 7th Armoured Division Workshop recalled:

'We were in Hemslo in the foothills of the Harz Mountains just outside a town called Diepholz which was the headquarters of the Nazi Youth training centre. On the night of 8 May it was snowing there and we were told that the war was over, so we then had permission to light camp fires for the first time ever.

'I was a bit of an artist and I did a drawing that night, I think it was probably the best I did because I did it on the spot, sitting there taking my time. I had almost finished the sketches when there was a rattle of machine-gun fire. And we thought, "Oh God, some silly arse from the armourer's shop! Go and tick him off!" So I had to run down to the armourer's and say "What are you lot doing?" "Oh, clear off!" they said. "We aren't touching the guns, war's over, didn't you know?"

'At that, there was a much louder clatter of machine-gun fire and some explosions from the tank park that was between two and three hundred yards away. We realized then we were being attacked. So we had to go down and investigate. We didn't know how many, we didn't know where they were, but we had been trained, commando-trained particularly, to keep quiet, take a pace or two, keep still. Unfortunately, being in the woods, it was easy to give yourself away by stepping on a stick. Fortunately, the youngsters that we eventually got did tread on a bit of stick and we rounded them up.

'They turned out to be young Nazis from Diepholz who had infiltrated the camp. They were shot under the terms of the Geneva Convention as they were not in uniform—they had Nazi armbands but that was not sufficient. They were shouting and screaming "*Heil Hitler*", "*Gott strafe England*". They had also been found setting fire to some parts of the forest to try and burn us out. And on this particular occasion, they were also armed, so they had to be disposed of.'

This incident was exceptional. By and large, the Allies treated their defeated enemy with reasonable compassion, although strict non-fraternization regulations were in force. David Niven, then an officer with the Rifle Brigade, described a strangely moving encounter on VE Day with an abject German officer trying to find his way home.

'By May 8th, the war in Europe was officially over, but people were still being killed and Hitler's werewolves were still hopefully stretching piano wire at head height from trees on either side of the roads. To avoid decapitation, the wiser jeeps now carried sharpened iron stanchions welded to their radiators. The routes west out of Germany were becoming clogged with an estimated eight million homeward bound displaced persons pushing their pathetic belongings on bicycles or dragging them in little home-made carts. One became hardened to the sight of people lying under trees or in ditches too exhausted or too hungry to take another step.

'On a country road near Brunswick, I drove through an attractive red-roofed village on the outskirts of which was a large manor house. Two tow-headed little boys were playing in the garden. A mile or so away, I passed a farm wagon headed for the village. I glanced casually at the two men sitting up behind the horse. Both wore typical farm headgear and sacks were thrown over their shoulders protecting them from a light drizzle. We were just past them when something made me slam on the brakes and back up. I was right, the man who was not driving was wearing field boots. I slipped out from behind the wheel, pulled my revolver from its holster and told the corporal to cover me with his Tommy gun.

'I gestured to the men to put their hands over their heads and told them in fumbling German to produce their papers. "I speak English," said the one with the field boots, "this man has paper—I have none."

'"Who are you?" I asked.

'He told me his name and rank—"General."

'"We are not armed," he added, as I hesitated.

'Sandhurst did it—I saluted, then motioned them to lower their hands.

'"Where are you coming from, sir?"

'He looked down at me. I had never seen such utter weariness, such blank despair on a human face before. He passed a hand over the stubble of his chin.

'"Berlin," he said quietly.

'"Where are you going, sir?"

'He looked ahead down the road towards the village and closed his eyes. "Home," he said almost to himself, "it's not far now only … one more kilometre."

'I didn't say anything. He opened his eyes again and we stared at each other. We were quite still for a long time. Then I said,

'"Go ahead, sir," and added ridiculously … "please cover up your bloody boots."

'Almost as though in pain, he closed his eyes and raised his head, then with sobbing intake of breath, covered his face with both hands and they drove on.'[4]

The German army in defeat and disarray was a pitiful and haunting sight. Nancy Wilson, aged 34, a Red Cross Welfare worker had encountered a column of tattered humanity on her way to Lüneburg. 'The sight of the bedraggled remnants of the defeated Germany Army slowly trudging towards our line of lorries was terrible.

'They had been disarmed and told to get home as best they could. Stumbling past, limping, bandaged, some supported by their comrades, totally broken and beaten. A terrible and amazing sight reminding me of the painting of the French Retreat from Moscow in 1812. I thought, this is history again, going by our transport windows.

'On VE Day, our hospital was settled in the Scharnhorst Barracks in Lüneburg, with the British 2nd Army also stationed in the area. It was a day of uncontrolled joy, relief and congratulations. On that day, the barracks were ransacked and rifled, chairs, tables, all kind of furniture, books, whatever, were dragged out into the open and set fire to in an enormous, joyous bonfire. But it was frightening in its intensity of vicious delight for our victory—understandable, I felt, but nevertheless, finally rather sickening, perhaps because I had so recently seen a beaten army in retreat.

'Although I joined in myself at one point, threw things into the fire and thought it was fun and then, having seen these broken enemy soldiers so recently, I suddenly ended the whole thing.

'There is one particularly nice memory that I have of VE Day in Germany—the sight of a German prisoner of war and a Tommy and they were talking to each other. I was in one of the wards, looking out of the Scharnhorst barracks and being barracks, there was a sort of exercising yard and it was across this exercising yard that I saw these two men, carrying a bed.

'Prisoners were made to work, so probably they were just getting the bed into one of the wards. I heard them just talking. The Tommy was saying, "*Kinder?*" And the German, who couldn't talk at all, just held up three fingers and they went on chatting a bit. There they were, two soldiers, far from home peacefully exchanging details of their domestic situations and fond interests.'

Across the border in Belgium, Mary Mulry, a twenty-four-year old Queen Alexandra nurse, who had arrived in Normandy to nurse the wounded and was stationed in Louvain by the end of the war, kept very complete diaries for those days and recorded a quiet moment of reflection on VE night:

'It was the 8th May 1945. I was looking out of the window of the Sacre Coeur Convent in Louvain, and wearing the scarlet and grey uniform of the Queen Alexandra's Imperial Nursing Service. It was almost dark, and as I watched a little old man hobbled along the cobbled streets lighting the gas lamps. It seemed strangely symbolical to me for this was Victory in Europe Day. Mr Churchill has announced peace. Germany was beaten. I had survived. It was a time of thanksgiving, a time to remember the personal friends who never made it. Six years is a large chunk out of one's life. I had seen so much death and carnage in those years. Would it be an uneasy peace to follow, or would it be the brave new world we hoped for?

'Germany had surrendered unconditionally, and there was a great excitement here in this pretty university town. There were flags flying from the windows. There were people in the streets running around excitedly and talking to each other in little groups. The church bells were ringing and the last "All clear" had just died down mournfully in the distance.

'This was a great day for the Belgians too. It was just a short time ago since the Gestapo patrolled along the streets where the flags were now flying so gaily. I could hear the sounds of hilarity and clinking glasses downstairs in the sisters' mess, but at that time I was glad to be alone—perhaps to pray. It was good to sit quietly in the evening twilight and try to realize fully how much this meant—no more waste of life—no more casualties—no more horror and destruction. It was wonderful too, to contemplate the lights going on all over London. It was a city which I had never known without the black-outs and air-raids.

'I went out to dinner with friends at the Hotel Splendide in Brussels on the night of VE Day. We were joined by Paddy, a major in the Royal Artillery. He requested to join us with such pleasantness and a beguiling brogue that we could not resist.

'We drank masses of champagne and Irish coffee and had a hilarious evening. Paddy was a great raconteur with the endearing ability of being able to laugh at himself. He reminded me of a young George Bernard Shaw with rather wild looking red hair, a tall and skinny form and that strong jaw line and stubborn chin that is so often typical of Irish physiognomy. His eyes were blue and full of devilment. His mother must have had an awful time of it when he was a small boy! He was the only British officer I ever knew who was drawing an extra shilling a day in pay because he spoke Gaelic! He persuaded the band that night to play some nostalgic Irish tunes. We talked about Ireland to a background of "The Wearing of the Green".'⁵

As Mary Mulry toasted peace with champagne, Ludovic Kennedy was heading towards Cairo and the Far East in a troopship, to join the destroyer, *Wheatland*, to which he had been appointed first lieutenant. The night of VE Day stands out particularly in his recollection: ' … all the scuttles and deadlights in our blacked-out ship were thrown back so that lights from every cabin and compartment blazed out triumphantly across the darkling sea—nothing else could have proclaimed more dramatically and with such certainty that the war was over.'[6]

The war in the Far East was to continue for three more months, and the troops out there felt distinctly remote from the celebrations in Britain.

Brian Aldiss, serving in India, laconically recalled that unit's celebrations comprised a five-minute cigarette break. The sergeant-major addressed the company and simply said, 'Right lads, war's over in Europe. Take five minutes!'

Elizabeth Milton, a WAAC officer who was twenty-one years old when the war in Europe came to an end, remembers VE Day as one of the most miserable in her life. In an advanced state of pregnancy with her second child, her husband away fighting in Europe, isolated in a house in a small hill station in Kasauli, in British India, she was in no mood to celebrate.

'The end of the war in Europe was a depressing time for me, for all of us. In the last few days of the war, I got a telegram announcing that the WAAC was to be disbanded. It wasn't a surprise as I knew this was only to be in wartime, a very temporary business, but it was distressing.

'We had very good communication with Europe, the BBC World Service was magnificent. I still erupt everytime they play "Lilli Bulero". It was our lifeline, we used to sit jammed to this tiny crackling little broadcast and kept very close to the news all the time and you knew exactly what was happening with the war in Europe.

'But for us in Delhi, it wasn't nearly over. We were geared to the Eastern Front and this was the terror that was held over your heads. Fighting the Japs was much more frightening for us and of course, much more on our minds. Burma was much closer to us in every way.

'VE Day was just another day of war for us, made rather worse for me by the telegrams that had arrived for me in that week—the one from the WAAC and then another from my husband, saying that he was hoping to see me but he was en route elsewhere and for the time being, there was no prospect of seeing me.

'When I heard the war in Europe was over, I was in tears. Some of it was relief, but I didn't have any neighbours I could celebrate it with, we were pretty sparse on the ground. You lived in these funny little houses in the hills and although the scenery was beautiful, isolation and loneliness were the worst of it and there were very few people to rejoice with.

'I was really sad I wasn't in Trafalgar Square for the celebrations there, I feel that more and more as I get older. I'm a patriot at heart. It is hard to be patriotic on your own.'

In a similarly remote location in the north west of India, Bruce Belfrage found himself charged with instilling a modicum of victory joy in the jaded hearts of Allied troops. 'When the war in Europe finished, I was in the North-West Frontier province and was asked to find out the general reaction of the troops to VE Day, and to broadcast on the subject.

'I was told to prepare a ten-minute talk, but found I could have done it in ten seconds. The only aspect of the news which was of the slightest interest to them was the knowledge that their families were no longer in danger of aerial attack. Otherwise the reaction was a complete apathy which the official issue of a few fireworks did nothing to dispel.

'One sergeant whom I asked for his views summed it up by saying: "When they tell me the day I set sail for home, I don't mind letting off one of their rockets if it'll give them any pleasure."'[7]

Further south, in Sri Lanka, then still called Ceylon, rumours of unconditional surrender, peace and VE Day had been circulating since the end of April—according to the diaries of Pamela Weeks, a Wren topographer based outside Kandy.

She wrote: 'Sunday April 29th Extraordinary day. Arrived at work to hear the war was over. VE Day in fact. My first reaction was wild, uncontrollable joy. I galloped like a mad thing and flung my arms around Gordon (a colleague). Then I felt terribly sad, kept wondering about my parents. Then we kept hearing it wasn't VE Day at all. And so it went on all morning.'

When the VE Day broadcasts finally came through, she remembers the moment with extraordinary clarity. 'I can see us all sitting in the day room in our "basha"—a hut with a gap between the top of the walls and the roof, to allow air to circulate and I can remember hearing it come crackling over the airwaves, I remember Churchill's words and the King spoke, too.

'We looked at each other and wondered when "our" war would be over. We weren't in London, we weren't amongst all these milling thousands on the streets. Nevertheless, I think we were pretty pleased about it. So there we were, listening to the cheering crowds in London, from halfway across the world.'

In her diary, she wrote: 'The German war is over' in huge letters right across the page. 'Heard the marvellous news during the night. We woke up having lived in suspense for two days. I felt dreadfully sad and happy all at the same time. It is odd not knowing what the folks at home are doing or saying.

'We went to a big lunch party with the ISTD (Inter Services Topographical Department). Dutch crowd there. Afterwards we climbed over the golf course. Had an amazing tennis party at 4 o'clock and then went out to dinner. Next day, had to go to work. Took a very dim view specially as we heard the King's speech at 1.30 in the morning. Sallied forth to Victory Parade. Great moment when we marched down the centre of an enormous arena and did "Eyes right!" to Lt Gen Browning. Very hot, masses of people, tons of flags and excitement but Oh! how I wish I was in England, to have all your friends round you and to hear all the cheering. This is all a little overdone—you must remember there is still a war out here and I am afraid a good many people will forget it, or forget us. Party at Air Command in the evening.'

Thoughts of what people were doing at home on VE Day preoccupied many people posted in the Far East, particularly the women. With essentially more time on their hands and less immediate danger to face, they had time to write letters and diaries and generally reflect on the significance of the end of the war in Europe—not that it would necessarily mean an immediate transfer back home.

One Wren Third Officer, Rosemary Gillet, based at a training establishment outside Colombo, was confined to camp along with the entire company on VE Day and spent much of the day either swimming or sleeping.

'The end of the war in Europe did not have a lot of significance for me, in Ceylon, I don't think. I was thankful for the people at home, my parents of course—I'd got a brother in the army who was killed right towards the end of the war, so I suppose it did bring some sort of release.

'But we were such a long way from any kind of fighting where we were, so I don't believe we thought about it very much.

'I was invited to a civilian party on the outskirts of Colombo, to which several WREN officers and Naval officers were also invited and other Services people were also happily eating, drinking and dancing. About midnight, four "volunteers" decided to ring the church bells to mark the occasion. The bell tower of the local church was a stone archway in the churchyard and having vaulted the church wall, all four swung on the bell rope and raised a cacophony of celebration for about five minutes. It naturally drew a big crowd, but everyone was good natured about the "peal".

'The houses and small palm-leaf huts all along the coast road from our camp towards Colombo were outlined by lamps made from half a coconut shell full of palm oil and a lighted wick. The night was warm and fine and the atmosphere of happy relief was memorable.

'I remember walking back to the Wrennery in the moonlight after a very happy evening—but next day, for us, the war went on!'

Wednesday 9 May

Mopping Up the Victory

Uri Levitan read out the 'Orders of the Day' over Moscow Radio and the city's public address system and his voice was as familiar to Russians as that of John Snagge or Stuart Hibberd in Britain. In fact he was so well known that Stalin, not famous for his sense of humour, once made a joke about him. Asked when the war would end, Stalin replied: 'Don't worry, Levitan will tell you.'

Curiously enough, he was right. Although most of Britain had spent the previous day celebrating the end of the war in Europe, no official announcement was made in the Soviet Union. When Churchill was broadcasting news of the victory in Britain, it was Children's Hour on Soviet radio and a woman was narrating a nice little story about two rabbits and a bird.

It was perhaps not unreasonable for the Russians to insist that the war was not ended until the surrender had been signed in Berlin or that they should view the ceremony in Rheims as something of a sideshow. But bureaucracy, confusion and incompetence contrived to delay the Berlin surrender to such an extent that this final act in the European war was not played out until almost midnight on 8 May.

Thus it was not until ten minutes past one o'clock on the morning of 9 May that Levitan finally came on the air to wake up Moscow with the glad tidings that 'in honour of the victorious conclusion of the Great Patriotic War' the day would be a holiday to celebrate the 'festival of victory'.

'The news quickly spread,' the Moscow correspondent of the *New York Herald Tribune* reported. 'Lights snapped on in residences and people many in night clothes—tumbled out into the streets, shouting and dancing. Some knelt on the ground and prayed.'

In Berlin, a party was already well under way. Kay Summersby had been allowed, as a treat, to join the SHAEF delegation of senior British, American and French officers the previous day. They arrived in the late morning at Tempelhof airport, the ruins of which were still smouldering. Correspondents accompanying the party were shocked by what they observed on the drive to an army engineering college in the suburb of Karlshorst, where Marshal Georgi Zhukov, the Russian commander, had set up his headquarters.

'This town is a city of the dead,' the Associated Press correspondent reported. 'As a metropolis it has simply ceased to exist. Every house within miles of the centre seems to have had its own bomb.

'The scene beggars description. I have seen Stalingrad; I have lived through the entire London blitz; I have seen a dozen badly damaged Russian towns, but the scene of utter destruction, desolation and death which meets the eye in Berlin as far as the eye can rove in all directions is something that almost baffles description. "The Blitz was a bank holiday compared to this," one of my colleagues remarked.

'Dozens of well-known thoroughfares, including the entire Unter den Linden from one end to the other, are wrecked beyond repair. The town is literally unrecognizable. From the Brandenburg Gate, everything within a radius of from two to five miles is destroyed. There does not appear to be one house in a hundred which is even useful as a shelter.

'The only people who look like human beings in the streets of what was Berlin are the Russian soldiers. There are two million inhabitants in the town, the Russian authorities told me, but they are mostly in the remoter suburbs. In the central part of the town you only see a few ghostlike figures of women and children—few men—queueing up to pump water.

'If Stalingrad, London, Guernica, Rotterdam, Coventry wanted avenging, they have had it, and no mistake about it.'[1]

Six hours after the delegation had arrived at Zhukov's headquarters there was still no sign of the surrender ceremony taking place. The delay, it was explained, was due to problems with the multi-language translation of the surrender document.

It was 10.30 in the evening before they were summoned to the room where the formal surrender was to take place. Kay Summersby takes up the story: 'The huge room was banked with klieg lights, blinding as we stepped in from the dim hallway. Everything seemed to be set up for the sole convenience of the Russian press, who numbered close to a hundred and swarmed around in shouting bedlam. Movie cameras were ready in almost every conceivable spot. Microphones sprouted from the floor, hung from the ceiling; they and the klieg lights created a veritable spider web of wires and cables.

'A long table at one end of the room commanded all attention; obviously this was for the biggest of the Bigwigs. From it stretched three other long tables, for Press and smaller fry. Set apart, under the balcony, was a short table apparently reserved for the surrendering Germans ... There was a momentary silence as Marshal Zhukov, a short-stubby officer with a stern expression, entered the room. Everyone stood up ... As we sat down, he called the conference to order.

'I was surprised at the way a civilian, later identified as Andrei Vyshinsky [Deputy Commissioner for Foreign Affairs], hovered over the entire proceedings, deferred to even by Zhukov. Even in this moment of Soviet military victory, the Kremlin was stepping in to take charge. Vyshinksy found no detail too small for his attention, whether it be a whispered conference with Zhukov or the location of a propaganda film camera.

'With final details arranged to everyone's satisfaction, the signal was given for the enemy's entrance. As a door opened just behind the empty table, a silence smothered the babble. Every pair of eyes in the room focused on a tall German officer in smart blue-grey Field Marshal's uniform, his chest covered with decorations and medals, his head poised high. He looked a little like Boris Karloff, this man; and his haughty manner was that of the born actor, the born Prussian. It was Field Marshal Wilhelm Keitel. He stepped stiffly to the table, jerked up his silver-headed baton in a curt salute and sat down. The noise rose again. No one seemed to notice as the other two German principals (Admiral von Friedeburg and Luftwaffe Colonel-General Stumpf) took their places beside Keitel …

'Keitel, I noticed, carefully pulled off one grey glove before taking the pen. He looked up contemptuously at the boisterous newsmen, then scribbled his signature across the surrender papers, moving hastily, as though anxious to dispense with a dirty job. Some of the reporters and photographers climbed on tables to get a better view; two had a brief fist-fight; all yelled and pushed. Von Friedeburg and Stumpf signed hurriedly while Keitel glared without seeing, the incarnation of the traditional icy Prussian …

'The Air Chief Marshal (Sir Arthur Tedder) arose and asked in an emotionless, high voice, "Do you understand the terms you have just signed?" almost exactly the same question which General Eisenhower put to Jodl and von Friedeburg back in Rheims.

'As the Germans nodded, Zhukov gave them the order of dismissal. The Nazis arose as at a parade-ground command. Keitel again jerked his baton in brief salute. They left the room with an exit equally as dramatic as their entrance … Now, even for the Russians, VE Day was official.'[2]

By then it was near midnight and the delegation was invited to re-assemble in the same room an hour later for a celebration party. When Summersby returned she found the room had been transformed into a banqueting hall, complete with orchestra on the balcony and a huge bar stocked plentifully with champagne and vodka. The meal lasted four hours and comprised a continuous round of toasts requiring glasses to be drained. At the end Summersby, who had persuaded her waitress to substitute water for vodka, was one of few still sober:

'By five o'clock in the morning, even the expert interpreter couldn't understand the toasts. The majority of the banquet guests were drunk, good, old-fashioned drunk … One of the Western Allies crumpled on the table after a last-effort toast. Several Russians literally went under the table. Another in our party disappeared.

The tables' strict seating arrangement was abandoned as everyone became neighbourly. Songs bubbled up in four languages, Russian predominating, closely followed by American. The orchestra, which had struck chords, for each and every toast, began to sour as vodka penetrated to the balcony.

'As the party broke up just before dawn [we women]—agreed there had been between 24 and 29 individual toasts, each requiring five to ten minutes for translation, plus the musical chord, and the final, deadly, bottoms-up. We all agreed we had been in on the VE party to end all VE parties.'[3]

There was partying, too, in Red Square, which by six o'clock in the morning was crowded with Muscovites as determined as Londoners to celebrate their own VE Day. 'The crowds were growing larger and larger and gayer and merrier,' the BBC reported. 'A British sergeant turned out to see the fun … they pounced on him, tossed him up in the air and shouted Victory! Victory! Then they asked for a song and he responded with "Tipperary". Before long the sergeant and some others in British uniform were singing and teaching the crowd "Pack up your troubles in your old kit bag".'

The Times correspondent was watching the victory celebrations from the safety of a rooftop: 'Hundreds of thousands of people since early morning have been streaming into the centre of Moscow. The crowds fill the broad street, two or three times the width of Whitehall, that runs below the western walls of the Kremlin past the university and the Lenin Library to the Moskva River. They line the river bank below the terrace. They are packing the Red Square … Crowds sweep each side of St Basil's Church towards the bridge over the Moskva River, away towards the theatre square, where a bandstand has been erected for street dancing, and into the dark streets of Chinatown. Wireless sets are broadcasting "Tipperary", sung by a Red Army choir. It is a homely, democratic crowd, in which generals and soldiers, commissars and workers, mingle.'

The veteran foreign correspondent Alexander Werth was similarly impressed: 'The spontaneous joy of the two or three million people who thronged the Red Square that evening—and the Moscow River embankments, and Gorky Street, all the way up to the Belorussian Station—was of a quality and depth I had never seen in Moscow before … The crowds … were so happy that they did not even have to get drunk. Under the tolerant gaze of the militia, young men even urinated against the walls of the Moskva Hotel, flooding the wide pavement.'

Dr Hewlett Johnson, the famous 'Red Dean' of Canterbury was visiting Moscow on behalf of the Anglo-Soviet Medical Fund and watched astonished as 'A dense crowd, enthusiastic and genial, released at last from the long strain of war, blocked our road and engulfed us, cheering every Englishman or American. They seized General Younger, a British officer in full uniform, and tossing him in the air, caught him as gently as if he were a babe. My turn came next.'

Mrs Churchill, also in Moscow on behalf of the British Red Cross Aid to Russia Fund, was fortunately spared such treatment. In the afternoon, she broadcast her husband's message to the Russian people: 'From the British nation I send you heartfelt greetings on the splendid victories you have won in driving the invader from your soil and laying the Nazi tyrant low. It is my firm belief that on the friendship and understanding between the British and Russian peoples depends the future of mankind … Here in our island home we are thinking today … about you all. We send you from the bottom of our hearts our wishes for your happiness and well-being and that, after all the sacrifices and sufferings of the dark valley through which we have marched together, we may also in loyal comradeship and sympathy walk in the sunshine of victorious peace.'

Marshal Stalin also broadcast a chillingly uncompromising message that day: 'Comrades, fellow countrymen and women, the great day of victory over Germany has come. Fascist Germany has been forced to her knees by the Red Army and by the troops of our allies … Being well aware of the subterfuges of the German leaders, who consider their treaties as mere scraps of paper, we have no reason to accept their word. Nevertheless, this morning the German troops have begun to surrender their arms en masse to the Soviet troops. This is no longer a mere scrap of paper. It is actual capitulation of the armed forces of Germany … The Great Patriotic War has ended with our complete victory. Glory to our heroic Red Army. Glory to our great people. Eternal glory to the heroes who fell in the struggle.'[4]

The Germans by then were getting their first terrible taste of life under Russian occupation. Dora Zimmel, the 24-year-old mother of three children, including a baby boy, was living on a farm on the outskirts of the village of Bobsien, near Hagenow, when the Russians arrived. 'The milk cart, which used to bring us all the news, also brought us the news that the Russians had arrived in the village. With that began our time of suffering.

'We knew we had to go out every day and work. They simply arrived one morning with fixed bayonets and drove us out onto the field. My mother stayed at home to tend the children, but my sisters and I had to go out into the fields to labour eight hours a day in the potato fields, bent double for the Russians.

'The farms lay outside the village, some distance from civilization, and every night we were invaded by the Russians. We women could simply not endure it, so every night we climbed on the milk cart and went down to the village on it and spent the nights sitting on stools in the homes of the estate workers and returned next morning.

'I had got my son and it was a blessing I had because when the Russians came to our farm at night, I took my baby Roland out of his pram and put him to my breast and they left me alone. They respected that. But otherwise, they behaved like animals, there was nothing they didn't do, I can't speak of it.

'We used wood ashes to wash clothes with and the tiny piece of soap we had left, well, everybody was allowed to wash themselves once a week with this piece of soap. We washed in the pigsty, with one of us on guard to keep the Russians at bay, so they didn't watch us getting undressed.

'We never thought of the future, we just lived from day to day, I never thought of it, I just thought about whether my husband would come back. How things would turn out, we simply didn't know.

'I don't really know if I felt "defeated" or not. We hardly knew of the the things Hitler had done, we knew nothing about the gassing of the Jews. If anybody had said it was happening, we would have said "impossible", but we didn't know at the time. Our only worry was, if my husband comes back, what will we do then? Where will we go?'

The ninth of May was also the day on which Guenter de Bruyn, the cadet who had joined the Wehrmacht at 17 and been wounded at 18, began his attempt to get home from Czechoslovakia. 'On the previous day I had fallen sick. Almost the last bit of business the doctors did was to operate on me. Next day the order was: anyone who could walk had to leave. I had spent five weeks in bed and had not eaten for five days but my legs could still carry me.

'The way home began in Rakovnik at 7 o'clock in the morning and lasted, with a few enforced stops, about three months. The journey was mostly on foot, but sometimes was speeded up by rides on freight trains, gun carriages, and goods trailers pulled by horses or lorries. Once my advance was boosted by the gift of a bicycle from a Russian, and which was then taken off me by someone else that evening.

'Despite fear, deprivation and hunger, these were happy weeks; I was, after all, free of the military. The fall of the Reich produced in me no similar sense of destruction; the feeling of belonging to a defeated people had no space to grow in my mind, rather I regarded the victors, who would spend a lot longer in uniform and carrying arms, with a certain sympathy. With the departure from the hospital, I felt all demands on me simply disappear. I had outlived the State which had had control over my destiny and felt freed of any regulations, my duty was now to myself and my need to get to my home.

'The external circumstances hardly reflected the internal sense of freedom that I felt. I was only able to get rid of my uniform piecemeal to begin with. The dispersal of those able to walk took a matter of minutes and so I had grabbed whatever clothing was to hand—a pair of grey military trousers, too short in the leg but which fitted round the waist and a blue and white striped hospital jacket which resulted in my being mistaken for a released concentration camp prisoner several times on the way. My head was still bandaged and on my feet, instead of the comfortable, supple boots which I had wanted for the journey home, I had a pair of worn-out slippers. I was able to abandon these on the next day as I stumbled upon a pair of walking shoes which fitted me, along with a collection of delicate ladies' shoes in a roadside trench. I had no luggage whatsoever. Apart from my paybook, a notebook, pencil and handkerchief, I had no possessions at all.'[5]

De Bruyn begged for food, did his best to avoid villages occupied by the Russians, and finally reached his mother's house, in the suburbs of Berlin, at the end of July 1945.

Churchill's reference to the liberation of 'our dear Channel Islands' during his broadcast on the afternoon of VE Day was not, in reality, supported by the facts.

It was true that two British destroyers, HMS *Bulldog* and HMS *Beagle*, had arrived off Guernsey at two o'clock on the afternoon of 8 May, to rendezvous, as arranged, with a German minesweeper. But the young naval officer, who had been rowed across from the minesweeper to greet them, announced that he had no powers to surrender and was only empowered to carry back the terms for a cease fire. Furthermore, he had orders, since the armistice did not come into effect for another ten hours, to warn both ships to move away from the shore as their continued presence would be regarded as a 'provocation'.

This went down rather poorly with the brigadier who had been sent to be military commander of the islands, but there was heavy artillery on the shore and he could not be certain that the German occupiers were not planning a last-ditch stand. The German officer was dispatched with a message saying that the British were not interested in 'terms', only in immediate surrender, and the two ships stood out to sea.

At midnight, as the war was officially coming to an end, they closed in to the shore once more. The war correspondent of *The Scotsman*, on board HMS *Bulldog*, described what happened next: 'Out of the darkness came a German armed trawler and, as we swept searchlights over the German vessel, there came into the rays a white eight-oared cutter. In her stern sat the same naval officer, but with him was a resplendent figure in light blue army greatcoat with red lapels. He was Major-General Heine, of the German Army.'

Heine was authorized to act on behalf of the commandant of the German occupying force. He was asked if he accepted unconditional surrender and he replied, '*Ja.*' It took some hours for the surrender documents to be drawn up and Heine signed at 7.14 a.m. Half an hour later, the German trawler on which he had arrived returned to to St Peter Port, this time flying the White Ensign and carrying a party of 20 men from the Royal Artillery and *The Scotsman* correspondent:

'The tiny force formed up on the docks, fixed bayonets and marched towards the dock gates. There behind the gates was a seething, cheering, crying mob of men, women and children. Over them the church bells of St Peter Port were clanging tumultuously … Then the crowd broke through the dock gates. In one second those gunners were marching like Guardsmen: in the next they were torn from the ranks, kissed, hugged, cheered. "You have been so long coming." "We have waited so long for you." "British, they're British," the islanders cried. Somehow the soldiers re-formed. Two girls with great Union Jacks led them into the town. People rushed from their houses to join the crowd.

'At the Old Court House the soldiers formed up on each side of the steps, at the top of which the officers of the landing party and Victor Carey, the Guernsey Bailiff, stood. As a command rang out, a halyard was pulled and the Union Jack floated out in the soft, sunlit breeze. One could hear the sob from the crowd, then, rising to a great volume of sound, they sang "God Save the King". Then they stopped, looked up again and cheered—that to us all seemed the real moment of the liberation of Guernsey.'[6]

On the neighbouring island of Jersey, the people were also waiting with barely concealed impatience, for the arrival of British troops to signify their nightmare was over. Jersey resident R.C.F Maugham recalled the moment when the British destroyers hove into view: 'On Wednesday, May 9, from an early hour, dense crowds thronged the port and water-front, every eye fixed on the direction whence the expected warship must make her appearance. They would have waited through-out the day rather than have returned disappointed to their homes. At length there came a burst of cheering and loud cries of "There she is!" as, rounding Noirmont Point, the grey hull and twin funnels of His Majesty's Flotilla Leader *Beagle* came steaming majestically to her anchorage beyond Elizabeth Castle, the white ensign of the Royal Navy flying out in the morning breeze. I think that that was the moment at which we realised, at which it came home to us, that the long years of German domination were over; that we were once more free ...

'When, some time later, the *Beagle's* picket-boat came ashore with two officers in uniform, the fervour and enthusiasm of the crowd's welcome were such that the greatest difficulty was experienced in extricating them from such an amount of hearty back-slapping, hand-shaking and merciless pressure as threatened at time to result in personal injury. Amidst roar after roar of delirious cheering, the welcome visitors at length reached a waiting car and, as it crawled at a snail's pace through the masses of excited people who pressed up to and even mounted the running-boards, the panting occupants were compelled to stand and shake dozens of hands through the windows. Soon, however, the car was forced to a standstill ... and finally the two officers were plucked forcibly from it and, show-ered with flowers, carried shoulder-high to the office of the Harbour Master, where, appearing at one of the windows, they were greeted by more vociferous cheering and a thunderous rendering of the National Anthem.'[7]

It is entirely appropriate that almost the last act of the war in Europe—the surrender of the German divisions on the island of Crete—should be witnessed by the dauntless war correspondent Clare Hollingworth, since she filed the first report in 1939 that Germany was about to invade Poland.

One of the few women correspondents to cover the war in Europe from beginning to end, Hollingworth was engaged in welfare work with refugees on the Polish border with Germany before the war. As the storm clouds gathered, she returned to Britain and persuaded the *Daily Telegraph* to take her on as a reporter. She was on the last flight back to Warsaw and immediately on arrival was sent on the night train to Katowice, which she knew well. She borrowed the consul-general's flagged car, the only vehicle allowed to cross the border, and went into Germany. Hessian screens had been put up on each side of the road.

As her car turned round to head back into Poland, some of the screens were blown down by the wind and she caught a glimpse of the massed tanks lined up ready to invade. Her story about an impending invasion was immediately denied; shortly afterwards the invasion took place.

By 1945 Hollingworth was based in Cairo. 'I was very close to Geoffrey Hoare, *The Times* correspondent, who I later married, and when we were told there would be an interesting story in Crete, we went together. I knew that the Germans had withdrawn five or six divisions from the Balkans to Crete, because that was the only place they could put them and I also knew that underground guerrillas had been very active.

'I think they wanted Geoffrey there as an interpreter. I do recall that he had German connections on his maternal side and I think, quite wrongly, the word has got around that he spoke German, which he didn't. He could only speak a few words. When we arrived in Heraklion, we were very well received and told the following day the German generals would all come and surrender. We were taken to the room where this was all going to happen and sat behind the table. Then the Germans arrived. One of two of them spoke a little English and there was a certain amount of confusion. They didn't seem to understand they had got to sign on the dotted line and surrender and Geoffrey was, of course, unable to interpret.

'Eventually I remember we put on the BBC in German so there could be no misunderstanding about what had happened and what they had got to do and after listening to the BBC they at last understood that everybody else had surrendered, so they all signed on the dotted line.

'Then someone managed to get hold of some junior person to interpret and there were discussions about the hand over and what they were going to do vis-à-vis the Communists. In the end it was decided to allow them, and this is the part I believe has never been published, to keep their weapons for a very limited period in order to protect the cities from the communists who were raging round in the mountains. I remember one of the senior British officers saying that letting the Germans keep their weapons was about the last thing in the world they wanted to do but there was no alternative. The fear was that partisans would come and steal everything if the Germans were not able to defend themselves. We, of course, were strictly enjoined not to publish any details of this strange agreement. It was really an extraordinary situation—a handful of British soldiers, no more than a battalion, containing a minimum of 12,000 Germans, most of whom were still armed.

'Geoffrey and I were both offered a German staff car each to drive round the island and see what was happening, which of course we accepted. We stayed there over a week. The condition of the German troops was generally good. They were demoralised in the sense that they had lost the war, but the weather was good and they were firing off their arms to get rid of the ammunition and that was fun.

On the whole the Germans were asking about when they could get back home, although some were saying don't let's hurry because the conditions were better where they were than in Germany.

'There was no real celebration of VE Day on Crete. There may have been the odd cheer and perhaps an extra drink in a café, but by and large the tiny British garrison was too busy to celebrate. Personally, I was very happy the war was over. I was longing to cover the peace negotiations and politics and so on. I was really looking forward to another kind of reporting.'

Thursday 10 May

After the Euphoria, the Reality

The price of victory was horrific, barely comprehensible. 300,000 British servicemen had died, along with 35,000 merchant seamen. 62,000 civilians were
killed, half of them in the Blitz of 1940-41. Some 3,300,000 properties were
destroyed, 92 per cent of them were private dwellings and half were in London.

In Germany war losses, up to 1 May 1945, were reported by OKW as 2,007,000
killed and 2,610,000 wounded or missing. No one could count the numbers of
refugees and displaced persons.

Before the fighting finally ended, some 20 million people were to lose their
lives around the world in pursuit, or defiance, of the ambitions of the madman
whose ashes lay under the ruins of Berlin.

It is said that every family in Britain lost someone. What is certainly true is
that no family was untouched by the war.

Nothing was the same after VE Day. There could be no return to the simple innocence of life before the war because everything, and everyone, had
changed.

Men who had spent nearly six years abroad fighting a war came home
changed. Some were not even sure they wanted to go home. 'I felt an incredible
sense of anti-climax,' said Major Peter Martin of the 2nd Cheshires. 'From the
age of nineteen the German war had always been there; and suddenly it disappeared. I couldn't see much point in my existence any more. The whole reason
for being had gone. I can remember weeping that night. And I don't think I was
the only person in the Division.'[1]

The sense of common purpose and the community that grew out of facing
a common threat also rapidly dissipated. This was the view of a housewife only
a few weeks after the end of the war: 'During the war I was secure in my receipt
of an allowance, my children had special advantages, life ran to a pattern, people were human. Now what is to happen? We have no economic security, our

children—what will become of them? Who knows what controls may be forced on us, what will shape our circumstances? Worst of all, the friendly spirit of common burdens and real goodwill has vanished in a flash—we are now neck and neck again after money, jobs, power, favour. Now we don't offer to get Mrs So-and-so down the road some tomatoes. We make sure we get our own first and then don't tell her where we got them. Peace to me means the return of old evils. I have lost my youth, and to what end? I was happier when I lay listening to bombs and daring myself to tremble ... '[2]

For many people the end of the war meant that the fear of dying was replaced by fear of the future. There was certainly a deep disquiet about what lay ahead. Would there be jobs for the demobbed, homes for the bombed out, a fair living wage for the masses?

Those who expected a sudden change for the better—and many did—were doomed to disappointment. Petrol and food rationing continued and, paradoxically, it became harder, if anything, to find the food that had been reasonably available during the war.

'People expected everything to be wonderful,' said the novelist Rosemary Ann Sissons, 'but it was not. VE Day was followed by the most terrible hardship, depression and gloom as rationing got worse. We got the feeling that we had lost the war, rather than won it.'

Few could be blamed for thinking the fruits of victory to be faintly bitter. Among a long list of defence regulations revoked on 10 May, it was decreed that blackout curtains could be removed at midnight. Street lights shone out gloriously, though not on full beam, as power still needed to be conserved. Weather forecasts were reinstated, as were place names in news bulletins. That tiresome phrase 'Don't you know there's a war on?', mainly used as a form of chastisement, was thankfully relegated to history.

There were many who could not wait to remove all traces of the war. 'Today, the last of the blackout curtains were taken down,' a former schoolmistress noted in her diary. 'They were not conspicuous, and I hadn't drawn them this winter, when we weren't so particular as we used to be. A jar of anti-mustard gas ointment was consigned to the dustbin. I wish we could be told what to do with our gasmasks. I'm tired of seeing then hanging in the hall.'[3]

Even the fact that the menfolk were coming home carried with it some concerns, not least a belief that the allocation of demob numbers was a swindle. In the absence of fathers and breadwinners, women had been forced to shoulder an extraordinary range of additional responsibilities. They dug the land, drove trucks, took hard and dirty jobs in factories. They changed. They became tough, independent and free-thinking.

A young Hounslow woman, who had delivered milk throughout the war from a horse-drawn float, celebrated the end of the war and struck a blow for equality by joining her father and brothers in the public bar of the local pub, from which women were rigorously barred. 'We were supposed to go into the saloon. The look on my Dad's face was comical. He just said, "You can't come in here with all these men." "Why not?" I asked. "I've worked among men for five years, kept the home fires burning, earned my money, now we'll celebrate," which we did, well and truly, with "Bless 'Em All".'[4]

Many women were reluctant to give up the independence that wartime had forced on them. They had risen to the challenges of war and had rejoiced in the female comradeship and sense of purpose that it had brought them. How could they resume their docile pre-war existence?

'I'm tired out tonight,' Nella Last confessed in her diary on 10 May. 'I feel as if the week's events are only just getting through to my real mind. It's been a long and often trying road, but I found comradeship, and it brought peace of mind when otherwise I'd have broken. The knowledge that I was "keeping things moving in the right direction", in however small a degree, steadied me, helped my tired head to rest peacefully at night, and have the strength to begin again when morning came. I wonder if it's the same feeling some of the lads have when they think of being demobilized!

'I love my home dearly, but as a home rather than a house. The latter can make a prison and a penance, if a woman makes too much of a fetish of cleaning and polishing. But I will not, *cannot* go back to the narrowness of my husband's "I don't want anyone else's company but yours—why do you want anyone else?" I looked at his placid, blank face and marvelled at the way he had managed so to dominate me for all our married life, at how to avoid hurting him, I had tried to keep him in a good mood, when a smacked head would have been the best treatment. His petulant moods only receive indifference now. I *know* I speak sharply at times, I *know* I'm not the "sweet woman I used to be"—but then I never was! Rather was I a frayed, battered thing, with nerves kept in control by effort that at times became too much, and "nervous breakdowns" were the result. No one would ever give me one again, no one.'[5]

For a young woman like Lucia Lawson who had known only the security of home, family and school and then joined the ATS, the future held understandable fears, which she recounted in a letter to her mother: 'After so many years of saying "When the war is over … " it seems almost unbelievable, and somehow I have a feeling of anti-climax. I don't know how I expected it to end, but I don't think like this and already I am scared—what's going to happen afterwards, what's it like when there isn't a war, what's going to happen to us in the ATS? Where will I be sent to? What will I do when I don't have to get up in the morning, don't have to dress the way I am told? Are all these questions to which I can find no answer questions which I feel people like me are asking all over the world? It is strange to feel lost, when I know I have a home to go to, but I can't just sit at home and do nothing, at least not after about a month of it. I suppose I could take up some good "works" or travel, but neither of them appeal to me. I could get married, but I suppose I'd better find someone I love before I do that … '[6]

The years of war had not always been kind to the women left at home to cope. Whilst strengthening their resolve and their will to survive, wartime had robbed them of many comforts. They no longer even looked like the women their husbands and sweethearts had left behind and romanticized from a distance. Hard work and deprivation had changed all that. Homecoming was to be an ordeal of getting to know one another again—on both sides.

Fortunately, Godfrey Winn, the prototype 'agony uncle', was on hand to give advice: 'Now, when you look anxiously into the mirror against his return, you are very conscious of the grey streaks in your hair, a thinness and a sagging that weren't there in the days of unrationed butter and eggs—and no queues. I dare say your first instinct is to try and cover it all up for him. Don't. Don't try to pretend that time has stood still for you, like the princess in the fairy story, waiting to be awakened with a kiss. Each time he came home on short leaves, you rightly tried to disguise from him the efforts entailed in keeping the home together, so that he would go back to his unit feeling every inch a fighting cock … But when at long last it is all over, let your side of the picture be placed alongside his, with not a detail, not a sacrifice spared. It is a story not of sadness, but of riches.'[7]

Despite Mr Winn, in the first few years after the end of the war, divorce statistics rose sharply. In 1940, less than 8,000 couples divorced. By 1947, the figures had risen to more than 60,000. It became plain that men and women had been affected too deeply by their experiences for their marriages to resume on any terms at all.

Alan Moorehead, chatting to two soldiers recently released from a prisoner-of-war camp in Germany, reported the following poignant exchange:

'"Well, it's all over now," I said. "You will be home soon. Are you married?"

'They said yes, slowly. Then one of them added: "My wife got killed in an air raid and his (indicating the other) has gone off with an American. She wrote to him about it."

'"I'm sorry about that," I said.

'They answered: "Well, we've thought about it and we're not sorry. How could we have gone back again after five years? It wouldn't work. No. It's better the way it is."'[8]

Those who could remember the First World War drew grim comparisons with VE Day: 'I thought of the sufferings and miseries of tens of thousands in Europe yet to come; I thought of the grim outlook for the future; I thought of my son in Burma. I compared my feelings with my feelings on Armistice Day of the last war, when I was on active service on the Western Front, and remembered how wild with joy and excitement I was then, how eagerly I looked forward to the New World that was to be built, how glad I was to be alive. My feelings on VE Day were something wholly different. Relief was there, enormous relief; but no triumphant excitement, no zeal about the future, no gladness to be alive. There was a sense of anti-climax in me, a curious deadness, a disappointment that I felt so different from what I expected that I should feel. This is due, I expect, largely to old age, because there is no useful work left for me to do, but partly because the future for Europe seems to me so gloomy. Everyone seems to be thinking in terms of force, violence, revenge and national interest. There seems no idealism anywhere.'[9]

There was no question that the spectre of what might happen in the Far East cast a shadow over VE Day.

'One had a tremendous feeling of relief, obviously,' said Ian Wallace, the opera singer and broadcaster. 'One saw pictures of people diving into the fountains in Trafalgar Square and that sort of thing, but the longer feeling was more sober relief, the sinking in the stomach that the Japs were still out there pitching. Of course, at that time, one had no idea that the war would finish in such a dramatic fashion. It just looked at that time like another great, big, grinding toil for the people concerned.'

Henry Treece, the author, had the same sense of unfinished business and foreboding: 'I am rather depressed at all this simulated gaiety. The war is only half-over, and many who are dancing and singing tonight will dance and sing no more. If one knew that this was the *real* end of the war, one might abandon oneself completely. But VE Day is only an incident in an already too long war'[10]

Yehudi Menuhin found the celebrations distinctly distasteful. He had travelled and performed throughout the war, playing for troops of all ranks—on the eve and aftermath of battle. If he was within a hundred miles of a camp, he would detour to give a performance. In the United States on VE Day, he nevertheless saw the pictures of celebrations in London and while he was sensitive to the nation's need to express its joy, he had grave reservations.

'I remember seeing the pictures of the jubilation in Trafalgar Square and the release of pain, effort, fear and hope. I can understand festivities as a form of release from anguish, but I cannot justify them in terms of crude victory. The celebration of victory, especially in the land of the vanquished, I find not only distasteful and immoral but also it compromises the future. By celebrating the fact that you have reduced your enemy, you are only inducing him to hope that one day he may do the same to you.'

In fact the majority of the defeated German people greeted the end of the war with as much relief as anyone, though their future could hardly have looked worse.

Dr Joachim Basedow was in a mounted medical unit serving in Russia and is proud of the fact that he never once carried any kind of weapon throughout the war. 'Naturally it was difficult to belong to a defeated nation, but in some respects not so difficult in that we always thought there was no possibility of us ever winning the war.

'It was a very remarkable feeling, to wage such an all-encompassing war for so many years, always accompanied by the feeling that it was a war that could not be won and that what one was doing was rank stupidity. I have often thought about it since then. In an authoritarian system there is no possibility to set yourself against things or, if you do, you risk your neck and you don't want to do that with a family at home waiting for you. You always had a spark of hope that things would turn out well for you, personally. In our company, that proved to be the case—we all made it safely through the war, although one was very much changed by it. You saw so much.'

In a prisoner-of-war camp in Southern Georgia in the United States, where he was for almost a year, the 34-year-old Dr Heinrich Fuerst despaired. 'We were about 5,000 miles from home, but we might as well have been on the moon, excluded for ever from the rest of mankind. Germany had vanished in utter disgrace as a nation and state. Still today, it hurts deeply to describe my conflicting desperate, and almost suicidal, feelings in a comprehensible context.

'To get rid of an evil tyrant is one thing, but to lose at the same time one's country in utter despair and disgrace is something else.

'There was an intense happy awareness that all was over, and that I had come out of the catastrophic débâcle with my body and senses all in one piece, but this was nearly the only positive fact. There was the intense moral backlash when the full horror of the concentration camps saw the light of day. For any decent German, the shame was inescapable. Years of endless suffering, all for nothing; and the only legacy a devastated and totally demoralized country—or what remained of it.'

Christabel Bielenberg, the British woman married to a German husband, understandably suffered conflicting loyalties: 'I suppose I was torn—joyous for Great Britain and weeping for Germany. But actual life was so near us at the time, I was just delighted that Peter was free and then I wondered, of course, whether my brothers, whom I knew had been fighting on the other side, were all right. I didn't know that one was a prisoner of war, I didn't know all those things, and the fact that I could communicate again with England was wonderful. I don't know that I felt very national—you know, how lovely that England had won. I can't say that I had any great feelings of victory. In waves, perhaps, but mostly I was just very glad the whole thing was behind us and that we had survived.'

Yes, survival was all. Victory held little joy for those with loved ones who had not survived. Dame Barbara Cartland's father was killed in the First World War and she lost two brothers in the second.

'We weren't feeling frightfully happy one way or another. It was no use saying you felt wonderful for people who were coming home, you didn't, you felt absolutely ghastly because you had lost the people you most loved.

'Nevertheless, I did not feel the whole war had been a waste, because you were fighting for England. You just did not want to think about it. It had been such a large part of one's life and so much had been lost. You really had to start your life again and I was starting my life again without my younger brother, the person who mattered most to me in the world. When he was killed, it was awful, it was like losing half of myself.'

A young mother called Megan Ryan unconsciously summed up the thoughts of many at the end of the VE Day celebrations. The day had had a particular significance for her: it was her 26th birthday and she had learned in the morning that Peter, her husband in hospital, was out of danger.

'That evening, after the children were asleep in bed, I went outside and sat on the low front wall before the house—the wall from which the ornamental iron railings had long since been taken for the "war effort". It was a warm, still evening and the long street was quiet. But from almost every window light streamed out, splashing onto the pavement. Curtains had been pulled aside and blackouts had been removed. For the first time in nearly six years we were released from the necessity of hiding out in darkness and people were reacting by letting the lights from their homes shine out.

'Too tired to move, I sat thinking about those six years. When they began, I'd been twenty, full of enthusiasms, ambitions, certainties and energy of youth. I'd married, borne children, but the war had stolen from us the simple ordinary joys of a young couple shaping a shared life. Our first home had been burnt to rubble and with it had gone many of the gifts which relatives and friends had given us and which should have been treasured for life, while what had been salvaged would always bear the marks of that night of destruction. We had known the agony of separation and the too rare, too short, too heightened joys of reunions. Apart, we had endured illnesses and dangers and fears for each other. As a family, too, we had been separated and now must learn to live together, overcoming the barriers set up by experiences which had not been shared.

'I thought of those who had been dear to us who had not lived to see this ... of John, who had stood at the altar with us on our wedding day, John who had been trapped in his cockpit when his plane sank beneath the waves ... Of Ron, constant companion of my brother since schooldays, who had vanished without trace when the troopship he was on had been sunk by the Japanese; of Peter, my girlhood friend's gay, kind brother, who had been shot while trying to escape from the prisoner-of-war camp to which he had been taken. They were all so young. The youngest died at nineteen, the oldest at twenty-four. I sat thinking of them ... and then went indoors to stand looking at the sleeping faces of my two little boys, whose lives lay before them in a world at peace.'[11]

Notes

CHAPTER ONE

1 BBC Sound Archives: Stuart Hibberd reads 'Hitler Is Dead', 1 May 1945.
2 Cross, Robin: *VE Day, Victory in Europe 1945*.
3 Flower, Desmond and Reeves, James: *The War 1939–45*.
4 Flower, Desmond and Reeves, James: op. cit.
5 Flower, Desmond and Reeves, James: op. cit.
6 Cole, J.A.: Lord *Haw-Haw: the Full Story of William Joyce*.
7 Olson, Stanley (ed): *Harold Nicolson. Diaries and Letters 1939–45*.
8 *Daily Telegraph*, London 2 May 1945.
9 Mass Observation Archive: Report on Victory in Europe, FR 2263.
10 Olson, Stanley: op. cit.
11 Mass Observation Archive: FR 2263.
12 Bielenberg, Christabel: *The Road Ahead*.

CHAPTER TWO

1 Dimbleby, Jonathan: *Richard Dimbleby*.
2 *Daily Mirror*, 20 April 1945.
3 Mass Observation Archive: TC Victory 1/A.
4 Mass Observation Archive: TC Victory 1/A.
5 Mass Observation Archive: TC Victory 1/A.
6 Mass Observation Archive: TC Victory 1/A.
7 Driberg, Tom: *Colonnade 1937–47*
8 Moorehead, Alan: *Eclipse*.
9 *Yank* 11 May 1945.
10 Ibid.
11 Mass Observation Archive: Report on Victory in Europe, FR 2263.
12 Moorehead, Alan: op. cit.
13 Romilly, Giles and Alexander, Michael: *The Privileged Nightmare*.
14 Schimanski, Stephan and Treece, Henry (eds): *Leaves in the Storm*.
15 Flanner, Janet: *Paris Journal 1944–65*

CHAPTER THREE

1 Montgomery: *The Memoirs of Field Marshal the Viscount Montgomery of Alamein KG*.
2 BBC War Report 6 June 1944–5 May 1945.
3 BBC War Report: op. cit.
4 Mass Observation Archive: Report on Victory in Europe, FR 2263.

CHAPTER FOUR

1 Sheridan, Dorothy (ed): *Wartime Women—An Anthology of Women's Wartime Writing* for Mass Observation 1937–45.
2 Moorehead, Alan: op. cit.
3 Montgomery: op. cit.
4 Summersby, Kay: *Eisenhower Was My Boss*.
5 Montgomery: op. cit.
6 Horrocks, KCB KBE DSO MG LLD (Hons), Sir Brian: *A Full Life*.
7 Deedes, William: 'When Peace Broke Out', *The Spectator* 27 April 1985.
8 Flower, Desmond and Reeves, James, op. cit.
9 BBC War Report: op. cit.
10 James, Robert Rhodes (ed): *Chips—The Diaries of Sir Henry Channon*.
11 Beaton, Cecil: *The Happy Years. Diaries 1944–8*.

CHAPTER FIVE

1 Broad, Richard and Fleming, Susie (eds): *Nella Last's War: A Mother's Last Diary 1939–45*
2 Donnison, F.S.V.: *History of the Second World War, Civil Affairs and Military Government in North West Europe 1944–6*.
3 Hodson, James Lansdale: *The Sea and the Land*.
4 Carmichael, Ian: *Will the Real Ian Carmichael …*
5 Moorehead, Alan: op. cit.

CHAPTER SIX

1 Patterson, Captain Joe: *Diary*, IWM 66/192/1.
2 Horrocks, Sir Brian: op. cit.
3 de Bruyn, Guenter: *Zwischenbilanz—eine Jugend in Berlin*.
4 Gerhardi, Helga: *Helga*.
5 Longmate, Norman: *When We Won the War*.
6 Ward, Edward: *Give Me Air*.
7 Longmate, Norman: *When We Won the War*.

CHAPTER SEVEN

1 Summersby, Kay: op. cit.
2 *Yank*, victory edition 1945.
3 Butcher, Captain Harry C.: *Three Years with Eisenhower.*
4 de Guignand, Major General Sir Francis. *Operation Victory.*
5 Butcher, Captain Harry C.: op. cit.
6 *Yank*, victory edition
7 Longmate, Norman: *When We Won the War.*
8 de Guignand, Sir Francis: op. cit.
9 Summersby, Kay: op. cit.
10 Butcher, Captain Harry C.: op. cit.
11 Summersby, Kay: op. cit.

CHAPTER EIGHT

1 Pocock, Tom: 1945. *The Dawn Came Up Like Thunder.*
2 Olson, Stanley (ed): op. cit.
3 Longmate, Norman: *How We Lived Then.*
4 Wheeler-Bennett, John W.: *King George VI, His Life and Reign.*
5 Summersby, Kay: op. cit.
6 Knightley, Phillip: *The First Casualty.*
7 Ibid.
8 Mass Observation Archive: Report on Victory in Europe, FR 2263.
9 Sheridan, Dorothy: op. cit.
10 Woolfitt, Susan: *Idle Women.*
11 Mass Observation Archive: Report on Victory in Europe, FR 2263.
12 Mass Observation Archive: FR 2263.
13 Mass Observation Archive: 'Diary for 1945, Holness, A'.
14 Walton, Gunner Ralph: 'Letter to fiancée', Document Dept IWM 88/211.
15 Anderson, Verily: *Spam Tomorrow.*
16 Broad, Richard and Fleming, Susie: op. cit.
17 Longmate, Norman: *When We Won the War.*
18 *Daily Mirror,* Tuesday 8 May 1945.
19 Sheridan, Dorothy: op. cit.
20 Mass Observation Archive: Report on Victory in Europe, FR 2263.
21 Longmate, Norman: *When We Won the War.*
22 Sheridan, Dorothy: op. cit.
23 Flanner, Janet: op. cit.
24 Carmichael, Ian: op. cit.
25 Courtneidge, Cicely: *Cicely.*
26 Benn, MP, Tony: *Years of Hope.*
27 Nel, Elizabeth (Layton): *Mr Churchill's Secretary.*

CHAPTER NINE

1 Lewis, Wynne: *Victory Day in Europe*, MS held by IWM.
2 Mass Observation Archive: DR VE Day 2575.
3 Sheridan, Dorothy: op. cit.
4 Ibid.
5 Mass Observation Archive: DR VE Day 1226.
6 Mass Observation Archive: DR VE Day 3650.
7 Mass Observation Archive: DR VE Day 3657.
8 Mass Observation Archive: 'Diary for May 1945, Holness A'.
9 James, Robert Rhodes: op. cit.
10 Wheeler-Bennett, John W: op. cit.

CHAPTER TEN

1 Longmate, Norman: *When We Won the War*.
2 Mass Observation Archive: DR VE Day, I.M.A. Naylor.
3 Nel, Elizabeth (Layton): op. cit.
4 Mosley, Leonard: *Backs to the Wall—London under Fire 1940–45*.
5 Gordon, Jane: *Married to Charles*.
6 Nel, Elizabeth (Layton): op. cit.
7 Thompson, W.H.: *I Was Churchill's Shadow*.
8 Letter from John Lowry to his parents, supplied by Lord Howe with writer's permission.
9 Brittain, Vera: *Testament of Experience*.
10 Transcript of interview for Sound Archives of the Imperial War Museum, ref 9820/5/2.
11 Olson, Stanley (ed): op. cit.
12 Hodson, J.L.: extract from *The Sea and the Land* taken from Norman Longmate's *When We Won the War*.
13 Lehman, John: *I Am My Brother*.
14 Beaton, Cecil: op. cit.
15 Churchill, MP, Winston: interview in *Sunday Telegraph Magazine*, May 1985.
16 Mass Observation Archive: Report on Victory in Europe, FR 2263

CHAPTER ELEVEN

1 BBC Radio Collection: 'Victory in Europe', King George VI, 8 May 1945.
2 Extract from volume II of *Portsmouth at War* published by Local History Group of Portsmouth WEA.
3 Mass Observation Archive: Report of Victory in Europe, FR 2263.
4 Longmate, Norman: *How We Lived Then*.
5 Mass Observation Archive: DR VE Day, 1644.
6 Longmate, Norman: *When We Won the War*.
7 Sheridan, Dorothy: op. cit.
8 Sheridan, Dorothy: op. cit.
9 Mass Observation Archive: Diary for May 1945, A. Holness.
10 Mass Observation Archive: DR VE Day 1651
11 Clark, R.W.: *Tizard*.

12 Mass Observation Archive: DR VE Day, Miss I.M.A Naylor.
13 Letter from LAC Brian Poole in RAF Rivenhall, Essex, to penfriend in Miami, Florida, held by Dept of Documents, ref 1075, at the Imperial War Museum.
14 Mass Observation Archive: DR VE Day 3320.
15 Dossett-Davies, John: from an unpublished MS. *A Dornier Flew over the Leys.*
16 Interview with Rabbi Blue in *Sunday Telegraph Magazine*, 5 May 1985.
17 Lambert, Derek: *The Sheltered Days: Growing Up in the War.*
18 Mass Observation Archive: Report on Victory in Europe, FR 2263.
19 Payn, Graham and Morley, Sheridan (eds): *The Noel Coward Diaries.*
20 Lyttelton, Humphrey: *I Play As I Please.*
21 Nel, Elizabeth (Layton): op. cit.
22 Driberg, Tom: op. cit.
23 Mass Observation Archive.
24 Hibberd, Stuart: *This Is London.*

CHAPTER TWELVE

1 Frost, John: Letter to his mother, written on 8 May 1946.
2 Ward, Edward: op. cit.
3 Longmate, Norman: *When We Won the War.*
4 Niven, David: *The Moon's a Balloon.*
5 Morris, Mary (née Muiry): Diaries, in Dept of Documents, IWM.
6 Kennedy, Ludovic: *On My Way to the Club.*
7 Belfrage, Bruce: *One Man in His Time.*

CHAPTER THIRTEEN

1 Prevratil, Rudolf and Richler, Karl (eds): *Witnesses of the Great Victory: World War Two in Reports, Epics and Memoirs.*
2 Summersby, Kay: op. cit.
3 Ibid.
4 Longmate, Norman: *When We Won the War.*
5 de Bruyn, Guenter: op. cit.
6 Longmate, Norman: *When We Won the War.*
7 Maugham, CBE, R.C.F.: *Jersey under the Jackboot.*

CHAPTER FOURTEEN

1 IWM 12778/20.
2 Mass Observation Archive: Report on Feelings about Peace, FR 2778.
3 Mass Observation Archive: Report on Victory in Europe, FR 2263.
4 Longmate, Norman: *When We Won the War.*
5 Broad, Richard and Fleming, Susie: op. cit.

6 Original letter lent to authors by Mrs Lucia Whitehead, copy in IWM Department of Documents.
7 Briggs, Susan: *Keep Smiling Through.*
8 Moorehead, Alan: op. cit.
9 Mass Observation Archive: Report on Victory in Europe, FR 2263.
10 Schimanski, Stephan and Treece, Henry: op. cit.
11 Longmate, Norman: *The Home Front.*

Bibliography

Anderson, Verily: *Spam Tomorrow,* Rupert Hart-Davis 1956.

BBC War Report 6 June May 1944–45, Oxford University Press 1946.

Beaton, Cecil: *The Happy Years. Diaries 1944–48*, Weidenfeld and Nicolson 1972.

Belfrage, Bruce: *One Man in His Time*, Hodder and Stoughton 1951.

Benn, MP, Tony: *Years of Hope,* Hutchinson 1994.

Bielenberg, Christabel: *The Road Ahead*, Bantam Press 1992.

Brittain, Vera: *Testament of Experience*, Gollancz 1957.

Briggs, Susan: *Keep Smiling Through*, Weidenfeld and Nicolson, 1975.

Broad, Richard and Fleming, Susie: *Nella Last's War: A Mother's Last Diary*, Falling Wall Press Bristol 1981.

Butcher, Harry C.: *Three Years With Eisenhower: The Personal Diary of Captain Harry C. Butcher,* William Heinemann 1946.

Carmichael, Ian: *Will the Real Ian Carmichael* … , Futura 1980.

Clark, Ronald W.: *Tizard*, Methuen 1965.

Cole, J.A.: *Lord Haw Haw: the Full Story of William Joyce*, Faber 1964.

Courtneidge, Cicely: *Cicely*, Hutchinson 1953.

Cross, Robin: *VE Day; Victory in Europe 1945*, Sidgwick and Jackson 1985.

de Bruyn, Guenter, *Zwischenbilanz—eine Jugend in Berlin*, S Fischer Verlag GmbH, Frankfurt 1992.

de Guignand, Major General Sir Francis. *Operation Victory*, Hodder and Stoughton 1947.

Dimbleby, Jonathan: *Richard Dimbleby*, Hodder and Stoughton 1976.

Donnison, F.S.V.: *History of the Second World War, Civil Affairs and Military Government in North West Europe 1944–46*, HMSO 1961.

Driberg, Tom: *Colonnade 1937–47*, Pilot Press 1949.

Flanner, Janet: *Paris Journal 1944–65*, Gollancz 1966.

Flower, Desmond and Reeves, James: *The War 1939–45*, Cassell 1960.

Gerhardi, Helga: *Helga*, Virona Publishing Aylesbury 1993.

Gordon, Jane: *Married to Charles*, William Heinemann 1950.

Hibberd, Stuart: *This Is London*, MacDonald and Evans 1950.

Hodson, James Lansdale: *The Sea and the Land*, Gollancz 1945.

Horrocks, KCB, KBE, DSO, MG, LLD (Hons), Sir Brian: *A Full Life*, Collins 1960.

James, Robert Rhodes (ed): *Chips—The Diaries of Sir Henry Channon*, Weidenfeld and Nicolson 1967.

Kennedy, Ludovic: *On My Way to the Club*, Collins 1989.

Knightley, Phillip: *The First Casualty*, Harcourt, Brace, Jovanovich, London and New York 1975.

Lambert, Derek: *The Sheltered Days: Growing Up in the War*, André Deutsch 1965.

Lehmann, John: *I Am My Brother*, Longman 1960.

Longmate, Norman: *When We Won the War*, Hutchinson 1977.

Longmate, Norman: *The Home Front*, Chatto and Windus 1981.

Longmate, Norman: *How We Lived Then*, Hutchinson 1971.

Lyttelton, Humphrey: *I Play As I Please*, Granada 1954.

Maugham, R.C.F.: *Jersey under the Jackboot*, W.H. Allen 1946.

Montgomery: *The Memoirs of Field Marshal the Viscount Montgomery of Alamein KG*, Collins 1958.

Moorehead, Alan: *Eclipse*, Hamish Hamilton 1978.

Mosley, Leonard: *Backs to the Wall—London under Fire 1940 45*, Weidenfeld and Nicolson 1971.

Nel, Elizabeth (Layton): *Mr Churchill's Secretary*, Hodder and Stoughton 1958.

Niven, David: *The Moon's a Balloon*, Hamish Hamilton 1971.

Olson, Stanley (ed): *Harold Nicolson, Diaries and Letters 1939 1945*, Collins 1980.

Payn, Graham and Morley, Sheridan (eds): *The Noel Coward Diaries*, Weidenfeld and Nicolson 1967.

Pocock, Tom: *1945. The Dawn Came Up Like Thunder*, Collins 1983.

Prevratil, Rudolf and Richler, Karl (eds): *Witnesses of the Great Victory: World War Two in Reports, Epics and Memoirs*, International Organisation of Journalists, Prague 1985.

Romilly, Giles and Alexander, Michael: *The Privileged Nightmare*, Weidenfeld and Nicolson.

Schimanski, Stephen and Treece, Henry (eds): *Leaves in the Storm; A Book of Diaries*, Lindsay Drummond 1947.

Sheridan, Dorothy (ed): *Wartime Women—An Anthology of Women's Wartime Writing*, William Heinemann, London 1990.

Summersby, Kay: *Eisenhower Was My Boss*, Werner Laurie 1949.

Thompson, W.H.: *I Was Churchill's Shadow*, Christopher Johnson, London 1951.

Ward, Edward: *Give Me Air*, The Bodley Head 1946.

Wheeler-Bennett, John W.: *King George VI, His Life and Reign*, Macmillan 1958.

Woolfitt, Susan: *Idle Women*, Ernest Benn 1947.

Index

If you are interested in purchasing other books published by Tempus,
or in case you have difficulty finding any Tempus books in your local bookshop,
you can also place orders directly through our website

www.tempus-publishing.com